SPREADING THE GOSPEL OF BOOKS

Terrebonne Parish residents arrive by boat to meet the Louisiana Library Commission bookmobile, ca. 1940. (State Library of Louisiana)

SPREADING THE GOSPEL OF BOOKS

ESSAE M. CULVER AND THE **GENESIS** OF
LOUISIANA PARISH LIBRARIES

FLORENCE M. JUMONVILLE

Louisiana State University Press
Baton Rouge

Published by Louisiana State University Press
Copyright © 2019 by Louisiana State University Press
All rights reserved
Manufactured in the United States of America
First printing

DESIGNER: *Mandy McDonald Scallan*
TYPEFACE: *Sentinel*
PRINTER AND BINDER: *LSI*

Cataloging-in-Publication Data are available from the Library of Congress.

ISBN 978-0-8071-7019-9 (cloth: alk. paper) — ISBN 978-0-8071-7259-9 (pdf)
— ISBN 978-0-8071-7260-5 (epub)

ℬ

To the librarians of Louisiana,
especially those who have served as state librarian:

Essae Martha Culver (1925–1962)

Sallie Farrell (1962–1975)

Thomas F. Jaques (1975–2005)

Rebecca Hamilton (2005–)

CONTENTS

ILLUSTRATIONS

Map

Photographs

PREFACE

In the 1920s, libraries were beyond the experience of most rural residents. To encourage their establishment and the spread of good books throughout rural America, in 1925 the Carnegie Corporation offered grant funding to a state deficient in library development. The purpose of the grant was to enable that state to create a model program, demonstrating to other states the benefits to be gained by an exemplary library commission with an aggressive, actively administered program of field work. This, in turn, would demonstrate to rural residents how libraries—and the books they lent—could enhance people's lives. Because Louisiana received the funding, its parish libraries evolved differently from county libraries in other states. Essae M. Culver, an experienced librarian who had worked in rural Oregon and California, was recruited to direct the project. She adapted the California plan of library development in ways that enhanced demonstration libraries' prospects for success, and, in time, the Louisiana plan became an exemplar for the nation and for foreign countries. *Spreading the Gospel of Books* chronicles the history of the Louisiana Library Commission and its successor agency, the State Library of Louisiana, from the commission's inception in 1920 through the administrations of the first two state librarians, Essae M. Culver (1925–1962) and Sallie Farrell (1962–1975).

When I was attending library school at Louisiana State University (LSU) during the 1971–72 academic year, Miss Essae, as she was widely known, was still living, and, among Louisiana librarians, at least, she was legendary. All of my teachers knew her, some had worked with her, and they spoke of her with combined respect and affection that verged on reverence. We students quickly learned the story of how she came from California to organize Louisiana parish libraries, spreading the gospel of books to the most remote areas of the state.

At the time, LSU held graduate-level library science classes in the library. One morning, word spread that Miss Essae was in the building. When the class had assembled, the professor—Thomas Shaw, formerly head of reference at the Library of Congress—entered the room smiling and announced that he had a surprise for us. He retreated into the corridor and returned a moment later, escorting Miss Essae on his arm. She spoke to us throughout the fifty-minute class period. I have forgotten what she talked about—probably her early experiences in Louisiana, with which I was familiar already. What I remember, all these years later, is that when class ended, she seemed to be sizing us up as we filed past her, appraising the aspiring librarians who would carry on the work. She died less than a year later.

In 1998 I attended a Louisiana Library Association committee meeting at the State Library. Two of my friends there, Judy Smith and Virginia Smith, invited me to join them for lunch after the meeting. In a nearby restaurant, they admitted to having an ulterior motive. "Did you know," they asked, "that we have Miss Essae's journals?" (No, I didn't.) Judy and Virginia thought that someone should use the journals for researching the State Library's history—and they had me in mind. Back at the Louisiana Collection after lunch, they showed me the journals, and they were right: the small volumes contained a wealth of information.

From the pages of those journals, and from correspondence, scrapbooks, reports, and comments of her contemporaries, Culver emerges as a woman of culture and diverse interests, an able administrator, a fun-loving chum, and a caring friend, as well as a devoted and dynamic librarian whose imagination, dedication, compassion, and tireless crusading spread libraries throughout rural Louisiana between 1925 and 1968. I drew upon the journals as I wrote a paper I presented to the American Library Association's Library History Round Table the next year. That paper led to another, and, two papers and one article later, I recognized that they should grow up to be a book. Thomas Jaques, Louisiana's third state librarian, approved the project and gave me total access to any file I wished to read and any employee I wanted to interview. His successor, Rebecca Hamilton, welcomed me equally. This research would not have been possible without Judy and Virginia, who proposed it; Tom and Rebecca, who supported it; and the State Library personnel who facilitated it, especially Judy in her capacity as Louisiana Collection librarian and her successor, Charlene Bonnette; Dorothy White; and the staff of the Office of the State Librarian.

Much of the writing occurred during a six-month sabbatical leave from the University of New Orleans, and I am appreciative of the support of Dean of Library Services Sharon Mader and my colleagues in the Louisiana and Special Collections Department, who made possible not only the sabbatical but also release time for months of trips to Baton Rouge every other Friday.

In addition, I am indebted to the late Honorable John C. Culver, former United States senator from Iowa, and his sister, Kay Baty, for generously providing invaluable information about their aunt Essae's childhood and Culver family history; also to Sonja Somerville of the Salem Public Library, for exhuming forgotten records of Miss Essae's employment there. Gracious assistance with the photographs that illustrate this volume came from Charlene Bonnette (State Library of Louisiana); Melissa Eastin (East Baton Rouge Parish Library); Fermand M. Garlington II and Laura L. McLemore (Louisiana State Library in Shreveport); Heather Pilcher (University of Louisiana at Monroe); Scott T. Jordan (University of Louisiana at Lafayette); Connie L. Phelps and James W. Hodges (University of New Orleans); Rebecca Smith, Heather M. Szafran, and Michael M. Redmann (The Historic New Orleans Collection); Sara Chetney (Claremont Colleges Library); Cara Setsu Bertram (American Library Association Archives at the University of Illinois at Urbana-Champaign); and Viktoria Mraz (McGraw-Hill).

Finally, I am grateful for the encouragement of Margaret Lovecraft, editor extraordinaire at LSU Press, and dear, longtime friends Jessica Travis, Catherine Kahn, Earl Hart, Faye Phillips, and the late Mary Louise Christovich. Jessica, Cathy, and Mary Lou read the original manuscript and offered many valuable suggestions. That Mary Lou liked it emboldened me to approach LSU Press, and Jessica has gone every step of the way with me.

SPREADING THE GOSPEL OF BOOKS

The sixty-four parishes of Louisiana. (Map by Mary Lee Eggart)

Prologue

From the Ladies of the Clubs to the Louisiana Library Commission, 1885–1925

I n 1885 the southwest Louisiana town of Jennings was young, vigorous, and growing. Its business district housed the depot, two stores, and a hotel, and its population included "a small group of cultured women" who, on February 7 of that year, had organized themselves into a society for mutual aid and social and intellectual development. Concerned about the cultural betterment of young men in the area as well as about their own, the clubwomen concluded that Jennings needed a library and reading room "for 'the boys.'" The following year they renamed their organization the Ladies Library Society of Jennings and began to acquire books, by donation and by purchase. This first women's club in Jefferson Davis Parish was just a year younger than the Women's Club founded in New Orleans by writer Elizabeth Bisland as the first group of its kind in the South.[1]

Women's clubs had burgeoned in the United States before the Civil War in small towns, possibly including New Orleans as early as 1859, and in 1868 in the large cities of New York and Boston. Following in the wake of the advancing frontier, they spread to cities, towns, and remote outposts across the country, many as outgrowths of post–Civil War soldiers' relief associations, benevolent societies, and church groups. Founded to provide women with opportunities for self-improvement through discussing literature and studying educational subjects, the organizations soon began to participate more actively in community life by advocating for legal rights for women and children, civic development of all sorts, formation of parent-teacher organizations, provision of kindergartens and night schools, conservation of natural resources, funds for scholarships, and library extension, to name just a few of the reforms for which Louisiana clubwomen campaigned.[2]

Organizing a community library proved to be an ideal project for clubwomen, for it entwined with the original purpose of literary discussion and extended their traditional roles beyond the thresholds of their homes while avoiding competition in male spheres. Other clubs took up the library cause, and across the nation and the state, women "gathered up [books] from the garrets of the best families," organized town libraries, and mobilized traveling collections. In Louisiana, different groups of Shreveport women, for example, formed the Shreveport Library Association and the Mechanics Library in the 1890s, merging them in 1901. Forty organizations for women jointly began a push for a free public library in 1918, but World War I had halted their progress; the Shreve Memorial Library eventually opened in 1923. Similarly, in Lafayette, the Five O'Clock Tea Club, based on study clubs described by a newcomer from San Antonio, began in 1897 to operate a lending library that survived for twenty years. In Baton Rouge, the Burroughs Club, its membership comprised of black women, established the Burroughs-Talbert Public Library, probably Louisiana's only subscription library begun by and for black citizens, and maintained it from 1923 to 1937.[3]

Just as civic-minded women discovered that they could accomplish more when they joined together in clubs, so did they find that the clubs made even greater progress when they united. In 1889 a group of prominent organizations formed themselves into a federation that welcomed the affiliation of clubs throughout the nation. By 1896 the General Federation of Women's Clubs had developed a list of societal improvements toward which its federated clubs should direct their energies. Libraries quickly became a high priority at the national level and a subject of mutual interest to many local and state organizations. In 1914 the federation defined five "library ideals" toward which affiliates should work: "1. A free county library in every county seat. 2. A county system of traveling libraries. 3. A book wagon to distribute books. 4. The use of the rural free delivery in getting individual books to individual borrowers. 5. The use of the rural telephone between home, school and library for reference purposes."[4]

Delegates to the convention of the Louisiana Federation of Women's Clubs pose for a group photograph following a session at Southwestern Louisiana Institute, Lafayette, 1927. (Photo by Edwin L. Stephens. University of Louisiana at Lafayette, Southwestern Louisiana Institute Photographs, 1923–1940)

Louisiana had not yet made progress toward reaching these ideals. William Beer, head of the Howard Memorial Library at Tulane University, had formed the Louisiana Traveling Library Association in 1897 "so that good books can reach every hamlet." As unneeded duplicates (or worse), the books probably were selected more on the basis of availability than on their desirability to the intended audience. The extent to which they circulated is not known; it is likely that they soon found their way back to the shelves of the Howard Memorial Library or to the discards bin. In 1915 the Louisiana Federation of Women's Clubs adopted the project as part of its educational program. The president appointed Harriet Daggett of Jennings to organize the traveling library, and she plunged into the assignment wholeheartedly.[5]

Daggett found herself overwhelmed by more requests than she could handle. "The family got pretty sick of seeing these boxes," she recalled in 1945. "But they proved one thing—the need, and the desire of people in the outlying regions for books." The project also revealed the need for more volumes. "Books continually traveled over the state, but our collection was so small that we could not meet many of the demands, either in number or in the kind of books wanted. The wide spread need for books and the inadequacy of traveling libraries to meet this need showed that the Federation should adopt some other method of spreading books and education throughout Louisiana." Daggett concluded, as had others before her, that Louisiana needed a library commission—a central state agency to stimulate public interest in libraries and to facilitate and supervise their development. Every obstacle to library development seemed to point to it as the best means of overcoming almost any impediment. Until a commission existed, library development depended on local initiative, which, in a largely rural state with the nation's lowest literacy rate, meant that "a great number of communities will have no library."[6]

Neither the idea of a library commission nor the provision of state aid to libraries was new. Rhode Island began in 1875 to give money to free public libraries to buy books. In 1890 Massachusetts initiated the first state library commission, constituting an example for commissions in New Hampshire (1891), New York (1892), Connecticut (1893), and other states. The Wisconsin Free Library Commission (1895) took the lead as a model for its region and the West. Lutie E. Stearns (1866–1943), a staunch "advocate for access" to free libraries, gave impetus to the drive to found the commission, which advised existing libraries, and communities that proposed to establish new ones, regarding the best procedures, book selection and cataloging, and other details. Stearns was instrumental also in establishing in Wisconsin 150 public libraries, 14 county traveling library systems, and 1,400 traveling collections patterned on those initiated in New York by Melvil Dewey, which she regarded as preliminary to permanent public libraries. She stationed these traveling libraries in post offices, farmhouses, and other isolated rural locations throughout the state. After leaving the commission in 1914, she began a new career as a free-lance writer and lecturer, continuing to advocate for free libraries as well as the suffragist movement and other social and political causes of the era.[7]

In 1897 Georgia implemented the first library commission in the south, but it initially functioned only in an advisory capacity. Seven states established commissions in 1899, and seven more did so within the next two years. Conditions varied among the states, but the commissions shared a common goal: to foster and encourage the growth of the library extension movement. By 1916 the "states having library departments have assumed, through them, at least ten general functions. . . . [At that time,] having a library commission [usually meant]: 1. The establishing of local libraries. 2. Aiding and improving local libraries. 3. Promoting helpful cooperation between libraries. 4. Raising the standard and quality of library service. 5. Providing aid to schools and to school libraries. 6. Aid to libraries in state charitable, penal and reformatory institutions. 7. Providing library facilities where no local library exists or can be maintained. 8. Selecting and distributing public documents. 9. Libraries for the blind. 10. Legislative reference work."[8]

Louisiana's library law of 1910, enacted by the Legislature at the behest of the recently formed Louisiana State Library Association, provided "for the creation, establishment, maintenance and equipment of libraries throughout the State," but it failed to appropriate funding, to require the employment of a trained administrator, or to authorize the formation of a state library agency. A decade later, Willie Chapman (Mrs. Albert F.) Storm of Morgan City, then president of the Louisiana Federation of Women's Clubs, spearheaded a movement to pass enabling legislation that corrected most of the earlier law's shortcomings. The campaign proved to be an arduous one. Storm spent most of the session in Baton Rouge to see the bill through the legislative process, for "the idea of a library commission for state library development in Louisiana was new, and legislators had to be convinced of its benefits." She recalled in 1950, "One of the happiest moments I can remember is the ripple of applause which went through the house of representatives in 1920, when, at an after-midnight session, the audible roll call vote on the library bill ended and the clerk announced 'The ayes have it.'"[9]

Signed by Governor John M. Parker on July 8, 1920, Act 225 authorized a Louisiana Library Commission, domiciled at Baton Rouge and comprised of five members, at least two of whom would be women. A provision called for the appointment of a secretary—a librarian with at least a year of training in a library school and a minimum of three years of successful experience as a public library head or high-ranking assistant. Storm submitted a list of five prospective Louisiana Library Commission members to Governor Parker, and he promptly commissioned all five. In addition to two New Orleans men, Rabbi David Fichman, director of the Jewish Charitable and Educational Foundation, and Professor R. W. Hayes of Tulane University, the group included three women, all of them mainstays of the library movement: Katherine Hill and Margaret Reed of Baton Rouge and

Harriet Daggett of Jennings. Hill and the two New Orleans commissioners held a meeting at which they elected Dr. Fichman as chairman and Hill as secretary-treasurer.[10]

All that the commission lacked was money to implement its plans. Largely thanks to the efforts of Reed and Hill, in 1921 the Legislature appropriated $1,000 to further the Library Commission's work. The two commissioners bought shelves and supplies, and they hired a librarian, Mrs. Owen Brown, who spent the spring of 1923 cataloging 2,500 books. Appealing for funds for continued support at several subsequent sessions of the Legislature proved fruitless. No matter their efforts, Hill and Reed found legislators to be "almost entirely ignorant about the Commission. Many of them had never heard of it, and those who had, thought it a 'women's fad.'" "The situation in regard to our work distresses me," Reed wrote to another commission member in 1922. "It is manifestly impossible to get such a librarian as we need with our present uncertainty as to future support. On the other hand, we cannot make much of a case to the legislature if we have nothing to show for the money already granted us. . . . I did so much, to me disagreeable work, in getting what we have . . . that I hate to see it die for lack of attention."[11]

By 1925, "club women and the few people of the state who were interested were fast losing faith that the Louisiana Library Commission would ever be able to function." Meanwhile, the commission was rapidly losing members. Hayes had left the state. Professional matters demanded Rabbi Fichman's time, while Daggett's family and a budding legal career consumed hers. Overwhelmed and discouraged, Hill and Reed felt unable to continue, and Hill submitted her resignation to Governor Henry L. Fuqua. He had not yet accepted it when the commission's fortunes took a surprising turn for the better, thanks to events that unfolded in other parts of the nation.[12]

CHAPTER 1

Essae M. Culver Answers the Call, 1925

F rom the last decades of the nineteenth century until the dawn of World War II, American culture increasingly became "'a culture of print,' that is, a culture that was knit together and defined by the printed word." As printed materials grew more diverse and more readily available, citizens relied upon them more and more to disseminate political, economic, and cultural information, "which circulated faster, more cheaply, and more widely than ever before" and contributed to the growing imperative to make books available to all the people through public libraries.[1]

Toward that goal, during a thirty-year period beginning in 1889, Andrew Carnegie, the Pittsburgh-based business tycoon who had made a fortune in the steel industry and focused his prolific philanthropy on libraries, contributed $41 million to construct 1,679 public library buildings. This program of beneficence continued after his death in 1919 under the auspices of the Carnegie Corporation of New York. During the next few years, however, Carnegie administrators grew increasingly disappointed that many municipalities had accepted funding to construct buildings but failed to move beyond bricks and mortar to engender meaningful library programs. Meanwhile, as the American Library Association (ALA) prepared to celebrate its semicentenary in 1925, the library profession's leaders acknowledged gloomily that national library development had progressed with distressing sluggishness—a circumstance mirrored in Louisiana. Members of another organization, the League of Library Commissions, shared this concern. The League, a group of some twenty state library agencies that came together in 1904 to work toward improved library service, stood ready "to help any of the states which, for one reason or another, had done little or nothing to help themselves," but its leaders hardly knew where to begin. "Little power or contact with those that were unconvinced" and lack of funds hampered both organizations.[2]

Shortly before the 1924/25 winter meetings in Chicago of the ALA and the League, news spread that the Carnegie Corporation "would entertain a proposal to put on a state demonstration in library service under the direction of the League. Before the Chicago conference adjourned, negotiations had gone far enough to make it fairly certain that $50,000 to be spent over a period of three years would be forthcoming for this purpose." In his capacity as League president, California state librarian Milton J. Ferguson subsequently accepted Carnegie funding in that amount to promote library development.[3]

Ferguson headed a committee charged with implementing this project. It began by tackling the question of where to spend the Carnegie money and League effort. Members "soon decided that the best results could be expected from concentrated sowing in one state, rather than dropping a few seeds in hopeful abandon throughout the nation." They sought a state deficient in library development, but one that presented a reasonable prospect for success and so positioned geographically that its achievements would constitute a model for its neighbors. Further, it should offer open-minded elected officials, at least a small group of influential and willing supporters, and a legal mechanism to perpetuate the League's work at the end of three years. Because library progress had lagged more in the South than in any other region of the country, selection of a southern state seemed likely—and the committee had at least ten to choose from. Louisiana, known to be among the states most deficient in the quantity and efficacy of its libraries, appeared to offer fertile ground for their nurture—and for demonstrating to the citizens how a centralized library agency could facilitate that effort.[4]

On his way home to California from the ALA mid-winter meeting, Ferguson visited the Pelican State to assess for himself whether Louisianians commonly held a statewide resolve to cultivate their libraries using intensive modern methods. There he found the general library law of 1910, which had not been actuated because of lack of financial support, and the 1920 law that had created the yet-unfunded Louisiana Library Commission. More

Milton J. Ferguson, ca. 1935, around the time he served as president of the American Library Association. (American Library Association Archives, 99/1/13, Box 2, Folder: Milton Ferguson, President, 1938–1939)

than 1 million people remained without access to library service. Some Louisianians, however, suspected ulterior motives. Governor Fuqua, for example, perhaps recalling post–Civil War American history textbooks from northern publishers that required schoolchildren to master regional trivia irrelevant elsewhere, mistrusted the plan "as a 'Yankee scheme to educate the heathen of the South'" but, upon receiving assurance that "success of the kind we were looking for would require local appropriations, he declared himself open to conviction." Fuqua agreed to appoint or reappoint the commission members under whose supervision the project would be carried out if Louisiana were selected.[5]

Ferguson considered Louisiana "attractive for several reasons: the people were enthusiastic and unbelievably hospitable, the ground was not encumbered by any structure which must be removed to make way for a newer edifice, and laws had been enacted so that money alone was needed to set the wheels in motion." Though the obvious frontrunner, Louisiana was not without competition. News of this "project of making a library 'demonstration' in states backward in library development" spread quickly, "and, in the spreading, the sum grew like the paper profits on a bull market." Thirteen states eagerly applied for consideration. Representatives of some of them, in addition to explaining why theirs merited selection, offered reasons why Louisiana should *not* be chosen. Meanwhile, local preparations were underway so that the state, if designated, would be ready. On March 9,

1925, Margaret Reed and Katherine Hill met with Governor Fuqua to discuss the prospect. While reserving the authority to use his own judgment, the governor asked them to submit a list of names of interested potential commissioners. Neither of the women wanted to continue in that capacity, but Ferguson had inferred that they would be expected to do so if Louisiana received the funding. They acquiesced, for they "felt that the sacrifice would be worth while if we can get this work started."[6]

On March 20, the governor named new members to the Louisiana Library Commission: two New Orleanians, G. P. Wyckoff, professor of sociology at Tulane University, and Eleanor McMain, head of a settlement house called Kingsley House, as well as Forrest K. White of Lake Charles, superintendent of Calcasieu Parish schools. As expected, the governor reappointed Hill and Reed. Unlike most governors, who strove for geographic distribution when populating commissions such as this, Fuqua chose appointees from the same region of the state (the southern section). He reasoned that because roads everywhere were deficient, geographical proximity facilitated getting together.[7]

Ferguson returned to Louisiana in April to attend the first meeting of a newly reorganized and reinvigorated Louisiana Library Association (LLA) and, on behalf of the League of Library Commissions, offered the state a fund of $15,000 per year for three years "for the purpose of making a demonstration of modern library service in the south." The commission accepted the grant and immediately voted to appoint as executive secretary "a librarian experienced in the best developments of Library Commission work." A decision on the exact forms of work to be undertaken was deferred until a suitable librarian accepted the position and arrived to take up the work. The commission planned to collaborate, meanwhile, with the LLA to educate Louisianians regarding the value of the commission's work and to organize local groups interested in founding libraries.[8]

Ferguson "had someone in mind for the job [of executive secretary], and there was never a rival candidate." As he wrote to Wyckoff, "The success of the work in Louisiana or any place else will depend very largely upon the ability, the understanding, the tact, and the skill of the executive secretary. I have thought all along that a southern person would be best for this position. I have in mind, however, a librarian who has great understanding, who has a most pleasing personality, who has had great success in work with clubs of all kinds, and who in short is what one might call a 'complete' librarian, but she is not of southern extraction. She is not offensively of one section or of another." Based on Ferguson's recommendation, Wyckoff wrote the next day to Essae M. Culver, offering the position of secretary. "Please," he implored, "do not decline the offer before consulting [Milton Ferguson] after his present visit to Louisiana."[9]

"The Great Need of the Rural People"

Born in Emporia, Kansas, on November 15, 1882, Essae Martha Culver was the youngest of five daughters and three sons of Joseph Franklin Culver (1834–1899) and Mary Murphy Culver (1842–1920).[10] Her unusual first name, which she fervently disliked, was pronounced like the word "essay" or the letters "S. A." Her parents creatively named her after an uncle called Sam; the sound of her first name, when coupled with the initial letter of her middle name, spelled SAM.[11]

In later years, Essae Culver described a seemingly idyllic childhood in the embrace of a close-knit extended family that included grandparents and cousins as well as parents and siblings, giving her opportunities to become comfortable with people of all ages. "We lived in a large house on a hill called University Place," she recalled. "The hill sloped down to a river and on the slope was an orchard, with apples, peaches, pears, plums, a vegetable garden and two grape arbors, and berries of every description. We had horses to ride and drive, dogs and cats to play with so that most of my time was spent out doors." Her mother "always insisted if we started any project we must finish it if at all possible and no matter how discouraging the outlook."[12]

Emporia had no public library when Essae was growing up, but the books that filled the Culver house stimulated her early interest in reading. The strongest influences in the youngster's life "were religion, education, and music," she reminisced. "Every member of the family either played an instrument or sang, and we were all given an opportunity to study. . . . My father said we could have all the education we could take but he would probably not leave us much in his will. He died before I was ready for college and there was never any question of my not going to college, for the whole family pitched in to see that I got a college education."[13]

After her father's death in 1899, Essae and her mother moved to Ari-

Essae Martha Culver in 1903, at age twenty-one. (Special Collections, Honnold/Mudd Library of the Claremont Colleges)

zona. Relatives on the Murphy side of the family already resided there, as did two of the older Culver daughters, who had followed their parents into the teaching profession. Essae resolved to do anything else. She graduated from Phoenix Union High School in 1901 and went on to Pomona College in Claremont, California, where she majored in piano and voice; she was a mezzo soprano. Although she did not consider herself a proficient pianist, "her mother cherished dreams of a concert career for her." The concert stage's loss proved to be the library world's gain, for Essae had decided, while employed as a student assistant in the college library, to make librarianship her career. Her brother Chester offered to pay her expenses to any library school in the country as a graduation gift, "so long," he added, "as you don't fly too high!" After receiving her degree in 1905, Essae worked for two years in the Pomona College library and for two weeks at the Detroit Public Library to see what public library work was like. Her sister Harriett predicted, "Being a librarian may be all right, but you'll never set the world on fire at it." Essae told her, "If I ever accomplish anything, it may very well be due to that remark!"[14]

Professional training for librarians was then in its infancy, and none existed yet in the West. Many prospective librarians from that area, especially those who, like Essae, held college degrees, selected the New York State Library School at Albany (later absorbed by Columbia University), which was noted for its high admission requirements. She enrolled in 1907 and left after a year's training, unaware she lacked one credit in bibliography and thus had not earned certification, a deficiency that came to light in 1931 when she contemplated pursuing an advanced degree.[15]

Graduates left this and other library schools of the day imbued with "library spirit," a sort of missionary zeal, enthusiasm, and esprit de corps that "provided them with a common, noble goal and a sense of cohesion." They shared a belief that libraries held tremendous potential to do good by reducing ignorance, promoting good government, and fostering conscientious citizenship. Such convictions helped them to withstand the disappointments and numerous responsibilities they encountered, as well as the isolation and homesickness that resulted from extremes of weather and long distances, not only from home and family but from everyday companionship.[16]

Upon completing her training, Essae received job offers from the Stanford University Library and the Salem (Oregon) Public Library. Library spirit may have influenced her decision, for, "choosing the challenge of pioneering in public librarianship, she accepted the Salem offer. She found there a small collection of donated books, gathered by the Woman's Club and kept in the City Council Room which served as their only library. The people wanted this converted into a city library, legally established and supported. Hers was the job of getting it done." During her tenure as its head, Culver "oversaw the building of Salem's first free-standing library—a Carnegie library built in 1911 and opened in September 1912. . . . She left the library less than a month after the new building opened and just days before it was considered 'really finished,' according to a newspaper article that referenced delays in completing the electrical work and getting furniture delivered." The library's annual report for 1910 described Culver as having "in every respect been an excellent librarian, caring for the city plant as carefully as if her own."[17]

Culver left Salem in 1912 to return to California, the state she had come to consider her home. There she held various positions at the California State Library and in libraries in Glenn, Butte, and Merced Counties during the next thirteen years. That state was then in the vanguard of county library service, and Culver gained experience that would be indispensable to her future. Under the progressive leadership of state librarian James L. Gillis, in 1909 the California legislature had adopted a comprehensive law that laid the groundwork for library service to all residents. This innovative legislation provided for a state library at the head of a system of county libraries that would provide the bulk of library services, complemented by the continued operation of city libraries. Strengthened in 1911 by additional legislation, the plan placed a central collection in each county, with highly visible local stations conveniently available to all residents and cooperation among all libraries to place books in the hands of every reader.[18]

Describing her experiences in California, in 1925 Culver addressed the League of Library Commissions on the subject of "A County Librarian at Work." California counties, she noted, compared in size more nearly to other states than to cities. Librarians there and in other western states ventured to remote outposts where they might spread "the gospel of books." This conscientious corps traveled on foot, by horseback, pack animal, team, stagecoach, and train. Culver described how "a librarian on horseback, with pack mule and Indian guide, ... [went] over steep trails, through an unfrequented country, taking with her the mental food for the remotest dwellers.[19]

"All pioneering sounds romantic when related," Culver continued, "even though not recognized as such during the experience.... If there is no fundamental difference in the demands in different types of library service, there is a great difference in the methods of extending it, and it is this library pioneering—so called—that differentiates county library service, very largely, from other types of service." For her, "the joy of the work came from the satisfaction of being able to meet the great need of the rural people in a service more extensive and more socialized than a metropolitan public would demand." Culver found pleasure in "the keen appreciation felt and expressed by the rural people. Perhaps it is because never before has such an educational and recreational advantage been extended and nothing is taken for granted." She attributed her accomplishments to the support of a central library agency of the sort that the Carnegie Corporation proposed to demonstrate in Louisiana.[20]

"Such a Splendid Undertaking"

In his position as California state librarian, Milton Ferguson was aware of Culver's work, highlighted by her extensive experience with rural libraries. During approximately the second week of March, he described the Louisiana Project, as it had come to be called, and, to her amazement, asked her to direct it. Culver had misgivings about the undertaking, citing Louisiana's high rate of illiteracy among her concerns, and wrote a letter declining the offer, but Ferguson refused "to accept it as final." He explained, "We do expect to give the state a three year trial and hope by that time to have convinced the people so thoroughly of the need of some type of library work that the service will be carried on at state expense. My thought is that if you should enter into this service you do so with the intention of turning it over to someone else after it was fairly well under way. You would by that time have pioneered the job and would have made converts to the library cause." To counter Culver's concerns about illiteracy, he reported that "many persons in the state of the very highest type of culture" supported the library project enthusiastically.[21]

Upon returning to California, Ferguson conferred with Culver again at his office in Sacramento. During her five-hour stagecoach ride home after the meeting, she thought seriously about the project, weighing its pros and cons. On April 29, she wrote to Wyckoff, "Just yesterday I returned from Sacramento where I talked with Mr. Ferguson about the position of secretary of your commission. As Mr. Ferguson seems not to have changed his mind about wanting me to accept and as he seems to feel that my experience here will enable me to initiate the work along the lines he hopes will be carried out there in Louisiana I have decided to accept your offer. . . . I shall look forward eagerly to my first glimpse of Louisiana and I know I shall greatly enjoy the experience to be gained from such a splendid undertaking."[22]

The annual salary of $3,600—roughly triple the average pay for state government employees at that time—may have been a factor in Culver's affirmative decision, for before filing Wyckoff's letter of offer, she attached to it a slip of paper on which she had calculated her monthly budget: sixty dollars for rent, forty dollars for food, ten dollars for an illegible expense that may be medical, and five dollars each for laundry and hair (Culver habitually visited a hairdresser), for a total of $120—well below her monthly income of $300. Although earning more money than she had in California, she found herself saving less because her expenses were heavier, probably including participation in the support of one of her sisters, who resided in a rest home in Alameda, California. The Culver siblings shared the cost of their sister's care, and the Louisiana salary's boost to Essae's income could augment her contribution.[23]

Despite the anticipated financial advantages, Culver immediately began to have second thoughts, fueled by a letter from Carl Milam, secretary of the American Library Association. "If I get any more letters about this opportunity for making or losing my reputation," she wrote apprehensively, "I think I won't risk either." Apparently, she committed herself to stay just for eighteen months, for about halfway through that period she suggested that it might be time to start looking for her successor. So dubious was she at the outset that she would last even that long, she had taken the precaution of purchasing a round-trip ticket to reassure herself that she could leave, if she found it necessary, at any time.[24]

As executive secretary of the Louisiana Library Commission, Culver was to focus on spreading books throughout Louisiana, a state that, in the 1920s, remained almost "bookless." Filled with "fear and trembling" because of the magnitude of the task before her, but armed with a stalwart "belief in the importance of books being made available and easily accessible to all," she arrived in Baton Rouge on the sweltering night of July 20, 1925. Her introduction to Louisiana did nothing to reassure her. The train discharged its passengers about 10:25 p.m., and she "registered at [the] Hotel Alvis. Conductor on train told me it was the best hotel," she wrote in her journal, "but I thought it was pretty awful. It was terribly hot & one could not sleep without the electric fan on. As it was a nickle [sic] in the slot affair I got up all thru the night each hour, 5¢ per h[ou]r, to keep it going." Surprised by the lack of closet space, she concluded, "Evidently people here don't carry many clothes with them." After several days, she moved to less uncomfortable lodgings at the Hotel Louisian, where "Miss Hill of the Library Commission came to call in evening [of July 24]. She asked me if I was a southerner. Said Mr. Ferguson promised he would send a southern woman—etc., etc."[25] Those et ceteras—often used in Culver's journals to indicate an unpleasant conversation that continued at length—suggest that

The Louisiana Library Commission's first home was on the ground floor of the State Capitol, shown here in 1937. (Photo by Louisiana Works Progress Administration. State Library of Louisiana)

Hill's welcome to her, as a non-southerner, might have been considerably less warm than the weather.

Worse than the uncomfortable accommodations in the local hotels, Culver discovered that the Louisiana Library Commission had made no preparations for her; indeed, no facilities existed to house its headquarters, not even a desk. Finding a suitable location was the first concern, and Hill arranged appointments for Culver to discuss prospective quarters with Superintendent of Education T. H. Harris, Louisiana State University president David French Boyd, and Governor Fuqua. Boyd proposed space in the university's library building, but the consensus was that the State Capitol, specified in the library law of 1920, would be "the logical and most desirable location," partly because the commission's mission included service to state officials and legislators. Also, aside from the convenience it offered, this location made clear that the commission was not an arm of the university, for its primary assistance would be to people outside of academia. No unoccupied space, however, could be found in the building. Culver appealed to Governor Fuqua, and Colonel Boyd, the governor's brother-in-law, exerted further pressure. As a result, the governor asked the bank examiner and the superintendent of buildings to vacate their quarters and turned their offices over to the Library Commission. Although "just one room with a little fireplace," it was advantageously located on the ground floor and had an exterior door. With relief, Culver accepted it.[26]

Culver found "the offices . . . so poorly furnished at the State Capitol you would think the State very poor." She borrowed a desk, chair, and typewriter table, and on August 26 set to work in the commission's headquarters. A delay in the delivery of permanent furniture postponed its official opening until November 1. While waiting, Culver surveyed library conditions throughout Louisiana and assessed the collection, in which she found outdated books—many of them, such as seventy-eight copies of *Cotton Growing in Egypt,* devoid of value for Library Commission purposes. Only rudimentary and incomplete records of the collection's contents existed, and no professional resources or publishers' catalogs facilitated the selection of new books.[27]

The purpose of surveying the state was "to reveal the extent of library development already made; to see at first hand the conditions under which existing libraries were working; to discover the type of organization which would most completely and adequately cover the field; [and] to study the type of people in the rural districts and their interests." What the investigation disclosed would enable Culver "to determine the most pressing needs and to adopt a project of work for the first year." She discovered that, aside from the long-established New Orleans Public Library, just four libraries—in Shreveport, Jennings, Lake Charles, and Alexandria—had been created under the provisions of the library law of 1910. In addition, approximately ten women's clubs sponsored some sort of book collection, but these were not organized in accordance with the library law and most required users to pay a small membership fee. "Everywhere," Culver noted, "the people seemed eager for the advantages of library service."[28]

Among the rural population were intermingled the descendants of French, Acadian (Cajun), and Spanish colonial settlers, as well as Americans of Anglo-Saxon descent. A substantial percentage of the citizenry was black.

Some Louisianians were highly educated, but others were illiterate. "While, in certain sections, Louisiana could rightfully claim an unusual degree of culture, unfortunately, as one writer expressed it, she stood in the basement in regard to illiteracy. Libraries, except for the private libraries of the plantation home and the limited libraries of the public school, were entirely outside the experience of the two-thirds of the population which was rural."[29]

To exacerbate Culver's tribulations, hiring additional staff proved difficult, for few professionally trained librarians resided in Louisiana. She had begun immediately to search for a staff assistant, preferably one qualified to succeed her eventually as executive secretary. At some point before 1924, Lucy B. Foote, a cataloger at LSU, had been brought to the commission's attention as a "prospective State Librarian," although at the time the position was executive secretary. Foote later became a nationally recognized authority on cataloging and especially on state documents, but in 1925 she had relatively little library experience, none of which involved spreading libraries into rural areas. Virginia Fairfax of New Orleans also was mentioned as a possible assistant to Culver, but family concerns prevented her from considering the opportunity.[30]

Lois Henderson of Shreveport turned down the position, and with no other eligible candidates nearby, the search moved farther afield. In October, Culver updated Milton Ferguson, "I have written to all the persons recommended by the A.L.A. and the Atlanta Library School that sounded at all possible for this work . . . and for one reason and another none of them can consider leaving their posts at this time although several would have if they had not been under contract or obligation. . . . I confess I do not know what else to do unless try out some of the people whose recommendations do not suggest they are quite fitted for this work and it might be an awful waste of our time trying them out." Katherine Hill sympathetically acknowledged to Culver "that with all the vexations, disappointments and delays in getting the work started combined with the extreme heat, you have been having the meanest kind of time."[31]

Fortuitously, a chance encounter between G. P. Wyckoff and the brother-in-law of Mary Walton Harris of the Fresno (California) County Library gave rise to the prospect of employing Harris. She possessed the necessary qualifications and was interested in the Louisiana work; indeed, had Culver declined the position of secretary, Ferguson would have "turned to her as the next best possibility." Culver immediately offered Harris the opportunity, adding, "We haven't much to work with as yet but there is something fascinating in the beginning of any undertaking and I really feel enthusiastic about the work down here in spite of a great many delays and disappointments and an unusually hot summer." On October 24, Culver happily informed the commission that Harris had applied for the job and recommended appointing her immediately. The new assistant secretary arrived from California on December 7, and Culver, who had "never felt more swamped in [her] life," greeted Harris with "a great relief." At last she welcomed not only capable help but also the warmth of a congenial friend in Baton Rouge.[32]

The unavailability of Library Commission members had consistently presented a problem. As soon as she arrived, Culver began trying to gather them together for a meeting, but not until October could more than three assemble at any one time. Reed and Hill continued to be mainstays, but Hill vacationed out of the country for months on end. Eleanor McMain, weary and busy with Kingsley House, rarely found it possible to get away. Ferguson noted, "She is a fine type of woman but I could see was not overly strong and had been hard driven in her own fine work. It is often a questionable expedient to appoint even such a splendid person when service on a board . . . amounts to a burden," as it clearly did for McMain. White concerned himself only with commission activities that impacted his own parish and interests. Although he spent two days at the Capitol on other business and passed the Library Commission doors several times, he ignored the opportunity to visit, to meet Culver, or to acquaint himself with current commission activities. Wyckoff, on the other hand, "[had] been great about trying to arrange his time to suit every one else," but his health interfered in November when he was stricken with a heart attack. "It is clearly up to me," Culver realized, "to get this Board interested enuf to *want* to come to meetings."[33]

Laying the Foundation

On October 26, the Library Commission met formally for the first time since Culver's arrival. The group convened, with Milton Ferguson present, at Tulane University in New Orleans to facilitate McMain's attendance.

"All [of the members] came but Mr. White, in spite of very heavy rain," Culver noted. "Miss Hill & Mrs. Reed rode down [from Baton Rouge about ninety miles away] & it took them five hours." Prior to the meeting, Ferguson reviewed with Culver the recommendations she proposed to present. The board adopted all six of her suggestions, and she hastened to begin implementing them. First and most significant was "that the Commission members and the Executive Secretary give publicity and encouragement to the organization of parish libraries throughout the State, since the parish seems the logical unit for organization in Louisiana, as the county is in other states." This accorded with the recommendation of the American Library Association, which had concluded two years earlier that "the county library system is the solution of the library problem for country districts." Culver further recommended "that as much supervision be given after organization as possible by the Executive Secretary in order to help make them successful. This supervision is especially important since there are no trained workers available to administer them, and upon the success of the first organized library depends, to a large extent, the future development in the state."[34]

Early announcements of the Carnegie grant anticipated structuring a model system of traveling libraries, but Culver had observed that "the traveling library at best gives a superficial service and cannot meet the needs of any community." Her experience in California had proven that demonstrations of library service yielded more permanent and more satisfactory results. She later explained that "the Parish was chosen as the unit for organizing, because it was the governmental units [sic] which could provide support for permanent library development, and also because other services, notably public schools, were organized with the parish as a unit. It would have been impossible I believe at that time for a new and practically unknown institution to contravene tradition and organize regions crossing governmental lines. It was suggested and carefully considered that the state as a whole be adopted as the unit and regional branches established, but the State at that time had made no appropriation to the Library Commission and funds were too limited to experiment." Although Culver probably was unaware of it, in 1805 the Legislature of the Territory of Orleans enacted a law that, had it been implemented, would have established libraries containing English- and French-language books in every parish, foreshadowing her designation of the parish as the unit for library development in Louisiana by 120 years.[35]

The second of Culver's six recommendations reserved large loans for the parish libraries that the commission set up, therefore limiting placement of books to the libraries initiated by the Louisiana Library Commission, because just a few existing institutions conformed to the library law. This second recommendation further provided that "an informational service be given to individuals living in districts without library facilities of any kind," suggested various ways in which the commission could support clubs and adult education programs, and offered to advise other libraries and help with administrative problems.[36]

Culver's third recommendation widely offered various other services to libraries, clubs, and individuals. Residents of parishes where the commission had not yet started a library could write directly to headquarters and receive books in the mail. Taken together, these first three provisions made some form of service available to every person in the state. Not only did they potentially make each citizen a reader; they also encouraged each reader to become a library supporter.[37]

From the inception of the service on November 1, 1925, through June 30, 1926, Library Commission personnel received three hundred requests for books or information. These queries covered a great variety of subjects, most of which reflected interest in Louisiana history and in practical needs such as child care, how to write business letters, and cookery recipes. The most pressing need appeared to be books as an aid to business. Years later, Culver still remembered "the very first request that we received. It was from a small boy on the western border of the state who wrote, 'I read in the paper where you have books free for nothing. Please send some quick.'" Next, a woman in St. Mary Parish asked for a book on prenatal care and another about stocks and bonds, while the third appeal came from an incarcerated young man who put his extensive leisure time to good use. Over the years, he borrowed many books and began to write, eventually having a story published. After his release from the penitentiary, he visited the Library Commission to express his appreciation.[38]

Culver required legal assistance to accomplish recommendation number four, "that an adequate library law be formulated for presentation at the next session of the state legislature." She turned to James O. Modisette, an attorney and a trustee of the Jennings Public Library. While traveling in California during the summer of 1925, Modisette learned that the Louisiana Library Commission had recently engaged a librarian from that state to develop library service in Louisiana. When he returned home, he wrote to Culver, saying he was ashamed that he had not known before about the Library Commission and that he wanted to help in any way he could to back the library movement. Culver, "a total stranger to the South, to Louisiana, her people, laws, and institutions, and . . . at a loss where to begin," welcomed Modisette's help. She immediately recruited him to rewrite the current library laws, which had failed to provide for financial support. On June 1, 1926, Culver summarized the need for the act and Modisette described its content at a hearing of the Education Committee, which "voted out favorably & unanimously." With Culver's enthusiastic support, the proposed law passed on June 26. In addition, the Legislature appropriated $5,000 for the commission's work during the next biennium.[39]

For the first time, Louisiana had a legal framework for levying taxes to construct and maintain a parish library. The new law also compelled the governing authorities of a parish or municipality, when requested by 25 percent of the payers of property tax, to launch a public library and to appoint a managerial board; and formed a Board of Library Examiners to certify public librarians' credentials. Additionally, Act 36 sanctioned the merger of existing libraries into parish libraries; authorized joint public libraries shared by two or more towns and/or parishes; and permitted libraries to serve towns or parishes having none. These provisions would be fundamental to the system of parish libraries that Culver aspired to build. When it was all over, Culver declared, "I have learned more about legislation and politics than I ever expected to know" and concluded that she would never make a good politician. Ferguson commended her, "Nothing could be a finer badge of honor and a greater recognition of your success in Louisiana" than these accomplishments.[40]

Culver's fifth recommendation, "that the resources of the commission be placed at the service of all state officials and the state legislature . . . at all times," resulted in the creation of the Legislative Reference Service, which she regarded as one of the commission's most important functions. With no library located near the Capitol, Culver recognized that legislators needed access to reference resources, and she initiated an informational service in time for the 1926 session of the Legislature. This convenience, introduced at the state level in Wisconsin by Charles R. McCarthy in 1901, constituted a new approach to legislative reference, actively and aggressively extending services to legislators to facilitate their efforts to draft solid laws. The idea, which stemmed from the new concept of information-based libraries rather than storehouses for books, swiftly spread to other states. In Louisiana, it benefited the library cause as well as the legislators, for it made them cognizant of the seven-month-old commission's existence. It also demonstrated yet another type of library service to an influential constituency: the one that voted on state appropriations. During the session, library personnel put forth particular effort "to obtain material on the subject-matter of the bills introduced and to bring this service to the attention of the proponents of the measures, so at the end of the session there were few members who had not learned of the help to be had from the library." Sixth, Culver recommended "that the commission give all possible cooperation and encouragement to the establishment of a training course for librarians in the state," for none existed as yet in Louisiana.[41]

At the midpoint in the three-year grant period, Culver summed up progress made to date. "The demands upon the Commission library for information grew daily," she reported, "as did the interest in parish libraries, but no new libraries were established," although several were in prospect. In 1928, as its work continued, the Library Commission defined its aims and purposes as follows: "the development of library service, the establishment and organization of new libraries and the improving of those already established, the encouraging of the library movement and the advancement of library science, the securing to the people of Louisiana library service through public libraries, maintained from the public treasury and supervised by trained and experienced librarians, and to further the cause of education and cultural development among the people, and particularly the rural populations through the establishment of libraries and library service." Making a good start was of utmost importance, for in the earliest parish libraries would be laid "the foundations for a permanent organization throughout the state."[42]

CHAPTER 2

Raising Funds for Parish Libraries, 1926

E xpressions of interest in the library plan came from all over Louisiana, including serious inquiries from twenty of the sixty-three eligible parishes. Encouraged by this enthusiasm, in September 1925
Essae Culver conferred with Mary Mims as to which parish might be the
best site for Louisiana's first rural library. As rural organizer for the State
Extension Department, established in 1914 to help people help themselves
in forests, wetlands, fields, and home activities, Mims's unparalleled familiarity with virtually every corner of every parish uniquely qualified her
to advise Culver. Mims, fondly known as "our Miss Mary" to thousands of
Louisianians, quickly became a fervent supporter of the library movement.
As a native of Louisiana and a longtime teacher in a country school, she
responded to the problems of the small community from the personal experience of an insider. Through her extension activities, she knew that the
people were eager for library service. At the time, she was working actively
in Washington Parish and thus arranged an invitation for Culver to speak
there. The librarian addressed an audience of twenty-five at a women's club
in Franklinton and then traveled to Bogalusa, a lumber town with a population of 18,000, where she visited the town library. Its collection of 3,800
volumes had an average circulation of 756 books per day.[1]

Culver, like Mims, saw considerable potential in Washington Parish
and spent the week of November 30 there to energize supporters. Upon returning to Baton Rouge, she described her experiences in a letter to Milton
Ferguson. "The organizing trip was exceedingly interesting," Culver wrote.
"When I arrived in Franklinton at noon on Monday I found they had sched-

uled me for at least two talks a day and sometimes three at different centers around the county and over the worst roads without exception I have ever seen. At three of the Centers none of the adults appeared and I was told it was customary for the High School students to take all information home to their parents who seldom came out to meetings of any kind. I therefor[e] explained as best I could to the H.S. students and found the school principals, without exception, enthusiastic over the very prospect. There were seven H.S. centers in the parish without library service and a very limited collection of books in the school library and there were 600 pupils in one of these H.S. alone so you can judge what the demand would be. [In response to Culver's evangelistic presentations,] these H.S. students, in several localities circulated a petition to send to their representative on the Police Jury."[2]

One of the idiosyncrasies of Louisiana government with which Culver had to familiarize herself was the police jury, which administers the general government of the parish in the manner of the county board of commissioners or supervisors in other states. It evolved from the establishment of parish government in 1807, when "administrative functions were vested in a body comprised of the parish judge, the justices of the peace, and a jury of twelve inhabitants appointed by [the judge]"; thus the origin of its name. Today, twenty-six of Louisiana's sixty-four parishes operate under home rule charters, but in the other thirty-eight, elected officials such as the sheriff share authority with the police jury.[3]

This system, which was more widespread in Culver's day, vests both legislative and administrative functions in the same group. Comprised of three to fifteen elected representatives, the number varying usually according to population, the jury "performs the legislative functions of enacting ordinances, establishing programs, and setting policy. It also is an administrative body in that it is involved in preparing the budget, hiring and firing personnel, spending funds, negotiating contracts, and in general, directing the activities under its supervision. Police juries centralize administrative responsibilities to some extent in various ways, but generally have no provisions for a strong executive officer." Among their more obscure functions, these bodies appointed boards of health; oversaw the care of prisoners, paupers, and delinquent children; exercised authority over charity hospitals; and funded libraries. Culver would work with them as she strove to establish libraries in the parishes they administered.[4]

As was often the case, the absence of financial support presented an obstacle. "Every time ... money was suggested in connection with [the library in Washington Parish]," Culver continued,

> the people shook their heads and said "it couldn't be done," with the exception of the Parish Superintendent. He simply said it was not the time to present it to the P.J. [police jury] because they had a delegation from all over the Parish that day swearing about the roads (And I didn't blame them) and the Banks had requested they pay up their loan and the Jury were turning down every proposition that called for money that day. The Parish Superintendent said that this is the first extensive road program they have had and just as soon as they realize they are going to have it with them for years to come and cannot let everything else wait until it is finished they would not be so hard to win over. He told them he had insisted that I explain to them what was possible for them to do under the law and what help the [Library] Commission would give just as soon as they felt they could support it and I must say they listened and seemed interested and since they did not vote it down there may be more prospect of their taking it under consideration at some other time.... There was so much of encouragement in the effort I cannot feel it was a failure and it has just made me realize it is going to take time[,] more time than I thought, to bring about the organization [in] other places.[5]

In her first years in Louisiana, Culver traversed the state, addressing meetings of community groups, parent-teacher organizations, service clubs, women's clubs, and agencies of local government to stimulate interest in demonstration libraries. After her presentations, she often reported favorable results. "People seemed enthusiastic," she noted after speaking to the Minden PTA on April 1, 1926. The following week she was so well received in Franklin that she was invited to return for a series of meetings, but later that year she was "supposed to speak at [the] P.T.A. [meeting in Elton, but] ... no one came out." Similarly, after an address about children's reading to the North Highland PTA, she "came home discouraged[;] little response indicated little interest. Several teachers got up and left before I got thru. May have indicated poor speech but likewise poor manners." Four decades later, she recalled that "I spent many more nights in hotels [during] my first years [in Louisiana] than I did in my own apartment." Colleagues marveled at her "amazing physical stamina," but occasionally, after grueling excursions like the one that took her to New Orleans, Franklin, and Lafayette during three days in April 1926, Culver conceded that she was "most weary."[6]

It was not, however, the physical rigors of her campaign for libraries or the occasional display of apathy that engendered the greatest weariness. Rather, it was overcoming antagonism toward minorities—groups defined variously as French speakers, black people, and strangers, especially those from outside the South. During a speech in Lafayette in early 1926, Culver complimented the state's inroads against illiteracy, attributing what remained to the French-speaking Cajuns and the black population in parishes where tax support was inadequate to fund the segregated dual school system. Following the talk, she was reprimanded for using the then pejorative term "Cajun" and for her analysis of the cause of illiteracy. Assailing her as an "outsider" who "did not understand," Henry Gill, head of the New Orleans Public Library, claimed that "Negroes were not capable of education and did not want it." He defended collecting scholarly materials but opposed the extension service that Culver advocated. After that session, she "returned home more weary than I have ever been & turned in at 6 p.m." Several weeks later, she "had much joy . . . in going over Acadia Parish which is . . . in the heart of the Acadian country and in hearing the word 'cajun' used over and over again by those people themselves both the educated ones and those who were not."[7]

In Louisiana, the newcomer found an insular citizenry that did not readily embrace outsiders such as a librarian from California. Lonely in the beginning, for she knew no one in Baton Rouge when she arrived, Culver spent her first Thanksgiving Day in Louisiana working at Library Commission headquarters. Her earliest friends included Mary Mims and other library advocates; Lois Shortess, the first professionally trained librarian in Louisiana and later the state supervisor of school libraries; and J. O. Modisette, the Jennings attorney who helped to draft the 1926 library law. As her staff increased, Culver also found companionship with some of her co-workers, notably Debora Abramson, who joined the commission in 1930 and became a dear friend. During the first PTA meeting that Culver attended, she recalled, "they asked all the Yankees to stand up. I inquired, 'How long do you have to be in the South before you're considered a Southerner?' The answer was ten years."[8]

It didn't take Culver that long to win acceptance, for she had a "capacity for sensing the local situation . . . [and utilizing] the proud traditions and spirit of the South . . . as a constructive force for library development." Confirmation that Louisiana had embraced her and her work came after just two years, when a newspaper headlined its report on her participation in the League of Library Commissions annual meeting, "Louisiana girl on the way north to make a speech." Lura Currier, director of the Mississippi Library Commission and formerly Culver's colleague in Louisiana, described in 1962 how the outsider had achieved acceptance: "Taking on the protective coloration of moonlight and magnolias, Miss Culver set about to become a Southerner. And that she did. Not a do-good 'professional Southerner' but a real one—understanding, sympathetic, loved and loving. No born-to-the-plantation Southern lady ever wore white gloves more becomingly, entertained visitors more graciously, brewed stronger coffee or produced more exciting café brulot, moved with more apparent leisure, paid feminine tribute to masculine superiority more strategically, smiled more advantageously, operated with less friction, or got her way more consistently than this 'do it yourself' Southerner." Culver countered, "They say that to be a native, one must either have been born, or re-born in a state. Well, I was re-born in Louisiana."[9]

Setting the Pace for the Rest of the State

Early in the new year of 1926, Culver visited the northern part of the state, and there, as purposeful momentum toward establishing the first parish library began, so did her rebirth. She attended a meeting of the Monroe Library Board in Ouachita Parish, which she pronounced "very unsatisfactory" because she found that the members of the board seemed to regard the "library [as] their plaything." But in Rayville, twenty-two miles away in Richland Parish, some seventy-five citizens, including a judge, a police juror, and representatives of every community in the parish, turned out for a meeting at the schoolhouse and left galvanized to spread word of the library plan among their neighbors. It was "just a splendid meeting," Culver commented happily. "Response wonderful." She estimated that running the library during its first year would cost at least $1,400 and supposed that funding would again be "a stumbling block." Culver informed Milton

Ferguson, "I have just returned from the northern part of the state and the prospects are very good that three Parishes will be established before the end of our fiscal year. People seem enthusiastic everywhere, but there is not so large a demand from Libraries, clubs, and individuals for books from our collection as I anticipated. We realize more every day how new an idea real library service is to the south."[10]

The northeastern Louisiana parish of Richland, with a population in 1920 of 20,860 and an assessed valuation of $11,347,340, enjoyed a comparatively low rate of illiteracy. Concomitantly, it was among the first to seek information about the Library Commission's plan. Cotton was the principal product, and Rayville, the parish seat, boasted but one paved street. A group of Richland women already had organized into a library association and, to the extent that its limited resources permitted, served readers from rooms in the high-school building. When the police jury met on March 2, 1926, a large delegation representing all parts of the parish was on hand to learn more about Culver's plan and, inspired by her vision, voiced support for a library. The police jury had already adopted its budget for the year and could provide little help, but the Richland Library Association contributed the money in its treasury. Funds from both sources amounted to $1,400, not enough to pay a trained librarian. Rayville resident Lillian Morris volunteered to fill the position at a very small salary and to enroll in the summer library course at Louisiana State University, and the school board offered rent-free housing. That afternoon the police jury unanimously passed a resolution establishing and funding a parish library in accordance with the library law of 1910. Well positioned "to set the pace for the rest of the state," Richland Parish would host the north Louisiana demonstration of library service. Richland citizens were "just pleased to pieces" that the Louisiana Library Commission selected their parish and moved ahead "by leaps and bounds."[11]

With the library in Rayville serving residents of the country as well as the town, "the machinery [was] already set up." The Richland Parish Library Board accepted the commission's help in strengthening branch services by lending a large collection of additional books and by publicizing the library throughout the parish and the state. In return, the commission cited this parish as an example of the "demonstration plan" it proposed to implement statewide. The library was officially established in May, but active operation was delayed until September while the librarian obtained train-

The branch library at Snake Ridge was one of two branches of the Richland Parish Library, in addition to the headquarters at Rayville, 1928. (State Library of Louisiana)

ing. Distribution centers—ten by September, and six more anticipated by June 1927—had already circulated more than 1,600 books to 700 borrowers. When Culver visited in December 1926, she noted, "The library in Richland has come before even the streets are paved and I waded in mud such as I never expected to see again when I was there. . . . It [is] quite remarkable that these people have done as well as that under the circumstances. Some of them told me with tears in their eyes how much the library meant to them."[12]

Library users universally praised the parish library. A police juror considered it "one of the best investments made by the taxpayers of Richland Parish." Never had he heard criticism of the library expenditure. The parish superintendent pointed out, "Schools educate the young, but they make no provision for the mental growth of adults, while a library provides means of lifelong education. . . . The library has a distinct function during vacation periods when boys and girls have idle time which might be devoted profitably to reading." Clubwomen fervently testified to the ease of obtaining materials and the difference it had made to them. "The general sentiment [seemed] to be that of a small boy who brought a friend to headquarters and was heard to remark: 'You just ought to join for it learns you a lot.'" Richland's enthusiasm spread throughout the northern part of the state and contributed directly to the emergence of centers of interest in three other parishes.[13]

Louisiana's First Parish Librarian

When Essae Culver arrived in Rayville, members of the extended Ellis family were among the first library supporters to greet her and to welcome her to their homes. Among them, she met Innes Morris Ellis, wife of district attorney (later judge) Carey J. Ellis. Mrs. Ellis had been administering a small collection of books kept at the schoolhouse, and Culver would later eulogize her as the "guiding spirit" of the Richland Parish Library. Innes Ellis's mother, Lillian Morris, became the first manager of the first parish library headquarters, setting a precedent of intelligence, dedication, and perseverance for the generations of librarians who would administer the Pelican State's sixty-three rural parish libraries. Lillian Morris's path to the library was an uncommon one that took her to Rayville from her native Brunswick, Georgia, by way of high echelons of New Orleans society.[14]

Born Mary Lillian Littlefield in 1864, at the age of twenty-one Lilly married Pendleton Stewart Morris (1858–1918), a native of Frankfort, Kentucky, who had entered the oil business in 1882 and moved to Brunswick two years later. They became the parents of three sons and their only daughter, Innes (1889–1936). Pendleton's employment with the Standard Oil Company necessitated that the family frequently move with him until 1908, when he accepted a position as special agent (later vice president) of the Standard Oil Company of Louisiana and settled permanently in New Orleans.[15]

In the Crescent City, Pendleton Morris soon established himself as a captain in the Louisiana National Guard and as a member of the Pickwick Club and several carnival organizations. At his death, he held the presidency of the Association of Commerce, in addition to his position with Standard Oil. Lillian, meanwhile, occupied herself with travel, active membership in the Daughters of the American Revolution, volunteering with the American Red Cross, a great deal of bridge playing, and attending luncheons and parties, especially during the 1911–12 social season when Innes, a Newcomb College student, made her debut.[16]

Shortly before her father's death, Innes married Carey J. Ellis (1888–1964), son of a prominent North Louisiana family. They resided in Rayville, where Carey practiced law and held the office of district attorney from 1916 to 1930, when he became judge of the Fifth Judicial District. Lillian Morris followed her daughter from the dance floors and bridge tables of New Orleans social clubs to rural Richland Parish soon after Pendleton died, but sporadic listings in New Orleans city directories indicate that she maintained a fashionable residence in the city as well. One of the Morris sons, Edgar, made his home in Monroe and worked as president of the Rayville Motor Company. Lillian's grief for his unexpected death in 1926 at the age of thirty-one may have motivated her to pursue the diversion of working in the library. She served as library manager at a salary the frugal Library Commission could afford and enrolled at Louisiana State University to earn the credentials that qualified her to hold the position. Her background suggests that she enjoyed both the financial security that permitted her to work for low compensation and the academic background needed to master the course work at LSU.[17]

Culver made several visits to Richland to help with technical duties at headquarters and to strengthen the work of the sixteen branches. After a tour in March 1927 to stir up even more interest in libraries, she wrote to Milton Ferguson, "I have just returned from Richland Parish where the demand for books is so great I had to get out or be mobbed. I visited all sections and in one small rural school we faced 100 of the healthiest looking children you can imagine and asked them about their library. They laughed and pointed to their book shelves where only a piece of a dictionary lay on the shelf. Really pathetic and you wonder how they can boast of their school system when that condition seems to be so general. Every child in the room wanted something to read. The teacher said she has been bringing the Western Story magazine for them since they had nothing at all and this for the first six grades—imagine. Mrs. Morris has circulated 11,000 books in less than six months and hasn't touched the surface yet. She has only about three thousand in her whole library. How is that for turnover."[18]

Flood!

Help with inculcating the reading habit in Richland Parish came from an unexpected and perverse source: the Great Mississippi River Flood, described by U.S. Secretary of Commerce Herbert Hoover as "the greatest peace-time calamity in the history of the country." In Cairo, Illinois, the river reached flood stage on January 1, 1927, and six weeks later at Baton Rouge. It remained at flood stage for a record 153 days. Not until July 14 did the flood waters subside at Baton Rouge, and the situation in other parts of Louisiana was worse. In May, Culver wrote to Ferguson of Louisiana's perilous situation and conditions in Baton Rouge: "I returned yesterday from the north and you just cannot imagine what a feeling of inadequacy comes over one to see water everywhere and only roofs of houses visible. The train 10 hours late crawled through four feet of water for about four miles near Alexandria and motor boats rode along side to rescue passengers I guess in case the train stuck anywhere. Refugees are pouring into Camp Beauregard at Alexandria by the hundreds. Delhi in Richland Parish has as many refugees as residents and only one dry ridge through the town. It's coming home fast. We do not know how much longer train service will continue but the telegraph is always available so you will know that no news is good news."[19]

In the same letter, Culver related apprehensively, "Our first parish library is probably under water by this time as the morning paper says another levee or two broke and inundated Rayville and the library was on the first floor of a house. Mrs. Morris purchased boots, moved the books to higher shelves and prepared to stand by but she is not young and should for health reasons get away." Later, Lillian Morris reported that "she was really having the time of her life, traveling around in a boat, being rescued by the Red Cross when with two friends she went for some milk and couldn't get back because of the current." Culver witnessed two persons, one of whom was a child, drowned needlessly in the Mississippi River. "They were on a pleasure ride and the boat upset in the current," she explained, "and only four out of the six managed to climb onto the bottom of the boat until rescued. The cries of the mother whose little son was drowned rang in our ears all night. Tragedy seems in the air these days."[20]

The inundation submerged ten thousand square miles of twenty Louisiana parishes. Despite the rising flood and no contact with the outside world

Flooded street in Rayville (Richland Parish) during the Mississippi River flood of 1927. A boat being paddled through the water can be seen at left center. (University of Louisiana at Monroe)

for days, sixty-three-year-old Lillian Morris waded through high water and paddled a boat through higher water to reach the library. It was one of two buildings—the other was the drug store—that remained open. "All of the books removed from the lower shelves in anticipation of still higher water filled all the chairs and tables, so that service was given under the greatest handicaps, and no invitation to linger could be extended, for four persons filled the remaining free space." Crowded conditions and floodwaters notwithstanding, patrons made their way to the library as best they could. Morris recounted that "everyone expressed their appreciation at being able to borrow under the circumstances, especially the mothers who said it kept the children out of the water."[21]

At the height of the flood, visiting the library meant traveling by boat. "As the waters came up to the floor of the porch, the steps were removed in order that the boats could more easily unload their passengers, and each boat took away books to supply not only all the members of the family, but usually the neighbors as well. Sixty books per day in a community of 1,499 population would be a fair circulation under the best of conditions, but under the difficult traveling conditions it is a record that is eloquent." A farmer credited the flood with interesting his neighbors in books. "With everything a lake outside," he said, "people just naturally took to reading. Mrs. Morris had the library open, and I've seen boys carrying books away in flour sacks." Often, four or five readers perused a book before returning it.[22]

Lillian Morris ran the Rayville library until 1930. Her daughter, Innes Ellis, died in 1936. Essae Culver recalled, "Mrs. Ellis wanted no credit or thanks for her efforts [on behalf of the library] . . . and said, 'My family and I will profit by such an institution and this institution is one established by representatives of the people for service to the whole parish and no one or two individuals should be given credit for it.' However, . . . it was . . . [largely] the enthusiasm and unceasing works of Mrs. Ellis that resulted in the establishment of the library." How long Morris remained in Rayville after her daughter's death is uncertain. By the time of her own demise in 1947, she had returned to New Orleans. Her obituary made no mention of her double life as New Orleans matron and Rayville librarian.[23]

One in the North, One in the South

Increasingly Culver recognized that the high demand for libraries, as exemplified in Richland, transcended flooding and poverty. But when the waters receded, the problem of inadequate funding remained—"an obstacle hard to overcome. Apparently," she concluded, "no parish had sufficient funds to adequately finance a library. The explanation was to be found in the state's antiquated tax system. A member of the Louisiana Tax Commission at that time said: 'The general property tax system as actually administered in Louisiana today is beyond all doubts the worst tax system known in all civilized nations under the sun.' Almost every parish in the state had already reached the constitutional limits in property taxation without having sufficient funds for already existing governmental and educational agencies, and no reasonable person could expect the police juries to appropriate an adequate fund from an already exhausted general fund or to reallocate funds to a library when they had never experienced the benefits."[24] Field work in St. Mary Parish would yield an advanced education in the peculiarities of taxation in Louisiana.

With a parish library flourishing in the northern part of the state, Culver turned her attention to south Louisiana. Along with Jefferson Davis Parish in the southwestern rice-growing region, St. Mary in the south-central part of the state was prominent among the parishes considered seriously to host a library demonstration in south Louisiana. When Culver had previously visited St. Mary on an organizing trip back in May 1926, it had a population of 34,458 and an assessed valuation of $19,800. Delegations from all over the parish attended a meeting of the police jury, bringing petitions bearing signatures of 250 library supporters, ten times the number required by law. The police jurors voted unanimously to establish a parish library if financing could be arranged, and they appointed a committee, chaired by John Caffery of Franklin, to find ways and means. Efforts got under way in July with a series of meetings in various towns, and citizens pledged two-thirds of the needed funding. The police jury then authorized Caffery's committee to request the commission's assistance in organizing a library just as soon as the total was pledged, without waiting for another jury meeting.[25]

While in St. Mary Parish, Culver discovered that Louisiana's incorporated towns did not pay into the parish's general fund. If funding for the library came from that source, none of the expense would be shared by the largest places. "This has not been brought to light in any other parish," Culver wrote to Ferguson, "and the people down there were as surprised as I was that they paid no County tax for general purposes—only for roads and Court House and health work, they told me. If this is the case generally we will have to make some provision in the law otherwise the organizing work is going to be very difficult if every incorporated town in the Parish has to be worked upon the same as the Police Jury and brought into a Parish system and the maintenance pro-rated. Perhaps when I organize a few more libraries I will discover more things about the law that I little dream of now."[26] Fortunately, this tax muddle did not manifest itself in other parishes.

"The Word Taxes Makes Them Shudder and Grow Faint"

Suggestions for raising the remainder of the funding confounded Culver. Of St. Mary, she wrote to Ferguson,

> I think the attitude there rather typical in the State and I am sure you could never find anywhere in the West a group of people of like training and wealth working so hard and diligently to raise $2,000.

The chairman of the Committee is a surgeon, highly trained and a charming gentleman, another member is son of an ex-governor and owns a large part of the Parish and the Police Jury member is a big sugar planter. These people seem to have everything in the world but ready money and the only way they could at first think of financing this, which they all agreed they should have, was by getting up a big entertainment. I convinced the Doctor that the plan was not favored by the [Library] Commission and he saw the light immediately and turned the whole movement in the right direction but you have no idea how hard it is down here to get a city of 6,000 people ... to appropriate $600 for a library. These people all ride around in the highest priced cars but the word taxes makes them shudder and grow faint.[27]

The same attitude prevailed in Claiborne Parish, where "new school buildings were every where in the Parish, two or three magnificent churches in every community, high priced cars and new homes on every hand and diamonds galore." Money for a library existed, Culver believed, if the citizens chose to spend it. As Ferguson pointed out, "The people down there have not been accustomed to buying library service but you are in the way of educating them on that subject. Some of these days they may be just as willing to spend a little of their money for books as they are now anxious to spend a lot of it for automobiles and nice houses. The main thing is that you are making progress." Before financial support for the library could be finalized in St. Mary, the sugar crop failed and a tornado tore across the landscape, halting library advancement. The parish remained on the list of prospects, and Culver continued to believe optimistically that "the final arrangements ... at any time may be carried through."[28]

While St. Mary Parish delayed, Jefferson Davis Parish had forged ahead. Talk of organizing the parish had begun in January 1926, probably fueled by J. O. Modisette. With his influence, on September 2, the police jury of Jefferson Davis Parish voted unanimously in favor of establishing a parish library. Two months later, voters considered a proposition to levy a one-mill, parish-wide tax annually for a ten-year period to support the library. "Never in the history of the South," enthused the Jennings *Semi-Weekly News,* "was such a forward-looking step taken by a parish board as was taken ... by the police jury of this parish in creating a parish library" and submitting the

A librarian helps children at the Elton branch of the Jefferson Davis Parish Library Demonstration, 1927. The library occupied the former waiting room of a doctor's office. (State Library of Louisiana)

matter of its support to the people. The Jennings Public Library was among the five public libraries operating under the provisions of the library law of 1910, and the plan was to consolidate it with the proposed parish-wide library, using the existing building.[29]

Culver spent much of the week preceding the election in Jefferson Davis, and she and Modisette covered most of the parish in an effort to spark support. To their dismay, they found a decidedly mixed reaction. In Lake Arthur, religious factions were quarreling and somehow "the library had gotten all mixed up in it in such a way that neither side were going to vote for the tax. . . . Many of the old 'Cajun' farmers didn't seem to know a thing about it and were agin anything that increased the taxes except . . . one who said he'd left school in the first grade (assessment $50,000) seemed favorable when Mr. M got through talking with him but we could not swear that he would vote for it." Assessments were important because of the requirement—unique to Louisiana—"that any measure involving property taxation must carry both in numbers voting and in as-sessed valuation."[30]

Even with these crusading efforts and the effusive support of the local press, the measure failed by a margin of 108 votes and a valuation of approx-imately $580,000. All except one of the communities voted affirmatively, but the proposal won little support in rural areas. When news of the failure reached the Library Commission, Culver wrote to Modisette, "Miss Harris said this morning 'it is just like a funeral around here' and I think we all felt sorry—not just because our hopes were defeated but sorry all your effort for the good cause was not rewarded. I certainly do not think the effort wasted for a good many more people know about library service than did before the campaign started."[31]

Modisette attributed the defeat to several factors. One was that library supporters neither mounted a campaign on behalf of the tax nor contra-dicted the wild stories spread by opponents, such as the notion of support for the library being unchristian and that, because both the number of peo-ple reading and the divorce rate were increasing, a cause-and-effect rela-tionship existed between them. Some voters misunderstood the size of the millage and believed the tax to be double its actual amount. Such confusion was particularly a problem in Jennings, where many voters thought they would continue to pay taxes on the municipal library as well as on the pro-posed parish library. In some communities, local controversies and preju-dices overshadowed all other considerations. Depressed prices for cotton and rice contributed to the defeat, as well.[32]

Convinced that rural citizens voted down the tax because they failed to understand what a library meant, Culver recommended that the Louisiana Library Commission establish a demonstration library in Jefferson Davis for six months, under the administration of a trained librarian. This, she felt sure, would convince everyone in the parish of a library's value. With success seemingly within reach, the commission concurred with her plan, and Ferguson thought it both "interesting and feasible." If it succeeded, demonstrations might be tried in other parishes, as well.[33] The original plan had required the parish to pledge funding before the library demonstration opened, as Richland Parish had done. Culver's innovative revision of that requirement contributed instrumentally to the eventual success of library demonstrations in Louisiana.

Headquartered at the Jennings Public Library, the Jefferson Davis Parish Demonstration Library opened on February 1, 1927. It established distribution points in eleven small towns, each housed in a convenient location such as the post office, gift shop, pharmacy, or physician's office, and each administered by a "custodian," a person who provided service to library users but lacked formal training as a librarian. Some received a small stipend; others served without compensation. The commission contributed 4,175 books, which, in six months, circulated approximately 26,000 times. School-children, especially those from French-speaking households in which books were all but unknown, proved to be the most avid users, and their teachers observed a distinct improvement in the children's reading ability. Parents who could not read English enjoyed studying the illustrations and encouraged their youngsters to read the books aloud to them. A high-school principal reported that as a result of the demonstration, nearly every pupil in his school earned a reading certificate, compared with just a handful in prior years. In one family, parents forbade their two teenagers—who, between them, had completed 108 books in about five months—to continue using the library, because they spent so much time reading that their schoolwork had suffered.[34]

Despite these successes and Culver's personal attention, the demonstration failed to garner the support necessary to maintain it. In the weeks preceding the August 23 referendum on the library, the Jennings *News* and other Jefferson Davis papers barraged their readers with editorials extolling the importance and negligible cost of the library. The *News* opened its columns to any taxpayer who wished to comment on the issue, and both supporters and opponents responded with letters. Opposition was thought to center in Jennings, where a city library had existed since 1908, because of reluctance to relinquish local control. But it was the unwillingness, shared by voters parish-wide, to increase taxes that led to the three-to-one defeat. In three of the seventeen precincts, just one voter supported the library tax; in six more, no one voted for it. A month before the election, optimism prevailed in all parts of the parish, "but from then on it began to look doubtful because the rice market was not good and a day or two before the price was below the cost of production and the blues spread like an epidemic. People who had supported [the tax] throughout and voted for it in the first election voted against it and it did not carry in those districts where we were assured before the election they were three to one in favor of it." In addition,

Jefferson Davis citizens anticipated expenses associated with the flood that had put two-thirds of Louisiana under water. Inundated parishes could pay neither for flood repairs nor even the interest on their bonds, and they had sought help from the state.[35]

Modisette suspected that "surely the bad rice situation has contributed materially to the defeat, but possibly it would have been defeated with [a] rising market, and whether or not Louisiana is ready for tax supported public libraries is yet in very grave doubt. . . . The odds were too great and defeat was inevitable. . . . This means a great loss to the cause for which we are all working." Culver blamed the pervasive reluctance to raise taxes. "The people saw more and more taxes coming their way and no income for this year's crop, a perfect combination to defeat any tax. A neighboring parish called off their school election after our tax was defeated and I wish I had even thought of it for ours and maybe saved it because now we will not be able to suggest library for some time to come. It indicates to me that there is no prospect that we can establish any libraries in the State this coming year that are dependent on the people voting a tax and we have slight hope that any can be provided for out of the budgets of the Police Juries for the coming year under conditions as they are now." She spent the last days of August and the first ones of September dejectedly packing up the demonstration library.[36]

Viewed in the most positive light, the demonstration proved "to the people themselves and especially to the Commission, that the people were hungry for something to read and would read good books if they were made accessible to them. As a demonstration the undertaking was a decided success, even though conditions at the time of its close made it impossible to vote the necessary maintenance tax for the library to continue the service. It cost the Commission in addition to the books something like $1,400 but it was well worth it, and as an investment in the library development of the State was one of the best the Commission has made." Culver explained that "many inquiries have come from neighboring parishes asking how a parish library can be obtained, indicating that Jefferson Davis parish has demonstrated far beyond its own borders." More than forty years later, the state library agency's first failure of a parish library demonstration would finally succeed when Jefferson Davis Parish assumed financial responsibility for its library in November 1969.[37] Meanwhile, Culver had sixty-one more parishes to conquer.

CHAPTER 3

Developing the Louisiana Demonstration Plan, 1927–1929

For most of 1927, the Mississippi River flood monopolized the public mind—dreading it, surviving it, recovering from it—and triggered a major setback for the Louisiana Library Commission. "It is not an exaggeration," Essae M. Culver reported, "to say that one year of the three-year demonstration period was lost because no new work could be started, no publicity could be given space in the newspapers, and no books could be sent through the mails during the period of the Flood." As Milton Ferguson observed, "It is hard to talk libraries to a man whose farm is under water, whose stock is drowned or scattered, and whose crops are destroyed." Both librarians manifested concern that Carnegie funding would end in one more year, and the prospect of the state taking it up was dim. Meanwhile, the library in Richland Parish flourished. "I would grow discouraged," Culver recalled, "but I needed only to visit Richland Parish, . . . and the enthusiasm of the people over their library would renew and encourage me."[1]

Culver derived encouragement also from J. O. Modisette, who had helped her to revise the library law. Commission members Eleanor McMain and Forrest K. White had resigned in late summer 1926, but Governor Fuqua told some of his cronies that he planned to postpone filling McMain's vacancy until after the November election. This delay suggested that he might appoint Modisette, who, though a Republican in an overwhelmingly Democratic state, had led the Fuqua drive in Jefferson Davis Parish during the gubernatorial campaign. Because of Modisette's party affiliation, his selection could be controversial. Governor Fuqua already had subjected himself to "all kind of criticism" for supporting a senatorial candidate who was unpopular with the press, and he would have wished to avoid more disapproval for appointing a Republican. Although Modisette had evidenced his desire for membership on the commission by actively seeking endorsements from his friends, and the other members generally welcomed him, Culver had misgivings. "Mr. Modisette does not want the appointment unless I stay on," she explained to Ferguson, "and I do not feel enthusiastic about his appointment unless he is interested enuf in the work to serve under any circumstances."[2]

On October 12, while returning to Baton Rouge from a conference in Washington, Culver received the shocking news that Governor Fuqua had died the day before. This turn of events was especially undesirable because O. H. Simpson, the lieutenant governor and a probable candidate for governor, had never been friendly to the Library Commission. If elected, he would replenish both vacancies. Simpson, who indeed filled Fuqua's unexpired term, rose above political affiliation, appointing Modisette to one vacancy and Hugh M. Blain of New Orleans to the other. Blain, a publicity expert, had established LSU's Department of Journalism and, more recently, had taught that subject at Tulane University. It was hoped that he would advise in the matter of publicizing the commission's activities.[3]

Modisette, whose commission arrived a month before Blain's, did not wait for the publicity expert. He launched his own promotional campaign by obtaining testimonials to the Library Commission's program, writing more than five hundred letters to influential Louisianians in the first year. T. H. Harris, the state superintendent of education, for example, responded by inviting Culver for a visit to discuss the commission's work "and then gave us a very strong letter endorsing the work of the Commission and especially commending the organization of parish libraries." Additional letters arrived from the attorney general, the state health officer, and the mayor of New Orleans. The governor's secretary telephoned Culver to ask her to write what she wanted the governor to say. At Modisette's second meeting as a commissioner, he stirred up his fellow members by presenting them with a list of propositions for their consideration. One was that commission members should do more to help the work along. He accompanied this proposal with a description of the endorsements he had obtained and set everyone else thinking of projects of their own. Although G. P. Wyckoff remained a commissioner until 1930, on July 2, 1927, the energetic Modisette replaced him as chairman.[4]

On September 20, Modisette, in his new capacity, explained the situation to Milton Ferguson: "Our state is in such a depressed condition owing to the agricultural depression since 1920 plus the flood disaster of this year that it will be very doubtful whether or not the Legislature can be induced to make an adequate appropriation for carrying on after July next. . . . The Commission feels it is impossible to try to plan for the future, unless aid may be expected from outside sources. . . . It is the opinion of Miss Culver and a majority of the Commission that the flood situation has so changed conditions that probably you and the League of Library Commissions and the Carnegie Corporation would all be favorably inclined toward an extension of the Carnegie support in Louisiana," rather than "to abandon the field under the present circumstances." Modisette requested a second grant of $50,000 for three years, specifying that Culver should receive a substantial increase in salary to entice her to remain with the project.[5]

Carnegie Corporation administrators concurred that Louisiana's dire economic condition jeopardized the progress made there to date and extended its grant funding for two years more. After early indications that no more than $500 could be added to the library's state budget of $5,000 in 1928, the persuasive powers of Culver and other library supporters resulted in an increase of $7,000 in its allocation, to $12,000 for the biennium. Culver wrote that, despite this large increase, "it would have been impossible to keep the work up to the standard without the additional aid from the Carnegie Corporation. The Commission took new courage from this generosity and faced the future hopefully" with the leadership of its new chairman.[6]

"Interested in Public Libraries"

Modisette's unabashed activism on behalf of libraries resulted from a childhood devoid of reading matter. Believing that "the best things besides human beings are books," he took every opportunity to advocate for libraries of all types, even including the phrase "Interested in Public Libraries" on his business card. Born on July 27, 1881, to Henry Harrison Modisette and Anne Eliza Vaughan (or Vaughn) Modisette, the sixth of twelve children,

J. O. Modisette, longtime member of the Louisiana Library Commission, 1930s. (State Library of Louisiana)

as a boy James craved books, but no libraries stood within a hundred miles of the family's Webster Parish farm. Pressed into helping with the chores, he intermittently attended elementary school (the highest level of education available in Webster Parish), "but so small was the aggregate result of these transitory terms of instruction that at the age of 14 years the boy was not able to read or write with practicable facility." Determined to obtain an education somehow, he studied at home and during short terms at country schools until, at the age of eighteen, he ventured out on his own.[7]

After a short stint as a book salesman, Modisette worked for several years in his uncle's store in Wynnewood, Oklahoma, while enrolled in high school in the neighboring town of Ravia. After graduation, he taught, first as a missionary to the Chickasaw Indians in Oklahoma and then at an Arkansas public school, concurrently furthering his own education. In 1905 Modisette graduated from the Louisiana State Normal School in Natchitoches and, with his new credentials in hand, found work as principal of high schools in the north Louisiana towns of Cheneyville and Campti. In addition, he took a correspondence course in law and received private tutoring from lawyers he knew. In 1908 he received LL.B. and LL.M. degrees from the Illinois College of Law at Chicago. He practiced briefly at Little Rock, Arkansas, and Shreveport, Louisiana, before settling permanently in Jennings. Modisette married Zada McDowell of New Orleans in 1909, and in 1911 he was admitted to the Louisiana bar. By 1926, when he joined the Library Commission, he had been regarded as a "successful and prominent" attorney for more than a decade.[8]

Modisette's first meeting as a commission member left him disappointed by the inadequacy of his colleagues' participation. "There were only three members of the commission present [himself, Wyckoff, and Hill]," he complained to Milton Ferguson. "One of the members came from Baton Rouge and was in a hurry to get back. She had done no thinking [about furthering the goals of the Library Commission], and the chairman didn't appear to have done much. I have since told Miss Culver in confidence that I considered the meeting was largely a failure, but she says it is better than some they have had." Modisette thought that too much had been left to Culver. "Instead of having cooperation, and assistance and encouragement, it seems there has been . . . apathy, indifference, and a 'Let George do it' attitude on the part of the entire commission."[9]

Culver reminded Modisette that the commission owed its existence to these members. "They have tried to do things in the past and doubtless will do more in the future when they are rouzed [*sic*] from the long vacation they have had from library affairs. I am sure they would be dumfounded [*sic*] if they thought anyone thought they were not doing anything and . . . it might spur them on to more effort but the best way to make them realize it is to have them hear suggestions from you that will show you have given more thought to this than they have. . . . After the next meeting I feel sure more cooperation and help will be given." As if confirming Modisette's characterization of the commission's lethargy, however, she mentioned to Ferguson, "Miss Hill has aged very much in the last few months and at the last two meetings she has had a very hard time keeping awake." Ferguson concluded that "a majority of the members apparently lack the interest. I am positive that old J. O. has enough enthusiasm for several commissions. One man like him is enough to make up for the failings of a great crowd and I am with him and you to the last ditch."[10]

"I Cannot . . . Desert a Sinking Ship"

One of Modisette's early activities as a commissioner was to dissuade Essae Culver from resigning. When the Louisiana project reached its first anniversary in July 1926, Ferguson told Culver that she had "accomplished wonders" in that year, not the least of which was completely winning over the prickly Katherine Hill. Just six months remained of the eighteen months for which Culver had promised to stay. Finding a successor was likely to take a while, and she suggested that the commission should begin to search for "a real live-wire southern girl to carry on." Mary Harris had been hired with the expectation that she would step into the secretaryship when Culver vacated it, but it turned out that she did not wish to do so. "On the other hand," Culver mused, "she seems just the one for the work here now because she is so familiar with the records we need and anyone else would have required so much direction it would not have helped me through these last months half so well." For her part, Culver was "not at all reconciled to staying on two years more but unless I find someone who will carry on our present policies I would not want to turn it over myself." Over the long term, the best solution seemed to be to hire an organizer who would be able to work into the position of executive secretary.[11]

By the end of Culver's second year in Louisiana, the flood had occurred and had jeopardized library development. "Miss Hill thinks I should stay until I had accomplished enuf organization to justify our plans and methods," Culver wrote, "and of course there is something in that because unless we can [have the work well under way,] the next fellow may turn everything up side down and start all over again. I am not anxious to stay on and especially as I should have to stay at least a year after next July if nothing can be accomplished this year and just now prospects are not bright and cheerful." Prophetically, Ferguson urged Culver, "If you could see your way clear to continue with the project a while longer, I know the work down there would advance much more rapidly and I believe, too, the reputation you would gain from originating and consolidating a new movement would be highly enviable."[12]

To tempt Culver to stay, Modisette began pressing the others to increase her salary. Although she appreciated their interest in raising her pay, the executive secretary doubted whether it was best for the commission that she continue; someone else—especially a man—might be more effective. "I am inclined to think," she told Modisette, "that anyone who would be in this position, in order to give him the proper standing with other library forces, should be on an equal footing with the other librarians in the State of important position—but as I have told you before I think there would be less objection on the part of politicians if that salary would be paid to a man and I think that a man would accomplish with one half the effort what we do with a supreme effort. I never was willing to acknowledge this before but I have seen with my own eyes that people seem to flock to the men for advice and help. . . . I would not want to stand in the way of the greatest accomplishment possible in the time before us." Modisette and Ferguson disagreed that anyone so well-qualified as she, male or female, could be found, and the commission concurred with the raise.[13]

Concluding that "I cannot of course desert a sinking ship," Culver resolved to stay and plunged even further into her work. Little library development could be accomplished during the first year after the flood, but progress might be made in other ways. To reach more people, the commission offered a new service: sending a collection of books to any group that formed a reading club and elected officers who would care for the books. Requests came from communities throughout the state. One application read, "I tell you it is needed out here. So many young girls and boys are out of school at 14 years and never read a line after." Within three years, some nine hundred Louisianians had joined twenty-three reading clubs. Another means of reaching a wide audience was through exhibits, which the commission utilized to highlight the variety of subjects on which books were available, the type of books recommended for children, and how books served the needs of clubs or business. An exhibit for the State Federation of Women's Clubs, for example, showed how books connect with and contribute to all phases of home life, and one for the Parent-Teachers' Association explained how to choose appropriate books in inexpensive editions for Christmas gifts and school libraries.[14]

Another means of outreach involved collaborative activities with community organizer Mary Mims, who strongly supported the commission's work. Each of the state's more than three hundred organized communities—which Mims defined as "any group of people, living within neighboring distance of one another, and having a common interest"—held monthly meetings. One meeting annually consisted of a library program intended to acquaint the rural audience with the Library Commission and its work. A typical program, interspersed with music, opened with a business session and a short song, followed by a paper on "What Everyone in the Community Should Know about the Louisiana Library Commission" and a presentation on the importance of books and reading. Next, twelve citizens described a book each had enjoyed, and someone read a story about the value of parish library service to a farm family. The program closed with a debate, "Resolved—That a parish library will help men and women more than it will help boys and girls." In addition, the commission received exhibit space and a place on the program of the annual short course for farm families, held at Louisiana State University. As many as 150 persons visited commission headquarters in response to each of these sessions.[15]

From the inception of the Louisiana Library Commission's plan for library development, publicity had been a key component. During the first two years, Culver or a commission member presented their program at a meeting of almost every organization in the state. Numerous articles appeared in newspapers and magazines, both in Louisiana and beyond it in towns just across state lines, such as Natchez, Mississippi, and Beaumont, Texas, and in national media. In 1928, the commission employed its first full-time publicity assistant, Rachel Violette, and she undertook a campaign designed to reach all 114 newspapers in Louisiana.[16]

To supplement these efforts, the commission commemorated Book Week, complemented programs of women's clubs, and instructed parents and teachers on how to select appropriate books for children. It also distributed posters and handbooks describing how citizens could obtain its services. Special publicity intended to sway voters to the library cause preceded tax elections, often contributing materially to their success, and Culver consistently responded by writing enthusiastic letters of thanks to cooperative editors. All the commission members and the executive secretary participated actively in publicity endeavors by obtaining letters of endorsement from prominent persons and organizations and by delivering addresses at club meetings and conventions, and Modisette gave weekly radio addresses on topics such as "Louisiana's Greatest Need—Free Library Service" and "The Influence of Good Books," which were defined nationally as "politically informing or culturally uplifting," unlike the popular dime novels, for example, which were deemed to lack merit.[17]

To publicize the Louisiana project among other librarians, the commission and the Louisiana Library Association invited the Southwestern Library Association to hold its 1928 meeting in Baton Rouge. Comprised of librarians from Alabama, Oklahoma, Texas, New Mexico, and Arizona, as well as Louisiana, the conference brought more than one hundred persons from those states and from the American Library Association. Culver further contributed professionally by serving as president of the Louisiana Library Association in 1928/29.[18]

By this time, Culver had become close, not only to J. O. but to the entire

Modisette family, including Zada and the five Modisette children: Marion Harrison (1911–1951), called Harry and, in some sources, mistakenly counted as a daughter; Mary Evelyn, nicknamed Mae (1914–2004); Zada (1916–2001); Gertrude Pearl (1918–2000), called Perk; and James Oliver, Jr., known when small as Jim-boy (1923–2003). As a four-year-old, Jim-boy developed a crush on Culver and ardently hoped that she would send him a valentine. Alerted by J. O., Culver obliged and made the little fellow very happy. It was with Mary Evelyn, however, that she developed the closest relationship, taking the teenager along on excursions to New Orleans and other points of interest and mentoring her when she contemplated a career in librarianship. Mary Evelyn stayed with Culver for two weeks in 1932 and sampled library work at commission headquarters to see if it suited her, but the experiment did not go well. Culver "tried Mary Evelyn out on reference. She gave every evidence of disliking it cordially. Finally put her questions on my desk half finished and offered to do no more." Culver became "strongly convinced Mary Evelyn is . . . staying here either to please her father or for a vacation lark & chance to be with her boy friend," but her protégé graduated from Louisiana State University's library school in June 1935. Over the summer, she worked at the Webster Parish Library and subsequently at the Hill Memorial Library at LSU.[19]

Filling a "Crying Need"

A decade earlier, aspiring librarians like Mary Evelyn Modisette would have had to leave Louisiana to prepare for a library career. One of the Library Commission's major accomplishments during its early years was stimulating education for librarians, for none existed in Louisiana when Culver arrived in the state in 1925. After just six weeks, she told Milton Ferguson, "We simply must get some kind of a library training school down here soon or our progress is going to be very slow indeed because we cannot give supervision all over the state. . . . I feel as if I wanted to stay a week or ten days in each place and one day is all I can possibly manage just now, if I do that much." The Louisiana Library Commission's difficulty in filling the assistant position exemplified the "crying need" for these professionals that would arise if more libraries were established, for the demand for the former increased in direct proportion to the growth of the latter. Culver recommended "that the commission give all possible cooperation and encouragement to the establishment of a training course for librarians in the state."[20]

Both Tulane and Louisiana State Universities expressed interest. Tulane announced the intention to establish a library school and, for several summers in the late 1920s, offered a six-week course. Commission member Margaret Reed advocated strongly for LSU, however, touting its lower tuition which would make the program accessible to more students. Culver, meanwhile, promoted the advantages of librarianship as a career for women. "'Suited as it is to the well-educated and cultured woman of today,' Miss Culver stated, 'librarianship has long since outgrown the stage when it was regarded as a refuge for the decayed gentlewoman whose genteel poverty necessitated her going to work. Today libraries are in charge of modern business women, thoroughly trained by special courses in library schools and holding degrees from recognized colleges and universities. Women who have worked themselves up in the profession through practical experience are valuable, of course, but no young woman of today may enter the field unless she is technically fitted to meet its demands.'"[21]

Twenty-one students "hungry for library knowledge" completed the summer 1926 session at LSU, and all who wanted library jobs obtained them immediately. Courses designed specifically to meet the commission's needs emphasized book selection and acquisition, cataloging and classification, reference services, and library administration. After a total of six intensive summer sessions, which gave the university experience in training for librarianship, in 1931 the program was expanded to a year-long (or three-summer) course. Over time, it evolved into LSU's current School of Library Information Science, preparing many librarians to work in the parish libraries that the Louisiana Library Commission would establish and in libraries across the state and the nation. In addition to supporting the establishment of the program, Culver lectured at LSU from 1928 to 1935. She also taught library science during summer sessions at the University of Wisconsin (1930) and Columbia University (1935–1938).[22]

"I Would Put It All in a Library"

In 1928, O. H. Simpson's brief tenure as governor concluded when he lost his bid for election in his own right to the popular, dynamic champion of the masses Huey P. Long. Perhaps because of his own humble background,

Long constantly sought to improve conditions for the poor, such as more and better roads and hospitals, and he may have recognized the Louisiana Library Commission's contribution toward that cause. Despite his reputation for using "deducts" from state employees' salaries to fund his campaigns and compelling state agencies to find well-paying positions for his supporters, "we got through those years that he was governor," Culver recalled, "without any deducts or any interference in any way. Nobody was ever put on our payroll, nobody was ever interfered with in any way at all during that five years."[23]

While serving as governor and subsequently as U.S. senator, Long visited New York repeatedly, including one trip when he ostensibly took with him a bartender from the Roosevelt Hotel in New Orleans to teach the barman's counterpart at the Hotel New Yorker how to concoct a Ramos Gin Fizz. During Culver's first summer at Columbia, some of her associates there heard that Long was in town, and they asked her, "'Why don't you invite him up to talk to the summer session?' Well, I knew, if we did that," Culver recalled, "we'd get almost anything from Huey after that, but I just couldn't make up my mind to do it, because . . . I didn't see him as such an outstanding, pure administrator that some people seemed to think he was," despite his support for libraries.[24]

For the rest of her life, Culver remained puzzled that neither Long nor any of his Democratic successors replaced the Republican Modisette on the Louisiana Library Commission. When Long took office, she recounted, Modisette went to see him and said, "'Huey, here's my resignation. You know, I didn't vote for you.' And Huey said, 'J. O., you're doing a fine job. Stay right where you are.' And because Huey had never fired the head of one of the state commissions, who was a Republican, then the other governors didn't do it 'cause they didn't know why and they were afraid to do anything about it, I guess. And so Mr. Modisette remained chairman of the Louisiana Library Commission for fifteen years."[25]

Long occasionally dropped in at commission headquarters. Culver remembered his first visit, on Saturday, July 21, 1928. "Sarah Jones and I were there alone, and suddenly the door—it was supposed to be closed, but the door burst open and in came Huey. And we were surprised as could be, but he said he'd come because somebody told him he was just like Napoleon and he wanted to get a book about Napoleon. Did we have one in the library about Napoleon? I said yes, we do, and he wanted to borrow it, so we gave it to him. And then he said, 'Do you happen to have Cellini's Memoirs?' And I said, 'Indeed we do, Governor,' and he said, 'Let me see the book.' So I showed it to him and he said, 'How much did you pay for it?' So I looked in the [accession] book and it was two dollars and eighty cents. I think we bought it at a remainder sale. And he said, 'Well, that's funny. I paid over nine dollars for my copy in New York.' And then he began talking about all the art works that were scattered over Europe that had been executed by Cellini. 'Well,' I said, 'you have a better memory than I have, Governor. I don't remember that. I remember his fine work, his jewelry and things like that, small art objects, but I didn't know he'd done any sculpture.' 'Oh, yes,' he said, and he told me all about it. He really knew, and from that time on, he never interfered or told us to do anything or not to do anything or put anybody on the payroll." Culver "always thought that he decided that we knew something about purchasing books because we had gotten one cheaper than he had. And also that he thought we knew something about books."[26]

About a month later, Long visited the commission again while just Culver's two assistants, Gretta Smith and Ivy Ritchie, were there. Smith reported, "He burst in the door *roaring* something about that he was still reading Ludwig's Napoleon but he had two other books which we could have back if we wanted them.... Then he paced madly toward the door and looked at the magazines.... Then he shouted out 'How many are there of you in this office?' Miss Ritchie said 'Three.' Then he dashed back in front of her desk and said 'What salary do you get?' and she told him and he asked me and I told him, and we both asserted absolute ignorance of yours.... I said 'Of course you know that our salaries come out of the appropriation from the Carnegie Corporation and that the state money all goes for books.' He alleged that *he* had got us a nice little appropriation this year." Now seated in Culver's chair, the governor tilted it back and made himself comfortable. Smith told him that "we had a new library in Concordia Parish which we were just opening and he said yes, there were several of them and they were good things!" Smith added that she "was quite glad to see him in the flesh and hear him roar."[27]

Whatever the reason, Long always supported the Library Commission—fortunately, because, as Modisette observed, "never a Governor in Louisiana has been so completely in control of the reins of government as is Governor Long." If he favored an appropriation for the commission, it enjoyed a strong chance of success in the Legislature, but "if he should be opposed to it, it would be dead before it was born." When one of Modisette's publicity campaigns requested a statement from Long about parish libraries, he replied, "In my opinion, there is nothing that can greater serve the cause of convenience, happiness and uplift of a community than a public library. It places within the reach of every child, as well as older people, the literature which enables them to become informed, and through which they may entertain themselves more delightfully, and to aid in their mental and spiritual development. If I had only a small amount of money to spend in public improvements, I would put it all in a library."[28]

"You Can't Imagine How Much the Books Are Really Enjoyed"

In the spring of 1928, flood recovery had progressed enough that Culver could resume talking libraries. Mary Mims wrote letters to all the organized communities, encouraging each of them to investigate the possibility of a parish library, and Culver traversed the state like a politician on the campaign trail (which, in a way, she was), spreading the gospel of books at meetings of various organizations in one small town after another. The first response came from the Tri-Parish Community Club of Tensas, Concordia, and Catahoula, an organization that grew out of the need for interparish cooperation after the flood. Culver explained the library plan to an audience of about 150 persons, who received the idea enthusiastically and endorsed it heartily. Ferriday, the largest town and situated centrally for all three parishes, would house the headquarters library in a room offered by the proprietor of the hotel, and distribution points would be placed in the centers of population. Both Tensas Parish, where post-flood crop conditions made it unlikely that funding could be found, and Catahoula soon withdrew. A demonstration went ahead in Concordia, a mid-sized parish of 714 square miles, located on the west bank of the Mississippi River opposite Natchez, with a population of 12,466. On June 17, 1928, the police jury passed a resolution of establishment and appropriated $1,250 for six months. With the demonstration now limited to a single parish, the main library should have been located at Vidalia, the parish seat, but the original plan of placing it at Ferriday persisted.[29]

Library headquarters opened on October 10, housed in the City Hall in

Concordia Parish Library headquarters, Ferriday, 1930. (State Library of Louisiana)

what had been the mayor's office; that he unselfishly moved into a former garage to make room for the library implies the extent to which he recognized the need for it. Five branches soon followed, and the collection grew to more than 3,800 volumes. At the end of six months, books had traveled to every corner of the parish. Everywhere, citizens praised the library and asked the police jury to appropriate more funds or to call an election for a maintenance tax. A teacher in New Era, for example, stated, "Unless you have lived in a country village, with bad roads and no entertainment, you can't imagine how much the books are really enjoyed." Another resident, who initially judged the library as "useless and futile," came to regard it as "the finest thing the parish was doing." The police jury scheduled a tax election on June 4, 1929, and the Library Commission began a multifaceted publicity campaign that barraged voters with circulars and newspaper articles emphasizing how much the library meant to the people of Concordia.[30]

As librarian-in-charge Bess Vaughan explained, "Everything seemed favorable until the spring rains in the upper valley began to swell the Mississippi. As the menacing waters crept up above flood stage, a terrible depression seized the people and there was much talk of a flood. Already backwater from the swollen bayous and streams of the lower part of the Parish had covered that section and was slowly creeping up toward the upper part. It became necessary to guard the levees night and day and officials called for volunteer guards." At one of the branches, the floodwater stood two feet, seven inches deep at the back steps and still rising. The custodian at another branch wrote, "The water is trying hard to run us out, but I intend to stay as long as I can." In the Concordia area, the river was expected to crest between June 4—the date of the tax election—and June 12. These circumstances necessitated postponing the vote until the flood scare had abated.[31]

When asked in July to reschedule the election, the police jury refused, explaining that backwater in the lower half of Concordia and seepage in the rest of it had ruined the crops everywhere, and no one could afford a new tax. Members of the Woman's Club and of the Rotary Club sped into action, circulating petitions that soon registered enough signatures to force a tax election, and it was set for September. "There were many days when things looked doubtful for there was much opposition due to the condition of the Parish," Culver reported. "There were many prophecies of failure and very few of the success of the tax." Despite the pessimistic predictions, the 3/4-mill tax passed—significant as the first tax adopted by Louisiana voters to support a library—with a good majority of both voters and property assessment. The editor of the Baton Rouge *Advocate* did not exaggerate when he wrote, "The passage of the Concordia parish library tax . . . marks a new era in the history of library development in Louisiana." It also proved dramatically that "taxes and poverty do not keep people from voting for library service if they really want it."[32]

Obviously, the people of Concordia really wanted it. In a study of publishing, bookselling, and library work, prepared for the Carnegie Corporation, *New York Times* reporter R. L. Duffus wrote, "A visitor from California or Massachusetts might have thought the supply of books inadequate and some of the stations and branches primitive in their arrangements. But the eagerness of the people to secure books was just as apparent as it is in states which have long had model library facilities. After going the rounds of the Concordia system, I found it impossible to believe that the residents of the parish would ever give it up." Glenn H. Holloway, president of the Concordia Parish Library Board, explained that the library "has become a living, breathing part of Concordia parish," proving "more effective and . . . giving a more complete service than was imagined possible before its establishment. . . . Not only does the collection of books include recreational, inspirational and informational material, but it has been democratized to meet the needs of the entire population." Holloway described the library as "the most practical tool which Concordia has ever found for community development."[33]

The demonstration in Concordia Parish, like its predecessors in Richland and Jefferson Davis, strove to place books "in every corner of the parish"—that is, in every corner occupied by white people. Caucasians, however, comprised less than half of Concordia's population of 12,466. "Plans for service to the Negro population [were] contemplated," Essae M. Culver reported, "but during the demonstration the book supply was not large enough to provide a separate book collection." And separate it would have had to be, for racial segregation was the law, upheld when the United States Supreme Court legitimized separate-but-equal railway cars in the Louisiana-based case of *Plessy v. Ferguson* (1896). This doctrine was rapidly extended beyond common conveyances to embrace schools, entertainment venues, recreational facilities—wherever people congregated in public, though the accommodations for black people seldom equaled those for white ones in quality or quantity. In the south, the social policy legislated by *Plessy v. Ferguson* had long been regional custom.[34]

"A Message of Service"

Education-deprived black southerners were not alone in regarding libraries as unknown territory. Although books had been familiar in some cities and towns, in the 1920s "a widespread knowledge of libraries [was] new" to residents of rural areas, no matter what their skin color. Many regarded the library as the realm of scholars and bookworms, not accessible to average citizens such as themselves. Aware that a demand for libraries had to precede their successful establishment, and that the populace had to want them before they would demand them, Culver and her colleagues knew that they had to instill a desire for libraries. Bookmobiles offered a tangible means of doing so, for they could carry a segment of the library, not just the illusion of it, to citizens' very doorsteps, thus making the library "a reality, and not just a newspaper article." For Louisiana's most isolated residents, "the book van driven all along deserted roads and stopping at the farm yard or gate is Pegasus turned into a Ford truck. It may seem less romantic at first sight, but it is no less magical, for it brings the whole world of books with it."[35]

Nationally, bookmobiles had evolved from a horse-drawn "book wagon" that traveled the vicinity of Hagerstown, Maryland, beginning in 1905. Its black color caused it to be mistaken for a hearse. Red paint eliminated the problem and initiated a custom of decorating libraries-on-wheels with eye-catching designs that doubled as an inexpensive means of publicity. Bookmobiles offered variety, for they provided turnover on a regular schedule, in addition to their ability to go wherever the roads were adequate for their passage. They went to their people, "seeking them out, not waiting for them to become library-conscious."[36]

For residents of the most bookless locations, bookmobiles may have been less intimidating than the permanent structures that townspeople worked so hard to build—smaller, more hospitable, and with individual assistance at hand, perhaps even staffed by someone from their community. "Men in overalls and grimy, too shy to go into a library building, come up to the truck to exchange and borrow books. The librarian knows not only what they read, but through her regular visits knows them personally, as well as their wives who borrow books when the truck is parked near the home— and the children who look forward with eager anticipation to the coming of the truck to the school."[37]

The first vehicle to be called a bookmobile traversed the country on a tour sponsored by the American Library Association, the National Association of Book Publishers, and others. This bookmobile set out from New York City on January 3, 1929, and reached Baton Rouge a little over a year later, having visited every state east of the Mississippi River except Wisconsin. It carried information pertaining to library work and bookselling, as well as a display of reference books, periodical indexes, and library furniture and supplies. The purpose of the tour was to assist librarians and booksellers with their work and to serve as a model for libraries considering the use of such vehicles, hastening the time when they would be considered standard library equipment.[38] Louisiana, however, already had one of its own.

On October 4, 1929, the commission announced the arrival of a book-mobile, a delivery truck purchased at a cost of $715.50 plus $66.21 for insurance. Shelves capable of holding five hundred volumes outfitted its interior, and, painted in bright colors on each side of the exterior at an additional expense of $61.00, were the words "Louisiana Library Commission" and the likeness of a shelf of books. This first bookmobile in the state was a Chevrolet, but vehicles from other manufacturers, mostly Fords, subsequently plied Louisiana's roads.[39]

The advent of automobile travel had been less meaningful to residents of Louisiana than to those of other states because cars had such a hard time getting around. Governor John M. Parker, who took office in 1920, sought to position Louisiana in the forefront of national efforts to construct a network of modern highways. When his term ended four years later, the state had built a system of 2,700 miles of gravel highways. As Culver knew only too well, when it rained they became muddy quagmires or flooded completely, such as the stretch between Kaplan and Lafayette where she drove "thru water way over [the] running b[oar]d" as she returned from a meeting, and when it didn't rain, the roads turned dusty. The state's terrain—red clay hills in the north, which made for treacherous passage in all kinds of weather, and swampy lowlands in the south—required expensive paved roads with built-up roadbeds. With few bridges across the numerous waterways, small, sluggish ferries further impeded mobility.[40]

Louisiana's first bookmobile, purchased for purposes of publicity rather than for transporting reading materials through one of the parishes, expeditiously carried "a message of service" to hundreds, even thousands of rural citizens. Staffed by Norris McClellan and Rose Egan, the bookmobile stopped first at the Vernon Parish fair in Leesville. Over the next six weeks, it visited a district parent-teacher meeting and ten more fairs, where McClellan and Egan answered questions and distributed posters and leaflets describing the commission's services. By the end of 1929, the attention-getting vehicle had captured the interest of fairgoers at all thirty-five parish and district fairs in the state. The editor of the Baton Rouge *Morning Advocate* praised the project as "one of the most important publicity schemes that the commission has yet undertaken" to give citizens "a clearer and more vivid idea" of its services.[41]

According to the bookmobile's log, "its initial trip . . . was fraught with adventures—adventures which were repeated on each succeeding trip. In each place [it] visited the bookmobile drew crowds—in many cases crowds that were pathetically eager to learn and know books, the like of which they had never before seen." Unquestionably, Louisianians greeted the bookmobile with enthusiasm. The titles it carried, carefully selected to touch on almost every phase of Louisiana life, mirrored those to be found in a small rural branch, but during this publicity tour, they did not circulate. Operating expenses slightly exceeded one hundred dollars per month.[42]

Like the library demonstrations, the bookmobile inspired a variety of amusing and touching stories illustrative of the relevance of books in individuals' lives.

In a little-populated section of the state, [for instance,] the bookmobile stopped at a roadside filling station, to be greeted by a worn but cleanly dressed woman with five or six children. Asked if she liked to read, the woman scornfully declared that she did not and that furthermore she had no time for such foolishness, and that she could not understand why anyone wanted to read. She added, however, that her husband read, and seeing that she quite evidently regarded reading as a man-sized job, the librarian in charge offered her a cook book. It was as if the word "cook book" had been a magic one, for the woman seized [the book] eagerly, further conversation developing that she was not quite certain as to the amount of baking powder that went into biscuits. Her joy when she learned that she did not have to pay for looking at the book and that she could secure others like it, or perhaps ones on sewing, housekeeping, and similar subjects, was unbounded and she immediately decided to write to the Louisiana Library Commission. In her enthusiasm and delight, she unbent enough to tell the librarian that her conception of libraries might possibly be wrong, since all of her husband's books dealt with gasoline engines. It was amazing, she declared, to think that libraries contained books on other subjects—books which would help her make her home a more comfortable and pleasant one.[43]

Youngsters, too, gravitated to the books. As a two-hour stop at a rural school waned, a little boy wept because he could not finish reading a biography of Charles Lindbergh before the bookmobile had to move on. Some connected the information in books with their own situations. "In a little school located in the French settlement of Louisiana, . . . [the children] received the bookmobile with open arms—indeed, so enthusiastic was this reception that they literally swarmed over the sides and it was with difficulty that the librarian in charge was extricated. She quickly restored order by promising the children the privilege of looking at the fascinating treasures if they would sit in a row across the playground."[44]

The children were charmed especially by a picture of a little Dutch boy whose finger plugged a hole in a dike, thus averting a flood. That this scene should so capture the attention of little French children in southwest Louisiana puzzled the librarian until, overhearing their conversation, she realized that they viewed the dike as a great levee threatened by the mighty Mississippi River. In the Dutch boy, they saw a small, wiry Cajun upon whom the safety of the whole countryside rested as his youthful finger averted the catastrophe of a Louisiana crevasse.[45]

For another child, books offered the potential to fill a poignant need. "A small youngster living on a farm in the Louisiana strawberry section . . . saw the bookmobile from a distance and tore pell-mell from the field where he was at work to investigate its delightful possibilities. Since he could barely read and write, and since he was the only one in the family who could do as well, the librarian found this interest in books quite surprising. A few questions soon resulted in the whole pathetic story, and it seemed that the small boy, deeply impressed with the family difficulties, when it became necessary to write a letter—a task which involved calling in the neighbors— had determined that he would learn to write in order that he might be the family's scribe in the years to come. And so through their intimate contact with the bookmobile, the citizens of Louisiana realize that libraries are no longer cloistered retreats for Latin and Greek scholars but that they are living, breathing parts of the community in which they are located, and that in library books the answers to everyday problems are to be found" by citizens at every level of society.[46]

The effectiveness of the tour soon became evident as the number of requests for information received at commission headquarters in October soared to 240 queries, sixty-one more than the largest number in any other single month that year. Queries pertained to subjects as varied as Louisiana cemeteries and monuments, folk tales, legends, early history, and art; American music; psychology; gardening, including tulips, flowering shrubs, and diseases of ferns; juvenile delinquency; establishing a chamber of commerce; bookkeeping; aviation; agricultural engineering; cattle; truck farming; interior decorating; achievements of women in politics; child care; and biographies of Victor Hugo, Thomas Edison, Carrie Nation, and Jane Addams, to cite just a few examples. Fair managers hastened to request return visits the following year.[47]

In 1930, the bookmobile hit the road again with a more narrowly focused mission: to bolster support for the establishment of libraries in specific parishes. Essae Culver must have made a startling impression that January when she alighted from the vehicle at a meeting of the Woman's Club in St. Joseph, in Tensas Parish. The next month, Norris McClellan and Bess Vaughan drove it through the southern and western sections of the state, and in March Vaughan and Culver took it to Monroe. While Vaughan exhibited it to schoolchildren there, Culver, at the invitation of the local Chamber of Commerce, addressed a mass meeting of civic leaders and citizens from all parts of Ouachita Parish regarding the purposes of parish-wide library systems and the success that other Louisiana parishes had already experienced. Neither Culver's customary eloquence on the subject dearest to her heart nor the prospect of Ouachita's own bookmobile, however, brought the desired result. A special committee of the Chamber of Commerce, designated to investigate the parish library project, subsequently decided to enlarge the scope of the existing Monroe Public Library, instead of establishing one parish-wide. The perennial horror of additional taxes contributed to the unfavorable vote, but it was not the only factor, for "the parish-wide plan . . . was entirely and heartily disapproved"; other reasons were not recorded. Meanwhile, the bookmobile continued on its mission of publicity at least until 1934 and also served soldiers at Camp Beauregard, near Alexandria.[48]

The Louisiana Library Commission and its successor, the Louisiana State Library, regarded bookmobiles as integral to rural library service. "The ideas in the development of libraries have been reversed entirely in the last 25 years," Culver explained in 1930. "Once it was just a question of a collection of books on shelves. Now it is a selection of books going out to find readers. That means that the books must be chosen carefully to fit the needs of the community into which they are going and that means also that the duties of a librarian have been changed from that of a custodian of books to that of a 'policeman' in directing the reading tastes of the clients into the literary channels most beneficial to their needs and surroundings.[49]

"With the aid of the bookmobile, 'a library on wheels,'" Culver continued, "those tenants who have little time to leave their homes and their farms, are furnished with wholesome and instructive literature. The highways, of course, have made such a feat a success and a possibility. Those people look forward to the arrival of the bookmobile as they would to a delivery truck containing food and clothing. It is the salvation of their 'mental diet,' which is the great element in the solution of their recreational problems and mental developments." Historian Winston De Ville, a native of Rayne, attested to that hunger for books when he recalled, "I was reared in an almost bookless household, so [I] read anything from labels to the *Beaumont Enterprise*. When the first bookmobile came, I approached it in awe, as if it were the Holy Grail. [For me,] it *was*." Ferrel Guillory, founder of the Program on Public Life at the University of North Carolina, grew up in Baton Rouge and concluded, based on personal experience as a regular visitor to the "lumbering van," that "an investment in a public institution—the library that sponsored the bookmobile—can pay off in touching young lives."[50]

"A Little Leadership"

Before Culver commenced her work in Louisiana, state library agencies did not include the establishment of rural libraries among their specific responsibilities. The programs in Jefferson Davis and Concordia Parishes, however, moved the demonstration method of library development to a different level of library organization. Under the auspices of the Carnegie Corporation grant, the Louisiana Library Commission demonstrated the benefit to be afforded by an effective library commission. In Richland Parish, it proved how an agency of its nature could support and strengthen the operation of a functioning library. But in Jefferson Davis and then in Concordia, the commission exemplified how a parish library could be established where none had existed before, the services it could give, and the options for providing its financial backing. Culver pioneered this aspect of library demonstration, originating a method "which has greatly influenced library development both in this country and abroad." Because of her work, supplemented by the contributions of Modisette and other early commission members and librarians, "Louisiana [added] the word 'demonstration' to the vocabulary of library development and the two have become almost synonymous." In all but four parishes, libraries in Louisiana were developed through the demonstration method that grew out of the unsuccessful tax election in Jefferson Davis Parish in 1926.[51]

Based on its constantly increasing experience with establishing parish libraries, the Louisiana Library Commission and its successor agency, the Louisiana State Library (later known as the State Library of Louisiana), evolved a set of policies and conditions that increased the likelihood of success. It chose demonstration areas based on local interest, leadership, and the reasonable probability of continued support. Services radiated from headquarters at the parish seat, located in a library building if one existed or, if not, the city hall or a vacant store. Branches were set up in other towns, with deposit stations or book depots in all other community centers. Staffed by branch assistants, these were situated conveniently in stores, post offices, and other locations where foot traffic was heavy.[52]

According to a manual later prepared for branch library assistants, that position was "usually [held by] an inexperienced person . . . without training in library work. However, with her knowledge of the place where she lives and its people, she can learn about books through handling and reading them, and she becomes a valuable library worker when she can relate books to her community's needs. . . . The ideal branch assistant is a leader in her community, and a participant in many community affairs." The Library Commission "resisted using civil service personnel chosen in Baton Rouge to be sent to the parish," recalled Sallie Farrell, who participated in various capacities in establishing libraries in forty-four parishes. "We insisted that local people be hired who were familiar with the parish. We felt that a complete staff of outsiders would not be accepted."[53]

In areas too remote to experience foot traffic, tiny branches, set up in a corner of a meat market, one-room post office, filling station, or even a farmhouse, served neighbors within a two-mile radius. In Winn Parish, for example, a farmer named Jim administered such a collection, spread in a row across the dining-room buffet in his home, "a little rough-plank

cabin,... the work of Jim's own hands.... The floors were rough and bare....
[Its furniture included] a weather-worn rocking chair with chicken wire
stretched over the back ... [and] a little vanity table hung with a scrap of lav-
ender sateen, the only patch of color in the cabin." Jim kept circulation records of the books—practical titles such as *Tomato Growing* and *Productive
Orcharding,* leisure reading that included *David Copperfield* and *The Secret
Garden,* and a large-print edition of the Bible—in a composition book.[54]

Under the plan, the library agency spent one-quarter to one-half of its
demonstration budget on a quantity of books which it placed in the parish on long-term loan. As the *Christian Science Monitor* noted in 1938,
"Instead of starting on a shoestring with a shabby, donated collection of
cast-off books which nobody else wanted, the Louisiana Library Commission brought the best books it could find—current, interesting books on
vital subjects which even a life-long reader would clamor for. Regardless of
the interest—long staple cotton, furniture making, or just a good western—
books hot from the publisher's griddle are supplied. With such excellent
reading people see how profitable library service can be." Any book in the
system, including demonstrations, was available for reference use by any
resident of Louisiana.[55]

"Late current publications" comprised most book collections, supplemented by "some classics . . . as well as older books always in demand by
some readers." Lack of prior access to reading matter impacted book selection because, to most residents, everything was new, although many
subscribed to the Book of the Month Club and similar services. Years of experience and many library demonstrations confirmed "that a more or less
popular type book collection is best suited for the first year," but utilitarian
books also found a wide audience. In 1928, when the commission's holdings
numbered ten thousand volumes, the most often used book was *Henley's
Twentieth-Century Book of Formulas for Home and Workshop.* Farmers
read about scientific agriculture methods, such as growing pecan trees,
vegetable forcing, and bee culture.[56]

Children's books were carefully chosen from "standard sources" and acquired in sturdy covers to withstand hard use. Animal stories enjoyed popularity with youngsters of all ages. Some of the picture books recommended
by the Library Commission in its early years were *Mother Goose* and other
collections of jingles and nursery rhymes, Kate Greenaway's *Marigold Gar-*

den, and *The Tale of Peter Rabbit* by Beatrix Potter. Suggestions for older children included *Bold Dragon and Other Ghostly Tales* by Washington Irving, Newbery Award winners such as *Hitty—Her First Hundred Years* by Rachel Field, and stories of heroism intended to reinforce Boy Scout principles.[57]

At library headquarters, "a good, basic reference collection" served "the entire system of branches when a branch assistant is unable to locate requested information in the limited reference volumes of the branch. Included in the collection are: encyclopedia sets, both adult and juvenile; dictionaries, unabridged, collegiate, and for lower grades; atlas, almanac; collections of verse and quotations; and standard works in the subject fields that are largely used."[58]

As time passed, the size of the initial collection grew larger—from about a thousand books in Richland in 1926 to more than 21,000 in the last demonstration in 1968. By the 1950s, the number of books was standardized at one-third of a book per capita, sent in an initial shipment of at least six thousand books that was supplemented by regular delivery of new publications and special requests. Books arrived fully processed and ready for use. They were "selected and bought with the greatest care and ability to insure the best on any subject, and the safest from the standpoint of educational and cultural values." The state offered some supplies; travel expenses for staff members; except in the earliest demonstrations, a bookmobile and its operational costs; and the salaries of full-time, professional librarians whom the state agency appointed and supervised. Early demonstrations lasted for six months, most later ones for one year, and a few for two years, especially in the presence of extenuating circumstances such as existed in Cameron Parish, which had been devastated by Hurricane Audrey just a year before the library demonstration began in 1958.[59]

For its part, the parish provided housing for the library, including maintenance and utilities, furniture, shelving, equipment, building and office supplies, and janitorial services. It also paid the salaries of part-time employees and the bookmobile driver. The police jury appointed a board of control, with terms that extended beyond the demonstration period, to represent the jury in matters regarding the library. Louisiana law required that the library board be comprised of five residents of the parish, plus the president of the police jury as an ex officio member. Before the demonstration period ended, the police jury took appropriate measures to ensure continued financial support through local funds, minimally at the same level of operation. Those funds might come from an annual appropriation by the police jury or from a specially voted library tax. At that point, the library became a local agency with local financial support and governance. Working toward securing this support was a major responsibility of the board of control, which also was instrumental in interpreting the library to the parish community to win its backing.[60]

The Louisiana plan of library development has been credited with greatly influencing other states and nations. As early as 1929, librarians from abroad expressed interest in and admiration for the parish library system. After World War II, the trickle of inquiries grew into a stream of visitors as the American Library Association began referring foreign librarians studying methods of library development. In 1950 and 1951, for example, visitors came from states as distant as Nebraska and as near as Mississippi, and from the Philippines, Egypt, Thailand, Morocco, Malaya, Germany, and Tasmania. In 1958, W. G. Buick, librarian-in-charge of the County Lending Service of the Public Library of South Australia in Adelaide, familiarized himself with the Louisiana system and returned home intending to institute there a similar plan of regional libraries, basing it on Culver's adaptation of the demonstration method. By the early 1960s, the U.S. Department of State, the Carnegie Corporation, and the Ford Foundation had joined the ALA in recommending that foreign guests visit the Louisiana State Library. More than sixty of them came in 1960 and 1961, including Dr. Osman Ersoy of Ankara, Turkey, who spent four weeks examining the State Library's plan of development and touring demonstrations as he planned nationwide public library service for his country.[61]

Librarians traveled from distant points to study the Louisiana plan because its methods succeeded. By requiring localities to provide facilities, furnishings, and some salaries, the state library agency ensured that these necessities would be in place when outside support ceased. To maximize the use of resources, the library agency avoided duplicating services provided by existing school libraries and moved books that failed to circulate in one community to another. Also, the Louisiana system was adaptable, capable of being easily modified to suit situations as varied as those in Louisiana, Australia, and Turkey.

Significantly, the Louisiana plan involved the people, first and foremost by placing books in their hands. Even before a parish established a library, its residents could obtain books from headquarters in Baton Rouge, delivered to their mailboxes. This attentive service led to widespread support, which was especially important at tax-election time and when it became necessary to pressure legislators to increase the budget. Legions of library supporters stood ready for mobilization when the library needed them. From the beginning, the library won the approbation of the press, and editors across the state cooperated splendidly in keeping the library's name and activities before the public.

The Louisiana method was innovative, employing many ideas and policies that were ahead of their time. In 1954 Gretchen K. Schenk, formerly state librarian of Washington, described, for example, "one of the earliest attempts to apply sociological techniques in analyzing library problems [which] occurred in Michigan in 1946 when a group of county librarians met in a workshop with rural sociologists to learn more about rural readers and nonreaders," but Culver had done much the same thing two decades earlier when she surveyed Louisiana and conferred with Mary Mims of LSU concerning the needs of rural readers. Using what would later be called needs assessment, Culver "compile[d] and analyze[d] basic data about [her] target group," obtained critical information and perspective from the citizenry, and employed community networking—techniques recommended in 2002 by the ALA Office for Literacy and Outreach Services. Under her leadership, the state library agency provided the people, wherever they were, with the books they sought, whatever those might be, "shift[ing] . . . emphasis from the importance of *book ownership* to that of *book use*." A quarter-century later, "a full realization of the impact of this shift [was] not yet apparent in all quarters." Today "the American Library Association believes that the sharing of material between libraries is an integral element in the provision of library service and encourages libraries to participate."[62]

Finally, and perhaps most important, there was Essae Culver herself. When she arrived in Louisiana, "the weakest point in the library situation in the South" was "state leadership in library extension." Recognizing early "that all states cannot be organized just like California," Culver provided the leadership Louisiana needed and created a blueprint for other states.

According to Schenk, "one of Culver's foremost accomplishments was to adapt the California library plan so completely to meet Louisiana's needs that it has really become 'the Louisiana plan' and is imitated by states throughout the country." Certainly, the demonstration method of library extension was not the right one for every area, but Culver showed the nation how it could be done.[63]

When the Louisiana Library Commission commemorated its twentieth anniversary, Milton J. Ferguson described the grants to Louisiana as "the best [investment] the Carnegie Corporation made in an experiment of [this] kind." Culver deflected praise for the library's success, attributing it to the people of Louisiana and their response to the idea. "*They* did it," she claimed, "the knowledge-thirsty Cajuns, . . . the book-starved cotton farmers," while modestly discounting her own role: "I only furnished a little leadership." When someone proposed writing her biography, she spent half an hour "persuad[ing] her it was not worth her time." She believed that "talkers are not doers; and that deeds and not words will provide an opportunity for librarians to work together toward the goal of freedom and opportunity to read for all the people."[64] In the early years, however, curtailed by funding shortages and Jim Crow laws, the opportunity to read was, more accurately, for all the *white* people.

CHAPTER 4

Two Case Studies in Success

Webster and Vermilion Parishes

I n 1929 the Louisiana Library Commission took the first steps toward its goal of extending its outreach to black Louisianians. By that time, the spread of American education was making readers of the American people. From 1880 to 1940, the number of seventeen-year-olds who had graduated from high school increased from 2.5 percent to 51 percent, and illiteracy had become rare. This growing literacy among members of the working classes, both white and black, inspired concern among men and women of culture regarding what members "of the new laboring classes would read and how they would interpret what they did read." The newly literate were encouraged to select "books that would make them better workers, learning to extract information from technical manuals and to draw inspiration from model biographies, the Bible, and tracts on good behavior." Rooted in oral tradition, literacy skills among black Americans were largely invisible to whites, many of whom presumed that the "Negro race" was inherently inferior to theirs. Law and custom required the Louisiana Library Commission to turn away blacks who sought to borrow books.[1]

After a *Times-Picayune* newspaper article about the commission's work appeared in 1928, J. O. Modisette received a letter from A. P. Tureaud, vice president of a New Orleans social, pleasure, and benevolent group called the Autocrat Club, inquiring about services to organizations. Tureaud, who would later distinguish himself as a civil rights leader, requested a conference with Modisette to discuss "plans for making our immediate community a larger reading community." Modisette did some checking and became suspicious that the Autocrat Club was "a colored organization." In his reply, he "left the matter open to them to disclose who they are without the color or race question being raised by me" and referred Tureaud to the New Orleans Public Library. He encouraged Culver to handle future inquiries similarly.[2] The episode implied that black leaders would be receptive to Library Commission services.

With shrinking tax revenues, voters' unwillingness to approve new taxes, the Carnegie Corporation grant money running out, and sixty of Louisiana's sixty-four parishes still without libraries, the commission needed additional sources of funding. Culver found one that would finance a fourth parish-wide demonstration and, through it, launch rural library service to at least a small segment of Louisiana's black population. In 1929 the Julius Rosenwald Fund, which had been established ten years earlier to advance the status of black southerners, earmarked $500,000 "for experimentation in county [parish] library service in the South. It was the hope that the program would stimulate the establishment of county libraries generally and at the same time demonstrate some desirable principles of support, organization and administration." Those principles required that the library would serve the entire population, regardless of color and whether urban or rural; that the total budget would equal at least fifty cents per capita; and that all library services in the demonstration county would be coordinated in a single system under the administration of a trained librarian. Like Louisiana Library Commission demonstrations, this program mandated the local provision of suitable facilities.[3] The program seemed ideally suited for Louisiana, and the commission moved quickly in its pursuit.

The Rosenwald Demonstration in Webster Parish, 1929–1934
"Within Reach of Every Resident of the Parish"

To host the Rosenwald demonstration, Culver considered several parishes known to encourage progressive education and selected the one that arranged financing first. In her letter of application to the Rosenwald Fund, she wrote, "I would recommend for your consideration Webster Parish, in the northern part of the State, for a number of reasons. Foremost, because the people of this parish are eager for the best educational advantages possible. . . . Eleven centralized school plants are provided for white children within easy reach of each and every child in the parish, and there are twenty-three Rosenwald schools for Negroes in this parish." (She did not describe the overcrowding at some Rosenwald schools, one of which packed about 1,000 children into a small building, with as many as 105 in a single classroom.) The president of the school board and the parish superintendent agreed that the city of Minden and the parish would join forces to provide suitable community headquarters for both the central white library and the central black library. Further support came from the superintendent of schools, E. S. Richardson, who promised full cooperation and stated his belief that "the people will welcome and approve the service to all the people, including the Negro population."[4]

Webster Parish, abutting the state line shared by Louisiana and Arkansas, was regarded as 58 percent rural-farm, another 22 percent rural, and just 20 percent urban. Culver emphasized to the Rosenwald Fund that her proposal would put library service "within reach of every resident of the parish." She estimated the annual cost of the program at $16,000 and requested that the Rosenwald Fund contribute one-half of the operating cost for the first two years, one-third for the third and fourth years, and one-fifth for the fifth year, with Webster Parish leaders bound by "the moral obligation to continue on an equal plane after the demonstration." Culver pledged the same support that the Louisiana Library Commission provided to its other demonstrations, including general supervision and the indefinite loan of one thousand books already prepared for circulation. Reference and interlibrary loan services also would be available. The application was successful, and the Rosenwald Fund selected Webster as one of eleven counties in seven southern states that received funding.[5]

Robert F. Kennon, who served as mayor of Minden from 1926 to 1928 and later as governor of Louisiana, recalled that "Miss Essae came to Webster Parish to speak to various community groups [about the prospect of a demonstration]. She was capable and well-informed, confident of the usefulness and workability of parishwide library service. An expenditure such as was required for the library from the local police jury, . . . although small in comparison to that of the Library Commission, was not normal at that time. But the eventual authorization of a parish library system for Webster Parish was a vote of confidence for Miss Essae." On June 4, 1929, the police

When the Webster Parish Demonstration Library opened in 1930, racial segregation prevailed in the South, and separate facilities were maintained for white and black readers. Shown here is the Negro Library Headquarters in Minden, ca. 1940s. The shelves were nearly empty because so many books had been borrowed. (Photo by William Grabill. State Library of Louisiana)

jury passed the enabling ordinance, providing that the library's financial support would be shared by the Webster Parish School Board and the city of Minden, which, as the parish seat, would host the library headquarters.[6]

Many residents of Webster Parish did their parts to get the library off to a strong start. Parent-teacher associations in several rural areas donated money that went primarily to purchase books for the branch libraries in those localities. Students at the Evergreen School brought cotton from their families' farms, which was baled and sold to raise money for the library fund. The Louisiana Library Commission sent Mary Harris, one of its most experienced and capable professionals, to serve as demonstration librarian, and Harris pointedly included black board members in all meetings. The Library Commission gave support and sent initial collections of 1,576 books for white users and 532 for black patrons. During the first seven months, the total number of books available in the parish grew to 6,445, which circulated

72,765 times. Of the 4,985 borrowers, 1,148 were black persons, who checked out more than 9,100 publications. White borrowers numbered 3,837 and circulated 66,375 volumes. Two years later, 8,974 readers checked out 195,455 books, or 6.5 per capita. Circulation to black borrowers averaged 2.2 books per capita, a disparity Culver attributed to "the fact that many of the older generation do not read, and that no branches have been yet been placed in some 25 schools." Harris reported in 1931 that "books have been provided for every person without regard to race or lines drawn in any respect."[7]

Webster Parish's demonstration differed from prior ones in the extent to which it coordinated with the school system, creating an important precedent for future library/school cooperation. The central library occupied a rented store in the heart of Minden, but soon the need arose for separate facilities for the "Negro headquarters." A library building, largely funded by the Rosenwald and Slater Funds and the General Education Board, was constructed on the grounds of the Webster Parish Training School, with all the labor and some incidentals provided by black residents of five communities in its service area. "The librarian in charge of the Negro service," Culver recalled in 1956, a black man, "had been trained as an agricultural extension agent in addition to a summer course in library science, and he combined this training very effectively[,] evidenced by a rural parish fair at which all the products of the area were exhibited and beside each article was the book or government bulletin use by the producer. The homemakers' exhibits of canned goods, quilts, dresses, etc., exhibited books from which they obtained the dress and quilt patterns and canning directions. So successful was the parish fair that the Superintendent of Education commented to the effect that if all the people would use books and printed information as efficiently it would speed progress immeasurably." The Rosenwald project credited this librarian with "bring[ing] to many of the vocational, recreational, and cultural activities of his people the knowledge and stimulation which make possible a higher grade of living."[8]

Despite the spirit of cooperation shared by personnel of the libraries and the schools, major problems arose. First, many residents of the parish doubted that adequate library service could be provided to Webster's 29,460 residents, dispersed over the parish's 609 square miles, while maintaining racial separation. There were predictions of failure and of racial trouble. With help from black leaders and the passage of time, the numer-

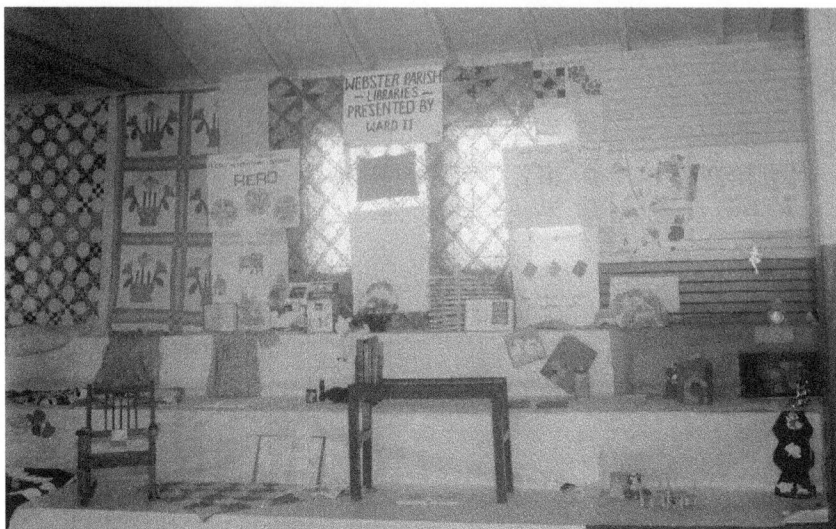

First Negro Parish Fair in Webster Parish, held at the Training School in October 1941. This exhibit, highlighting the library's role in community service, won first prize. (State Library of Louisiana)

ous rough spots were smoothed out. Second, concern arose over the ability of the libraries to serve both the schools and the community, while maintaining school accreditation requirements. The Department of Education found, however, that as a result of the parish library's work, several schools had come up to standard, and commended "most highly . . . the zeal and the efficiency with which [the library] has functioned." Third, people had to be convinced that the successful operation of libraries depended upon the work of trained librarians. Slowly they recognized that "a librarian is to the library what the pharmacist is to the drug store, the diagnostician to the hospital, or the trained teacher to the class." Before the library commemorated its third anniversary, it had "made a place for itself in the hearts and minds of the entire population, both white and black. As evidence of this fact, . . . when the parish school board was forced to reduce the entire budget 20 per cent, the appropriation for the library was not touched."[9]

Culver regarded this demonstration as "outstanding in the South, both from point of view of organization and of service." One of its innovations was an agreement, unique in Louisiana, whereby the schools turned over all of their book funds to the library, which administered them and provided the books. Where schools housed library branches, teachers served as library managers. An early model of a bookmobile carried books to outlying sections. Emblazoned on the sides for all to see as the vehicle rolled past was the library's slogan: "Books—Service—Free to All." It won the parish-wide slogan contest because it included the word "free."[10]

The "Apple Box Years"

The bookmobile helped to nourish residents of the parish physically as well as mentally. A severe drought in 1930 caused most food crops to fail, bringing the imminent prospect of famine. Rainfall that came late in the growing season was sufficient for the cultivation of peas, turnips, beans, okra, and greens, and farmers managed to produce these abundantly—but they would not survive the first frost, and the surplus was at risk of going to waste while people elsewhere were starving. School superintendent E. S. Richardson and home demonstration agent Julia Cooksey developed an emergency plan to press into service all the steam cookers from homes throughout Webster, to be used by volunteers at canning centers, hastily set up mainly at the home economics departments of schools.[11]

Black citizens contributed hampers of foodstuffs and participated enthusiastically when "canning day" was held at the Webster Parish Training School for Colored. The parish library supported this effort by lending its bookmobile to transport vegetables from farms to the school-based canning centers, which produced fifty thousand cans of vegetables and meats during an intensive two-month campaign. Superintendent Richardson reported, "This calamity has taught us two important things. First, the real need of the spirit of cooperation that is necessary to make any community worth while; second, hundreds of persons have learned how to operate steam pressure cookers."[12]

Richardson's interaction with the Library Commission extended beyond borrowing the parish bookmobile and advanced less smoothly. In the first year, misunderstandings arose from the unfamiliarity of the cooperative arrangement between the school system and the commission. Initially unaware of the time and effort required to order books and to ready them for use,

When food shortages threatened parts of Webster Parish, canning programs were set up in the home economics departments of high schools. The Webster Parish Library's bookmobile transported vegetables from the fields to the Training School, which hosted one of the parish's nine branch libraries for African Americans, 1930. Note the Webster Parish Library's motto, painted on the side of the bookmobile: "Books. Service. Free to All." (Photo by William Grabill. Earl K. Long Library, University of New Orleans, from *The Nation's Schools*, July 1931; and Northwest Louisiana Archives at LSUS)

Richardson believed that the Board of Education's appropriation exceeded the value of services that the schools received and told Culver he didn't like the librarians' attitude toward the schools and toward him. Some principals contended that they, rather than the parish librarian, should supervise the teacher-librarians. Those problems were soon worked out, and especially in the rural schools, students received vastly improved library services.[13]

Other disadvantages could not be overcome so easily. When school-based libraries also served the community, some adults avoided visiting during school hours. Teacher-librarians lacked familiarity with the book collection at the main library, which curtailed their ability to assist patrons to make selections. Also, when schools closed for the summer, most teachers left the area and had to be replaced. During the school year, forty-five buses transported far-flung students to school. That the buses did not run during summer vacation deprived students of library access if they lived too far away to walk. In the summer of 1934, a group of youngsters arranged with the driver of a school bus to work in his fields in exchange for rides to the branch library on Saturday afternoons, but small-scale solutions yielded only limited benefits.[14]

By the end of the first year, the Webster Parish Library operated eleven branches for white people and nine for black ones, eight of the latter situated in Rosenwald schools. Black schoolchildren's reading interests proved to be the same as those of children of other races, and library books ignited some rural students' interest in their schoolwork. Adults asked for books on popular science, cookery, all phases of agriculture, animal stories, games for recreational purposes, carpentry and simple house plans, and Bible stories, church manuals, and missions. "On the advice of the older Negro teachers themselves," however, book selection for some of the school-based libraries omitted "books that describe the emancipated Negro," and it is likely that an effort to avoid controversy that might have antagonized any potential voters contributed to the library's acquiescence. Rural preachers obtained material for their sermons and urged their congregations to read the books they mentioned. Publications pertaining to what would now be called black studies enjoyed popularity, with Frank Caldwell's *Wolf, the Storm Leader,* Howard W. Odum's *Rainbow Round My Shoulder,* and James Weldon Johnson's *Book of Negro Spirituals* requested often. Among novels, *Porgy, Mamba's Daughters,* and *Scarlet Sister Mary* triggered the most extensive interest. Rosenwald Fund personnel regarded the Webster demonstration as "outstanding" in its effort "to adapt the book collection to what are judged to be local needs." The plan also saved money and won praise from the schools.[15]

As the Great Depression worsened, so did funding problems. In 1933 the Minden bank collapsed, taking with it not only the library's funds but those of the school board and parish, as well, and jeopardizing the project's survival. The Webster Parish Library saw its funding halved, and some City Council members wanted to close it. An emergency grant of $2,000 from the Library Commission helped, but not enough to permit expenditures for furnishings. Crates intended for packing apples sometimes doubled as shelving, and those hard times were remembered as the "apple box years."[16]

Despite the shoestring budget, Webster, like other parishes, motivated

Readers enjoy the yard of the Couchwood branch of the Webster Parish Library, 1930s. (State Library of Louisiana)

many testimonials of the library's impact on citizens. A black farmer wrote that his community was being helped to raise its standard of living and was obtaining practical information about farming techniques. Another learned to keep farm accounts; yet another, how to terrace his land. Library bulletins and books aided the women to improve their methods of food preparation and child care. An old man who had fathered many children, none of whom had attended school, drew inspiration from a community meeting and decided to educate his youngest. In Minden, a wheelchair-bound former teacher found a new source of camaraderie and intellectual stimulation as the leader of a reading club. Men who had been laid off from their jobs used the library for the first time to prepare for new employment, and a businessman sought to improve his methods and awareness of current trends by reading on the psychology of salesmanship and on economics. Black leaders praised the library as "a great help in the advancement of living conditions for their race."[17]

When the five-year Rosenwald-funded program ended, library service to black residents of the demonstration counties was judged "greatly superior" to that which was available at its start, but it remained unsatisfactory. "The progress which has been made under favorable conditions leads to the conclusion that intelligently planned and executed library service has much to offer for the improvement of the economic, educational, and cultural status of the Negro, and that the facilities for this service should be expanded so as to bring its benefits to increasingly large numbers." Noting that "Negro service represents to most of the libraries a relatively new and very inadequately developed type of service," the final study of the Rosenwald project advocated that "interest among Negroes should be cultivated and stimulated in every way possible." Recommended means of achieving that outcome included expanding the book collections, improving the physical facilities, increasing training for custodians through courses and county-wide meetings, and employing a field representative for libraries that served black citizens.[18]

Library services to black communities remained minimal in most of the ten demonstration counties in other states, largely because the program was administered locally and was channeled through the schools. Louisiana, however, enjoyed the advantage of the already established, professionally staffed Library Commission to contribute experience and expertise, and the Webster Parish program flourished. It was so successful and offered so much potential that Rosenwald trustees extended their financial assistance for two years more, for a total of seven years. Since 1936, an ad valorem tax has provided support. When the Webster Parish Library commemorated its tenth anniversary in 1939, it reported not only extended and increased service, but, with the greatest support per capita of any library in the state, gave the most extensive service. Its steady growth and varied services positioned it as one of Webster Parish's important institutions.[19]

Perseverance in Vermilion Parish
"No One Could Question Its Success"

Interest in libraries had existed in Vermilion Parish since early in the twentieth century. Seventh in size among the state's parishes, Vermilion covered some 1,200 square miles. Low and swampy where it met the Gulf of Mexico, it supported a flourishing rice industry and some of the world's largest game preserves. In its towns, as in so many localities nationwide during the decades surrounding the turn of the twentieth century, clubwomen blazed the way to the library. Members of the Women's Club in Abbeville had organized a small circulating library in their town in 1907, but lack of funds forced its closure four years later. It reopened in 1916, after a visit from Lutie Stearns kindled renewed interest. Spreading the same message that Culver would soon repeat throughout Louisiana, Stearns spoke first to a Women's Club convention in Monroe in November 1915 and shortly afterward to a large and receptive audience in Abbeville. An impassioned advocate for the right to information, Stearns recounted experiences in Wisconsin that ignited the idea of a parish-wide library movement in Vermilion. Town libraries existed already in Gueydan and Kaplan, and supporters there shared their Abbeville neighbors' enthusiasm for a cooperative effort of the sort that Stearns advocated.[20]

Shortly after arriving in Louisiana ten years later, in mid-November 1925, Essae Culver attended a Louisiana Federation of Women's Clubs convention, and it was probably there that she met the president of the Little Library Association of Vermilion Parish. Culver explained the potential workings of a parish library system and encouraged the club officer to "help create sentiment for a library to serve all the people of the parish." The people of Vermilion took full advantage of the commission's books-by-mail service as an ever-widening circle of library users encompassed teachers, students, clubwomen, and businessmen, and other readers throughout the parish. Because of their enthusiasm, Culver received invitations to speak at school commencements and to advise how school and club libraries in Abbeville, Gueydan, and Kaplan might be improved.[21]

Vermilion Parish had been settled largely by descendants of the Acadians who were deported from Canada in the eighteenth century. They found in Louisiana a hospitable home among others who, like themselves, adhered to the Roman Catholic faith and the French language. Ninety percent of the parish's population still spoke French, and probably little English, even in the 1930s. As Culver explained to the *New York Times,* "We never think of these people as illiterate when we meet them. . . . Their social life is polished, they dance well, they converse well. But through a lack of schooling their pronunciation, even of French, has become confused, and they have reached a state where, although they can converse, they cannot read or write either French or English." Culver found that, "although their background of culture and wealth of tradition equals that of any of their more literate neighbors," this linguistic confusion factored into pushing Vermilion's rate of illiteracy to 37.3 percent, one of the three highest among Louisiana's sixty-four parishes. It made their eagerness for a library all the more poignant.[22]

Despite the citizens' apparent enthusiasm for libraries, more than five years passed before Vermilion's demonstration library opened in early 1931. Using much the same strategy that it had previously implemented four times (in Richland, Jefferson Davis, Concordia, and Webster Parishes), the commission proposed to set up a parish library financed for the first year largely by the state. In addition to paying the salary of a librarian qualified to supervise the project, it would send more than four thousand books; parish and local governing agencies would provide facilities, supervisors at the branches, and operating expenses estimated at $1,500. Prior to the September 1930 meeting of the police jury at which the library demonstration was on the agenda, Culver had been forewarned of resistance, although library supporters had plied their jurors with entreaties. New libraries meant new taxes, and the Great Depression had made times hard. After the demonstration year concluded, local funding had to take over—and that required more than $1,500. A Vermilion politician who had been elected on an economy platform was predicted to lead the opposition.[23]

Culver explained the program to an audience that included the president of the police jury, the superintendent of schools, and the head of the Chamber of Commerce. Although she expected to see friendly faces in the crowd, she did not anticipate Lenora Vaughan. When Culver finished speaking, the white-haired woman, attired in the style of the nineteenth century, stepped forward from the rear of the room. She had come by boat and on foot from Pecan Island, walking the last two miles of the journey, to appeal on behalf of her four hundred fellow islanders for a library. "I have lived on Pecan Island for 50 years," Vaughan told the crowd. During those years, access to good books would have meant a great deal to her. "When I got married I realized that I would be an ignoramus if I did not learn to read. Gentlemen, the only reason I'm able to talk to you now, is because of the scraps of papers and magazines I found lying around that I picked up and read. Today, I'm writing the story of my life so that my grandchildren will have something to read."[24]

Fourteen miles long and half a mile wide, Pecan Island is not so much an island as a ridge of high land jutting out of the marshes of Vermilion Parish. Accessible only by water, Pecan Island remained in 1930 almost as remote as when its first settler arrived nearly a century earlier. The mail boat, its only contact with the world beyond its borders, came once a week. Many inhabitants of the self-sufficient settlement earned a living mainly by fishing, trapping fur-bearing animals in the winter, and serving as guides to hunters from the mainland. They built the schoolhouse themselves. No policeman, doctor, or dentist lived on the island. Isolated Pecan Islanders needed the printed page to substitute for the educational, recreational, and inspirational opportunities that city dwellers enjoyed, and Lenora Vaughan's eloquence ensured that they got it. When she finished speaking, the economy-minded politician leaped to his feet and pledged to appropriate as much money as the library needed. Culver left Abbeville convinced that "books mean just as much to the uneducated as they do to the most scholarly."[25]

A field representative employed by the Louisiana Library Commission selected books and equipment. She worked with local supporters to identify a headquarters site and, in each town, branch locations where pedestrian traffic was greatest. Opening day was set for February 16, 1931. When a truck carrying the first three thousand books arrived at the headquarters in Abbeville, the parish seat, "the farmers around came to help unload them," Mrs. W. P. Edwards, a member of the Vermilion Parish Library Board, told the Louisiana Library Association a few months later. "The books were put on the shelves during the morning. That night not a book was left. Every one had been loaned to someone eager for a book. There are 34,000 inhabitants of the parish. The circulation of the books amounted to 11,000 the first week.[26]

"Men who hadn't read for 20 years are reading constantly now," Edwards continued. "One merchant I met going home one evening had three books under his arm. . . . At first, one town councilman said this was just the scheme of some book company to sell a lot of books in Vermillion [sic]. But that man is reading all the time now." While school was closed during the summer, the principal, "realizing how much reading meant to the whole community, drove miles each Saturday to issue books from the branch library in the school house." One little boy, a habitual Saturday borrower, walked five miles to the school to get his books, even with a sore heel. The mail boat delivered books to Pecan Island.[27]

In the 1930s, this mail boat, the *Crescent,* ran between Abbeville and Pecan Island in Vermilion Parish. For isolated Pecan Islanders, it was the only means of leaving their high ridge of land. That it was also the Louisiana Library Commission's only means of sending books to the branch library there exemplifies the rudimentary nature of support services available to the commission in rural Louisiana. (State Library of Louisiana)

Librarians responded to special requests on such diverse topics as Louisiana history, the Spanish-American War, radio advertising, retail merchandising, the importance of the world's great rivers, old quilts, china, pottery, violin makers, astronomy, abnormal psychology, radio telegraphy, stocks and bonds, incorporation law, literature for children, and elementary-school teaching. During the first year, seventy-six thousand volumes circulated in Vermilion—an average of about nineteen times per book, a deceptively low figure because as many as four or five readers perused some of the books before returning them. "The good that has been accomplished thereby," proclaimed the editor of the Abbeville *Meridional,* "cannot be measured in dollars and cents."[28]

But it took dollars and cents to fund library operations. When the demonstration period neared an end and the time came to vote on an ap-propriation, the library board declined to call for a tax election because the prevailing economic hardships made passage hopeless. Banks were shut-tered, the police jury was $39,000 in debt, and people struggled financially. The initial allocation carried the library until September 1932, when its nine branches closed. With monetary help from the Abbeville town coun-cil, the library there continued to operate until 1938, when housing prob-lems forced it, too, to shut down. The failure of the Vermilion Parish Library Demonstration could not be attributed to disinterest, for, "from the point of view of service rendered, volumes circulated, and number of people bene-fited by the service, no one could question its success." Many of the books went to Sabine Parish for use there in the next library demonstration.[29]

A Second Chance

A few years later, Vermilion got another chance at library service when the Louisiana Library Commission scheduled a second one-year demonstra-tion. Headquartered at Abbeville again and housed in the Masonic Temple, the new Vermilion Parish Library Demonstration opened on March 3, 1941, with more than eight thousand books (the total later exceeded ten thou-sand, the most the Library Commission had yet provided to a demonstra-tion) and a bookmobile to serve smaller communities and isolated fami-lies. Improved economic conditions and a larger budget made possible a better-organized and more extensively equipped library. State funding in the amount of $15,000 offset most of the cost, supplemented by federal as-sistance. Vermilion's share of $2,000 for operating expenses came from the police jury, the school board, and the towns of Abbeville and Kaplan, which appropriated $500 each, with smaller contributions from three other towns and from individuals and organizations.[30]

Vermilion's citizens "had not forgotten the joy of having books available all over the parish to be read for the asking," and evidence of the library's impor-tance to them soon poured in. At the Kaplan branch, patrons set a record by checking out 125 books in the first two hours the library was open—an average of more than one per minute. Even the routine transactions filled real needs. The library "help[ed] the unskilled, unemployed man preparing himself to hold a job in essential industry; the skilled worker, either in re-education

Library personnel unpacking books and preparing them for the formal opening of the Gueydan branch of the Vermilion Parish Library, 1941. (Photo by Stroube's Photo Department. State Library of Louisiana)

or preparing for greater responsibility; the research worker in every field, [and] the farmer who must adjust to new economic conditions." The bookmobile, staffed by a French-speaking librarian and a French-speaking driver who "knew every man, woman and child [in the parish] and was related to a large number of them," was widely called the "blue bus" or, by the French speakers, "le bookmobeele." It proved to be a resounding success. One of its patrons, a fifteen-year-old girl, had never attended school because her mother, who was chronically ill, needed her at home. Using easy books from the library, her little sisters began teaching her to read.[31]

French-speaking members of the older generation, educated in the years when Vermilion schools were conducted in French, had long lacked books in their language. Both along the bookmobile route and in the branches, they welcomed the opportunity to renew their familiarity with the printed word.

Vermilion Parish residents traveled by buggy to meet the bookmobile, 1950. Those whose primary language was French knew the vehicle as "le bookmobeele." (State Library of Louisiana)

Popular topics among all borrowers reflected the growing concern with war industries and, after the Japanese attack on Pearl Harbor on December 7, 1941, America's entry into World War II. Demand soared for books about the war and about the history and geography of places where local soldiers were fighting. When resources in the parish could not answer patrons' questions, librarians obtained books from the Library Commission—692 of them by year's end. Total circulation in Vermilion during that period reached 107,438, or about 2.8 books per parish resident. That the number compared unfavorably with the national average of 4.3 suggests that not everyone had flocked to the library.[32]

Nevertheless, when Lenora Vaughan and a large delegation of other citizens called on the police jury on January 6, 1942, to ask that a tax election be scheduled, little persuasion was necessary. Although some areas still suffered from the effects of a flood in 1940, generally the parish was thriving. Educators and other leaders acknowledged the library's value in raising the literacy level by providing an informal means of continuing education that appealed both to adults with little formal schooling and to those who had long ago left the classroom. On February 14, voters approved the millage decisively, with 563 in favor (assessed valuation: $1,557,578) and 250 opposed (assessed valuation: $791,607). In the town of Gueydan and on Pecan Island, no one voted against the library tax.[33]

By 1947 the library headquarters in Abbeville had outgrown its rented facilities in the Masonic Temple, and no building could be found that was large enough. At the library board's request, the police jury scheduled a vote on a bond issue to construct a new one. The result was overwhelmingly favorable—339 for (assessed valuation: $1,009,714) and 94 against (assessed valuation: $209,920). Construction of the new library soon began, and it was dedicated on March 12, 1950, as a memorial to Vermilion members of the military who lost their lives in World Wars I and II. Much interest in improving library facilities existed around this time. Other localities that constructed their own branch libraries included Erath (1948), Kaplan (1952), and Gueydan (1953).[34]

Even isolated Pecan Island had a library facility of its own, housed in the Vaughan-Copell Memorial Building, appropriately named in honor of Lenora Vaughan, who had campaigned so effectively for a library and had become esteemed as the matriarch of Pecan Island. Plans and fundraising had been under way for years, with $1,000 from the school board, generous contributions from oil companies drilling in the vicinity, and whatever the inhabitants could raise. Those with no money to spare gave a day's work, or two or three. They and other local volunteers constructed the library themselves on land donated by the school board, and the parish library supplied equipment. Doors opened in 1949, and during the first year, circulation to Pecan Island's 450 inhabitants reached 7,105 volumes. After the novelty wore off, borrowing hovered around four hundred books per month. Westerns were popular, not surprising in a center where ranching had become a common occupation and where community butcherings provided sporadic opportunity for conviviality and fresh meat.[35]

A native of the island, Olga Conner, ran the library with a few departures from standard practices. Because she also worked right next door in the Conner General Store, she could open the doors whenever anyone wanted something to read, as well as during the scheduled hours of 1:00 to 3:00 each

Young women reading at a table at the Vaughan-Copell Memorial Library, the Pecan Island branch of the Vermilion Parish Library, 1952. (State Library of Louisiana)

afternoon. New books arrived on the mail boat, which now came twice a week. Conner occasionally took time off from the store and the library to travel the forty miles to Abbeville to pick up special requests. Once, when she realized that many books were overdue, she offered the schoolchildren a nickel for each volume they found and returned. The results amazed her: the children brought in several hundred books.[36]

The Vermilion Parish Library demonstrations illustrate something of the professional expertise and the human drama behind efforts to establish rural library service in Louisiana. Between 1926 and 1968, similar scenarios played out across the state as the Louisiana Library Commission and its successor agency, the Louisiana State Library, worked with citizens to establish libraries in the sixty-three rural parishes.

CHAPTER 5

The Depression Years, 1930–1941

W hen the Carnegie-funded demonstration of what a state library commission could do for rural citizens concluded in 1930, successful libraries had been launched in three parishes— Richland, Concordia, and Webster, with Vermilion to open in February 1931—and Louisiana, along with the rest of the nation, struggled in the grip of the Great Depression. Rampant unemployment had idled many workers, and those fortunate enough to keep jobs earned low wages. Everywhere, agricultural and industrial production dropped, but the latter had relatively little effect in the Pelican State because not much industry existed there. Its residents may have suffered less than most Americans because their economic situation had long been worse than that of the nation as a whole. The average income of Louisiana families in 1930 fell below half the national average, and especially in rural areas, people were accustomed to hard times. To many, walking ten miles over unpaved roads to school or to the crossroads store was a familiar part of everyday life. The Great Depression affected Louisianians by perpetuating these harsh economic realities through ongoing joblessness, low agricultural yield and prices, and cutbacks in plans for industrial expansion. Farmers continued to be the most beleaguered of all.[1]

The consequences of the depressed economy extended to Louisiana libraries, both by curtailing their development and by presenting opportunities for them to contribute to relieving citizens' distress. One of the first and most apparent results was the collapse of the first Vermilion Parish

Library Demonstration. For much of 1932, the Richland Parish Library could not meet its payroll, and in Concordia the library's income dropped from $6,000 in 1933 to $3,536 in 1937 because of the decrease in assessed valuations. No new parish demonstrations could be started between 1934 and 1936, primarily because of inadequate funding, although requests had been received from thirty parishes. Nevertheless, only Richland was compelled to reduce weekly hours, and all maintained or increased the number of distribution points from 1934 through 1937. Culver reported at the end of 1937 that, "while the showings made by the parish libraries of Louisiana are very creditable, not one of them has reached its potential usefulness, due to lack of funds. Not one library in the state has reached the standard set by the American Library Association, which says that the appropriation for quality library service should be $1.00 per capita."[2]

Monetary problems plagued the headquarters library, too, where a 10 percent cut in its appropriation led to "retrenchment" and layoffs in 1930. In April 1933, Essae Culver reneged on agreements with two publishers, Longmans, Green & Co. and Macmillan, to host displays of their new books for children because the Library Commission could not afford to pay the shipping costs. She explained to both companies, "Just now our banks are closed, two here [in Baton Rouge], two in New Orleans, and elsewhere, state funds are tied up, and we do not know whether we shall have even postage for the next few months. The libraries have nothing to spend for books just now and could not even pay transportation." In 1936 the American Library Association's Section for Library Work with Children organized traveling exhibits of children's books that libraries could receive free of charge, and the Louisiana Library Commission eagerly took advantage of the offer. To afford maximum opportunity for librarians, teachers, parents, and children to peruse the books, the commission routed them to schools, libraries, and clubs throughout the state. The purpose of the exhibit was to create a demand for good books and to highlight innovations in the production of children's books, and recipients examined the displays so enthusiastically that the commission continued to obtain them. When no longer needed for exhibit, the books became part of the Library Commission's collection.[3]

In another effort to spur a demand for good books, in 1932 the commission issued reading certificates to thirty-three persons who had read twelve "good" books during the year. "Reading is contagious," library personnel reasoned, "and when a good book is read, enjoyed and talked about by one person, a dozen others wish to read." The number of readers aspiring to earn certificates increased approximately 400 percent in 1933, and thousands more citizens read some of the books. Culver reported, "When unemployment, financial difficulties of major magnitude, and enforced leisure were everywhere, the libraries gave a valiant performance,—proving to be sources of spiritual comfort, factual information, and professional advice. The response that such service earned has been an increased good-will, and the effects will long be remembered." Reading certificates grew in popularity, which justified continuing the program. "The [mental] stimulation that comes from diversified reading," Culver stated, "seems to be as good for the people as some balance in their physical diets, and the response to the reading certificate lists and awards has been gratifying."[4]

The depression did not impede the construction of the new, thirty-three-story State Capitol. Since Culver's arrival in 1925, commission headquarters had occupied cramped rooms in the State Capitol (today known as the Old State Capitol), its operations increasingly hindered by the inadequacy of its facilities as demands upon its services grew. While the new Capitol building was in the planning stage, Culver "called the architects and asked them what provision was being made for the Louisiana Library Commission, [and] they said they didn't know there *was* such a thing as a library commission. But they were interested, I must say that, so they gave us space in the basement for a work room," where the Extension Department repaired books for the demonstrations, as well as the entire eighteenth floor. Later the work room was "taken away from us for a barber shop."[5]

On Monday, May 16, 1932, Culver attended ceremonies dedicating the new building and inaugurating Huey Long's successor as governor, Oscar K. Allen (1932–1936). Later in the week, the commission moved to its new accommodations. Culver boasted that the move required just two days, with no interruption of library services. The Baton Rouge *Morning Advocate* predicted, "When the Louisiana Library commission [is] in its new headquarters at the new capitol where space for storing books, and large roomy offices have been provided, a new era will dawn for the commission—but it will continue to bring inspiration, service and romance into the lives of individuals in remote districts, and to others as well."[6]

Spacious, airy quarters housed more shelving, which released many

Essae Martha Culver (center), Louisiana's first state librarian, with librarians Sallie Farrell (left) and Debora Abramson (right), in Louisiana Library Commission offices in the State Capitol, late 1930s. (State Library of Louisiana)

volumes from storage. Among the new furnishings that greeted visitors throughout the offices were comfortable chairs and eight tables that permitted readers, for the first time, to consult books at commission headquarters. Another innovation was a rare book room with a fireproof vault, intended to house valuable books and documents owned by the commission and to accommodate future donations and historical materials that private owners deposited for safekeeping. Increased space made it feasible to offer new services, and in July, the commission launched a series of reading courses sponsored by the American Library Association. By August, when the commission began exhibiting reproductions of famous paintings, its new accommodations had generated so much interest that scores of people toured them each day. The staff settled in and tackled the increased demands occasioned by the extensive publicity and by preparations to demonstrate library services in another parish.[7]

"Enough Interested in Providing Good Books"

"As conditions are at present," Culver had written to Governor Huey Long in 1931, "there is no aid, federal, state, or local, to parishes starting a library service." Explaining that "without doubt, more parish libraries will mean students better prepared for public school and university education, more business progress, and, certainly, better community development," she appealed for additional revenue, but to no avail. When a request for a demonstration came from the library-minded citizens of Sabine Parish, the commission's annual appropriation of $18,900 was insufficient to encompass such an endeavor along with regular expenses. Again, the Louisiana Library Commission approached the Carnegie Corporation, and again, Carnegie funding made the demonstration possible, providing $4,922.91 for the salary of a professional librarian and the purchase of books. The police jury pledged $1,500 toward local expenses, such as travel within the parish to distribute books. Also, a small balance left from the Carnegie grant enabled the commission to reorganize and strengthen the Richland Parish Library, thus helping it to attain a higher standard of service.[8]

Although Long failed to increase the commission's budget, he was, as Culver reminded him in 1932, "enough interested in providing good books for the people of Louisiana to favor the State's appropriating a fund that might be spent in bringing about the establishment of parish libraries in order to reach the rural population as well as the urban. . . . Thinking you might know of some way to help us out of this difficulty of providing what the people really want and need, I am asking you again if you can assist us in any way to secure funds for this purpose." By that time, Long had been elected to the U.S. Senate. Although his boyhood friend and handpicked successor, O. K. Allen, held the governorship, Huey continued to run both the state and O. K. Allen. Neither of them came through with the hoped-for library funding, and the commission, which had requested $50,000 per year, received $18,500. The coarse and powerful Long, to his credit, expanded access to medical care for the poor, elevated the status of Louisiana State University, provided free textbooks to students, and built new schools, highways, and bridges.[9]

Long's road-building program had coincided nicely with the arrival of the state's first bookmobile, making it possible for libraries on wheels to make their way through rural Louisiana as efficiently as they did. In 1928, the year Long became governor, the state had just 331 miles of paved highways and three major bridges, none of which spanned the Mississippi River. He promptly instituted a program of highway construction that proved to be the most immediate and most apparent of his public works projects. Governor Allen continued the work, and by 1935, 2,400 miles of concrete highways, 1,300 miles of asphalt roads, and 4,000 more miles of gravel roads wound through Louisiana. In addition, two bridges across the Mississippi River, one at Baton Rouge and the other at New Orleans, were under construction, and more than forty new spans crossed the smaller rivers—and all the roads and bridges were toll-free. This improved network of highways and bridges, one of the best in the nation, did more than open the byways to bookmobiles; it opened rural Louisiana to greater contact with the outside world, which also brought improved commerce, medical care, and access to modern conveniences.[10]

On Sunday, September 8, 1935, Culver recorded in her journal, "Senator Long shot by Dr. Carl Austin Weiss—Eye Ear Nose & Throat specialist . . . at close of session of Legislature in halls just before door to Gov[ernor]'s office." For three days, as the senator hovered near death, the state and the nation held its collective breath, and Culver made daily notations regarding his condition in her journal. On September 10, she wrote, "Senator Long very low. Slight hopes for recovery," and on September 11, "Senator Long died at 4:10 a.m. today." On the twelfth, Culver, Mary Harris, and Lois Shortess went to the Capitol, where he lay in state, "to pay our resp[ec]ts to Senator Long. [We] were told 2,200 people passed the bier all night long." Library Commission headquarters closed at noon "out of respect to Sen. Long." His funeral that afternoon, according to a biographer, was "the most lavish and best attended that Louisiana ever knew." Shortly before it began, Culver, overlooking the Capitol grounds from her window, speculated that "20,000 people are on the grounds," but other estimates (including people watching from rooftops and other nearby vantage points, as well as the Capitol grounds), reached 175,000.[11]

In 1937, in an extension of the textbook legislation, the state spent $250,000 in revenues from severance taxes to buy library books for schools in thirty-eight parishes—thereby, stated school library supervisor Lois Shortess, positioning Louisiana as the first state to purchase school library books without requiring matching funds to be raised locally. But it remained for Allen's successor to find more money for the Louisiana Library Commission.[12]

"In Trying Times like These"

In January 1933, the most extensive demonstration library to date opened in Sabine, a large, north Louisiana parish with a population of thirty thousand, of whom twenty thousand were white. The Sabine Gas Company lent the headquarters building, and fifteen distribution points were set up throughout the parish. To administer the demonstration, the Library Commission sent two of its most capable librarians, Sarah Irwin Jones and, as her assistant, Mathilde ("Tillie") Abramson. Some of the seven thousand books were left from the failed Vermilion Parish demonstration, but they were selected in consideration of Sabine citizens' interests and abundantly supplemented by new purchases. Books for children represented 60 percent of the collection, with the remainder divided about equally between adult fiction and informational books, including history, biography, travel, hobbies such as hunting and fishing, music, art, homemaking, and how-to-do-it. Patrons asked specifically for books on ways to farm, the training and care of bird dogs, how to construct a creosoting plant, the power and control of the Gulf Stream, the effect of climate on the history of the world, bass fishing with fly and bait casting, building a pottery kiln, writing collection letters, landscape gardening, studio art studies, radios, and disaster relief. Not surprisingly, considering the prevailing circumstances, many readers requested a book entitled *Hard Times: The Way In and the Way Out.*[13]

Residents of Sabine greeted their new library with the same enthusiasm with which residents of other parishes had welcomed theirs. "When we announced the opening of our library in Sabine parish," Culver said, "there were more people on hand waiting for the books than we had books to supply. Some of the children cried in disappointment. We sent post haste for more books to satisfy this demand." At a distribution point in Pearson, a former sawmill town in which half of the houses sat vacant, children lined up for half a block to await the arrival of the books and checked out ninety-six of them in the first hour. Michael Carrol, a rural letter carrier, observed, "You see people from the 'silver haired daddy' down to little tots, hurrying around every corner from every direction with books under their arms, headed as straight to the door of the library as a martin to his gourd."[14]

A disproportionate number of Sabine borrowers were women, whose reading interests centered on their homes and families: child rearing, quilting and embroidering, interior decorating, meal planning. Culver, perhaps reflecting on her own culturally rich upbringing and fulfilling career, found herself deeply moved by "the plight of rural women in a few of the more backward or isolated communities.... 'They have so little to interest them [that] their minds get rusty from lack of use. I asked someone what they talked about, and he smiled ruefully and said: "Marriage, birth and death." It is incredible that there are so many grown women who are starved for reading matter.'" She hoped someday to "have more money, enough to carry good books to every settlement in the state." In December 1933, a resolution of the Sabine Parish Police Jury established the library as a permanent agency, thereby ensuring that its services would remain available to residents of the parish.[15]

Praising the expansion of parish libraries to Sabine, the editor of the Baton Rouge *State-Times* noted that "especially during these times [of unemployment], when many have undesired leisure, library service is a boon." Another corollary of the Great Depression was shortened school terms, for school boards—at least eighteen of them—lacked the money to pay teachers, utility bills, and other expenses. Children filled their new-found free hours with reading, and freshly out-of-work adults began studying subjects that might enhance their value to future employers. Consequently, more patrons found their way to the Louisiana Library Commission's reading room or borrowed books by mail. The Baton Rouge *Morning Advocate* editorialized, "The importance of good books for leisure hours cannot be over emphasized.... It is in trying times like these that the value and the necessity of books is demonstrated to a remarkable degree.... The works of the masters, handed down to us from generation to generation, as well as the many worthwhile modern books, provide inspiration and information to persons without a job to do at this time." Library usage under the prevailing conditions confirmed an observation by writer and editor Louis Untermeyer in an address on "What Americans Read and Why": "people read either to escape life or to understand it more fully."[16]

In 1937, Concordia Parish, like Richland a decade earlier, experienced flooding. Although spring routinely brought high water, that year there was enough of it to be disruptive. Backwater from the Mississippi River covered a large section of the parish and necessitated closing every school in Concordia. Library headquarters moved temporarily, from the first floor of the Ferriday City Hall to the second, in case of rising water. In scenes reminiscent of Richland, some of the branches that remained open could be reached only by boat and took the precaution of sending about half of their holdings to Ferriday. One of the two branches that closed completely, in New Era, did so because it was needed to house evacuees from flooded areas. The manager wrote to Sarah Jones at commission headquarters, "Very much to my regret I am having to send in the books. The people that are staying here are in great need of the library room. I mailed 11 boxes of books yesterday but they will not all be delivered at the same time as the mail is being carried in a small speed boat."[17]

Similarly, the custodian of the Acme branch reported, "I'm mailing you several boxes of books. I am reserving a few books for adults as quite a few are staying here and you know it will mean a lot to have a book to read in order to forget the desolation around us. Water is now three feet deep in my house, built as you know on a knoll." Unwanted leisure caused by flooding, like that created by unemployment and by school closures, impelled people to turn to reading, just as their Richland neighbors had done a decade before, and the Concordia Parish Library circulated 4,840 books in a single month. Distribution of books to the branches was suspended, but Ferriday residents contributed magazines for evacuees' use. Those containing plans for constructing boat models were in high demand.[18]

"The Profession of Librarianship"

The administrative librarians of the Sabine and Concordia Parish Libraries, like those of all the demonstrations and libraries established under the auspices of the Louisiana Library Commission, possessed education for and experience in librarianship. To ensure this standard, Culver and Modisette had provided in the Library Law of 1926 for the establishment of a State Board of Library Examiners, comprised of three trained and experienced librarians appointed by the commission, who would certify the credentials of those seeking "to practice the profession of librarianship." Culver moved expeditiously to establish the board, which has met at least annually since 1927 to administer written tests and oral interviews to applicants who offered the appropriate combination of education, experience, and temperament.[19]

At the time, Henry M. Gill, whose unenlightened attitude toward literacy among minorities had reduced the newly arrived Culver to unprecedented depths of weariness, had served since 1906 as New Orleans city librarian. The appointed position, long considered a "political plum," had been exempted since 1924 from the civil service system within which the rest of the New Orleans Public Library, along with the city's other agencies, operated. New Orleans also was excused from the certification requirement for library administrators. Gill and his next two successors, Daniel D. Moore (1928–32) and Edward Alexander Parsons (1932–35), could not have been certified, for they lacked the required library training and, "whatever their educational attainments, . . . were as innocent of public library practice as the brawniest stevedore on the waterfront." Rather, they fit the description of the "gentleman scholar," a man of refinement who devoted his time to intellectual pursuits and generally believed that the library, as Gill declared in 1926, "should build up coll[ections] to which serious people would come. . . . Others," Culver inferred, "not wanted in effect."[20] Nothing could have been more inimical to her philosophy.

A pervasive lack of confidence in the city library's administration and a groundswell of support for hiring a professional librarian had existed as early as 1928, when Gill was removed from his post and library advocates urged that the library board "secure a trained and experienced person, [so] that the public may receive the best service possible." D. D. Moore, a member of the board, took over the management of the library without compensation until March 13, 1929, when the board—from which he had recently resigned—named him to the position permanently at an annual salary of $4,500. Moore's appointment did not quell calls for a professional librarian, "skilled in his profession, and free of political bosses." Indeed, they grew louder during the administration of Edward A. Parsons, who was appointed city librarian on March 4, 1932, after Moore resigned amid Mayor T. Semmes Walmsley's extensive reorganization of the library. Qualifications that Walmsley sought in a librarian included the absence of "bigotry or narrowness." Further, the mayor "recommended that a man selected as librar-

In contrast to the opulence of the New Orleans Public Library, shown here between 1932 and 1934, the utilitarian buildings that the Louisiana Library Commission spread throughout rural Louisiana emphasized access over architecture. City librarian Edward A. Parsons can be seen in this photograph of the lobby, a small figure in black standing near the circulation desk against the left wall. (Williams Research Center, The Historic New Orleans Collection, Edward Alexander Parsons Collection, Mss 665, Acc. No. 91-77-L.20)

ian must be capable and 'know books.' 'A man,' he said, 'who while learned must have tolerance and patience with those who have not had the benefits of higher education and who will be able to direct the reading of people who seek proper direction from it.'"[21]

Parsons (1878–1962), a native New Orleanian, personified the gentleman scholar. He offered credentials superior to those of his counterparts because of his lifelong love of books and an extraordinary personal ambition to collect them. An attorney who practiced his profession until his death, Parsons participated actively in numerous cultural and historical organizations, including a lengthy tenure as president of the Louisiana Historical Society; served on the Board of Education and the Board of Curators of the Louisiana State Museum; and wrote nine books and many articles. He began collecting books as a fourteen-year-old, walking to school to save streetcar fare, which he combined with his allowance to fund purchases, and he cultivated a talent for sneaking the volumes into the house to conceal their quantity from his parents. This was the genesis of his personal collection, which came to be known as the Biblioteca Parsoniana. When the University of Texas bought it in 1958, it occupied ten rooms of the sixteen-room Parsons residence and was regarded as one of the three finest private libraries in the nation.[22]

Hints of Parsons's impending designation as city librarian became public even before the board that elected him had been legally constituted. Objection to his appointment began immediately, with emphasis on his salary: $3,000 more than his predecessor's. At $7,500, it would account for 10 percent of the library's budget and result in an equivalent reduction in money available for services to the public—"and," the editor of the *Times-Picayune* exclaimed indignantly, "just as the mayor and Commission Council are moving to reduce, by 5 to 15 percent, the salaries of all municipal employees!" Dissatisfaction peaked at the beginning of 1935, when Parsons announced that a budget cut had necessitated curtailing branch library hours and eliminating ten jobs that, in total, paid $7,172 annually—less than his own remuneration, which remained unchanged.[23]

Organized by the Woman Citizen's Union, members of more than thirty civic and professional groups, like their nineteenth-century ancestors who had crusaded for a library commission, led the public outcry. Stressing that their interest was not "in the removal, appointment or promotion of any individual . . . [but rather] in the development of the public library system in New Orleans," they formed the Interorganization Committee for Better Library Service to work toward that end (it subsequently reorganized as the New Orleans Library League, to work permanently for the library's betterment). The first outcome of the group's involvement was that Parsons reinstated some of the curtailed hours, subsidizing them with a voluntary 10 percent reduction of his pay. Second, in response to the committee's "agitation over a long period . . . for a study by a group of professional Southern librarians of the needs of the library system," the board hired two nationally recognized librarians recommended by the American Library Association, Joseph L. Wheeler of the Enoch Pratt Public Library in Baltimore and Jesse Cunningham, Memphis city librarian, to conduct a "survey"—that is, an evaluation—of the library system.[24]

After studying the New Orleans Public Library for three days, Wheeler and Cunningham submitted their report. They devoted eleven of its eighty-four pages to a scathing criticism of Parsons, who, they wrote, should be removed "because of his inability to direct the library, indifference to employees, ignorance of library methods and waste of public funds." Among other points, they criticized his general incompetence, nepotism (one of his daughters worked at the library), his practice of buying rare and costly books that were of dubious interest to the reading public, the excessively high salary, and his continuation of his law practice, which curtailed the amount of time he spent at the library. Further, the librarians stated that "in 25 years of professional experience we have not heard of a situation in so large a city where conditions are so bad as we find them here. . . . The people of New Orleans have never had a chance to get adequate book service." They recommended various reforms, including the "appointment of an outstanding librarian, in his prime, college and library-school trained . . . of recognized administrative ability, and experienced in previous administrative positions," and the reduction of the librarian's annual salary to a maximum of $4,800.[25]

In a sixty-one-page, item-by-item rebuttal, Parsons disagreed vigorously, accusing Wheeler and Cunningham of attacking him personally and of an "ill-concealed hatred of bookmen or collectors and their deliberate, ignorant or wicked statement that the book collector is not a librarian." Asserting that he "has devoted his life to the cause of books," he denounced the survey as "partial, preconceived, purpose-serving, prejudiced, inconsistent and wholly destructive." One of the surveyors, upon receiving a copy of the rebuttal, claimed that "it furnished additional evidence of the correctness of the surveyors' report." At a meeting to consider both the survey and the rebuttal, the library board voted to reduce Parsons's salary to $4,800. "Immediately upon the passing of this motion Mr. Parsons, who was seated on the platform near the members of the board, arose and declared that he 'would not be interested' in the position of librarian at such a [low] salary."

The board summarily declared the position of city librarian vacant as of June 1 and subsequently invested Mildred Guthrie, head of the circulation department, with authority to act temporarily as librarian.[26]

Although the library board immediately announced its intention to base its selection of a new city librarian on the Wheeler and Cunningham recommendations and began to accept applications, a year-long interregnum ensued while civic groups continued to press for professional training and segments of the public argued against the necessity for it. A major obstacle was the preference for a librarian who resided in New Orleans, for none of the trained applicants did so. At the beginning of 1936, however, an appointment seemed imminent until Edward Estalote, an Algiers attorney who claimed to represent unnamed individuals and groups, filed suit to restrain the board from appointing a nonresident, even though a qualified librarian. He condemned the survey report as "a document full of damned foolishness and stupidities." After Judge Walter L. Gleason of the Civil District Court ruled "that the public library board has the right to appoint any librarian it finds competent," the board began considering applicants.[27]

The Interorganization Committee brought in Essae Culver to discuss "the ways in which a trained librarian in New Orleans could aid the state in its program of library development." "'This plan would be greatly aided by a strong library system in New Orleans,' she said, 'and appointment of a trained librarian here would have a marked effect on the remainder of the state. The most forward step that you could take would be to appoint as librarian a person of training with large vision and a knowledge of methods which would give the best service. It would be a waste of your money,' she continued, 'to put in the library someone who must learn by experience. Other cities have found that a trained librarian gives better service than an untrained person.'" An appreciative audience received Culver's address favorably, but they were supporters already. The conflict continued. Milton Ferguson called it "the second battle of New Orleans."[28]

Opposition festered within the library board's own ranks, manifested by two members who continued to resist considering a librarian from out of state, regardless of qualifications, and objected to paying the travel expenses for an applicant, Edmund L. McGivaren, to come to New Orleans for an interview. Though a native of Baton Rouge, McGivaren worked as assistant supervisor of library services for the Tennessee Valley Authority at Wilson Dam, Alabama. A vote on the candidate had to be postponed when adversaries, apparently urged on by the tenacious Edward Estalote, repeatedly interrupted a public meeting of the library board with catcalls, boos, and the specter of imminent fisticuffs. The board agreed to consider additional Louisiana applicants. Nine aspirants came forward, including two library employees and former city librarian Henry Gill. Two of the nine offered some level of professional training. On April 2, in another stormy public meeting, the library board elected McGivaren to the position of librarian at an annual salary of $4,000. Although his tenure would be brief—barely two years later, he died of pneumonia at the age of twenty-nine—he set the precedent for professionalism at the helm of the New Orleans Public Library and began a tradition of cordial cooperation with the Louisiana Library Commission. "The controversy," Ferguson noted, "has served to awaken the city and the state to the fact that a librarian is expected to know something—besides the political boss—and to give honest service to the public."[29]

Just three years after the trained librarian supplanted the gentleman scholar in Louisiana, a parallel drama played out on the national stage, but with a diametrically opposite outcome. On June 6, 1939, despite the American Library Association's two-year campaign for the appointment of a librarian of Congress who possessed library training, President Franklin D. Roosevelt nominated poet and scholar Archibald MacLeish. Culver described him as a "man who has never been identified with the administration of any library and who has had no library training or experience," and Ferguson, completing his term as ALA president, spoke on the organization's behalf when he posited that MacLeish's accomplishments as a poet no more qualified him to be librarian of Congress than "chief engineer of a new Brooklyn bridge." Nevertheless, the U.S. Senate overwhelmingly approved MacLeish on July 29.[30]

"More and Better Libraries"

On an unseasonably warm day in October 1928, five months after Huey P. Long took office as governor, Essae Culver encountered him at the state fair in Natchitoches Parish, "tearing across the campus" as she strolled along. "What are you doing up here?" he asked her. "Well, Governor," Culver replied, "I'm doing the same thing you are. I'm meeting the people"—just as she had been doing since she arrived in Louisiana, for involving the citizenry with the establishment of parish libraries was one of the cornerstones of her program. She took it to a new level in 1931 by introducing to Louisiana the Citizens' Library Movement (CLM), a national organization formed to crystallize the efforts of persons and groups advocating for strong public libraries.[31]

The CLM began in North Carolina in 1927. Its underlying philosophy was that in the development of libraries, as in civic movements generally, *"permanent growth and improvement must grow out of an informed public opinion, and that the duty is upon those assuming leadership to create such informed public opinion."* When library supporters in the Tar Heel State undertook to persuade their unconvinced neighbors of their "obligation to place books within the reach of every man, woman, and child of that state, the response [reportedly] was electric." North Carolina attributed its library progress to the interest aroused by this initiative, and officials in other states hastened to launch their own programs.[32]

At the American Library Association's mid-winter meeting early in 1931, Essae Culver learned about the movement from O. Max Gardner, the governor of North Carolina, who acclaimed it as the best thing his state had done to foster library support. Further discussion with librarians in New York and Georgia convinced Culver that "their plan seemed sound and certainly workable in Louisiana, where libraries were desperately needed and where there was widespread interest . . . but no organized citizens' backing for library projects." Enthused, she began immediately to lay the groundwork for a similar campaign to consolidate and focus library support in Louisiana.[33]

Just three weeks after returning to Baton Rouge, Culver obtained the Louisiana Library Commission's endorsement of the movement and of the idea of enlisting cooperation from the Louisiana Library Association (LLA). At that group's next meeting in April, Glenn H. Holloway, president of the Concordia Parish Library Board, recommended the movement, and LLA formed a committee to support it. The following year, the committee elected Colonel J. Fair Hardin, assistant U.S. attorney at Shreveport, as chairman. For the next four years, however, activity apparently was limited to annual meetings scheduled in conjunction with LLA conferences.[34]

The campaign finally got under way in 1936, when some sixty representatives of interested groups, educators, and supportive citizens attended a "pre-organization" meeting at Louisiana State University. They agreed unanimously "that Louisiana needed more libraries, that books as a means of education had an inestimable value—and that an organization of citizens dedicated to library support was desirable." Toward that end, the assembly adopted a resolution endorsing the formation of a statewide Citizens' Library Movement "for the purpose of securing and promoting adequate library service to the entire state." As an immediate result of the pre-organization meeting, state officials awakened to the need for state funds, even if they did not fill that need.[35]

An important element of a CLM was its chairman, ideally "a man who has many contacts, who talks well, who has vision." This brief description fit J. O. Modisette perfectly, and, appropriately, he was elected temporary chairman. By this time, Essae Culver had been associated with him for close to a decade, and certainly she had learned that the most effective way to get something done was to put J. O. in charge of it. True to form, he invigorated the campaign with an organizational meeting in April 1937, in Shreveport. Some 150 library advocates, representing groups from all over Louisiana, established the organization's objectives: "the creation of interest throughout the state in libraries, state aid for existing libraries, and the promotion of the general welfare of all Louisiana libraries." They adopted a slogan, "More and Better Libraries," and elected officers, headed by Modisette as permanent chairman. The group designated Governor Richard W. Leche as honorary president and, as honorary vice presidents, T. H. Harris, state superintendent of education, and Dr. J. M. Smith, president of LSU.[36]

Membership in the Louisiana CLM was open to any citizen of the state, upon payment of dues of twenty-five cents. Organizational memberships cost one dollar, but many groups contributed as much as ten dollars. A membership drive in the fall spread enthusiasm, and units soon formed in localities throughout the state. In the Grant Parish town of Rochelle, for example, all 125 members of the school faculty joined. Although children were not specifically encouraged to join, the fifth- and sixth-graders eagerly wanted to emulate their teachers. Most of them came from families too desperately poor to spare a quarter, and the resourceful youngsters paid their dues with money they earned by working at a picnic. During the first year, statewide membership reached 200,000 individuals and seventy-two groups.[37] They soon had an opportunity to show what the power of the people can do.

The Louisiana Library Commission or the Schools

Although thirty parishes—more than half of those still without libraries—clamored for demonstrations, the impossibility of raising enough money for even one more meant that the demonstration in Sabine would be the last until the economy improved. As early as 1930, Culver had recognized that "because some of the parishes of the State are too small to maintain a library service on a reasonable tax, it seems highly desirable that a demonstration of cooperation of several parishes in one library system should be made." During the Great Depression, "the difficulties encountered in finding local funds sufficient to adequately support the parish libraries [made evident] that it will be necessary to organize a regional library unit made up of several parishes. In order to prove the value of such co-operation, a demonstration should be made in some selected area by the Louisiana Library Commission, in which event state aid will be necessary, because the present funds are too limited for field demonstration." The opportunity to test this idea occurred sooner than Culver may have anticipated. By the time Richard W. Leche succeeded Allen as governor in 1936, the financial situation had begun to ease. Leche took a special interest in efforts to extend access to books to the 80 percent of the rural adult population without library service, and he wanted to find out how that might be done more effectively: through the Louisiana Library Commission or through the schools.[38]

It was Superintendent of Education T. H. Harris who, when approached by the governor about this dilemma, proposed an experiment. "He suggested that one demonstration be put on through the 56 high-school libraries in ten parishes for which $10,000 would be spent for purchase of books of adult interest. He further suggested that the Louisiana Library Commission also purchase $10,000 worth of books for a general library service in two parishes [later expanded to three]. Since the Louisiana Library Commission lacked sufficient funds for the entire expense of a demonstration, the State Board of Education came to the rescue and offered to provide

$10,000 for the purchase of books."[39] The purpose of these parallel demonstrations was to ascertain whether the school-based collections for adults or the parish libraries reached the greater number of readers. If the schools proved to be more effective, the Louisiana Library Commission's future would be grim indeed.

Harris told the Board of Education that, in his opinion, "the most effective plan for supplying the adult population with library books was through the establishment of libraries in charge of well-trained, enthusiastic librarians, but that it was true that parish libraries could not be established in many parishes of the state for many years. For these, he recommended the use of high schools as distribution points. 'We believe,' Mr. Harris told the board, 'that this plan of using the high school as a basis for supplying library materials to the adult population will prove at least fairly successful in the poorer and more isolated country parishes. We would suggest that before spending a great deal of money upon this untried plan that the state authorities make available a limited list of library books and have these supplied to all of the high schools in not more than 10 of the country parishes. In this way we shall be able to try out the plan without the expenditure of large sums of money. If it should be successful, as we think it will be, additions may be made to the number of high schools handling this phase of the library work and to the number of titles used in the libraries for adults." The experiment involved nine high schools each in Livingston and Vermilion Parishes; six each in Allen and Evangeline; five each in Caldwell, St. Helena, and West Carroll; four each in Catahoula and LaSalle; and three in Cameron.[40]

Each school library received a collection of approximately one hundred volumes. Oakdale High School accepted the first shipment, which contained popular and memorable titles such as *The Bounty Trilogy* by Nordhoff and Hall, Dale Carnegie's *How to Win Friends and Influence People,* Edna Ferber's *Show Boat,* and *Lost Horizon* by James Hilton, as well as books that enjoyed temporary usefulness but failed the test of time, such as *Any Girl Can Be Good Looking, How to Ride Your Hobby,* and *Your Telltale English.* Prospective borrowers sent lists of first, second, and third choices to the school with their youngsters, who carried the volumes home to their parents and later returned them. School buses transported books to households without schoolchildren. The Louisiana Library Commission assisted the school library project, supplementing the one hundred books assigned to each school by lending informational and nonfiction volumes specially requested by individual readers.[41]

For the library side of the experiment, "the parishes of Winn and Grant were chosen because both of these parishes were working [through the CLM] for a parish-wide library service and public sentiment was entirely favorable. Winn Parish citizens had a library organization with a slogan 'We Want a Parish Library,' and Grant Parish organizations had sent the Governor's Office and the Louisiana Library Commission 29 petitions for help in starting parish-wide library service. These parishes were ready to cooperate in every way possible. After Winn and Grant Parishes had been chosen, [contiguous] Jackson Parish petitioned to be included in the region to be organized and the Louisiana Library Commission voted to add $5,000 to the $10,000 provided by the State Board of Education for books and make it a Tri-Parish Library." The commission sent eight thousand books to the Tri-Parish Library in time for opening day, June 1, with more shipped subsequently. As the editor of the Baton Rouge *State-Times* noted, "Development of parish libraries has been retarded by the inability of smaller parishes to finance such institutions alone. The regional plan may well be the answer to the problem." Success would again focus the national library spotlight on a Louisiana innovation.[42]

The Louisiana Library Commission committed "to make provision for all of the books required in the demonstration, secure the necessary physical plants required to take care of the project, furnish the services of a trained librarian, and such other clerical help as may be necessary; make provision for a bookmobile for delivery of books; and do all other things necessary in the administration of the demonstration," just as it had done for the others it had implemented. The difference was that the plan would save money by establishing a single central library to administer branches in all three parishes, rather than placing a headquarters in each of the cooperating parishes. Culver hoped, of course, "to prove that through the tri-parish unit more books will be read by more people than are read through the circulation of books by the school libraries in 10 parishes."[43]

In the competition between parish libraries and libraries-in-schools, the outcome was clear: "After about six months [of the three-year demonstration], use of the regional service showed overwhelmingly that the public library best reaches a rural population." Parish libraries issued 101,236

The Louisiana Library Commission bookmobile made books accessible to residents of isolated areas of Winn, Grant, and Jackson Parishes, served by the Tri-Parish Library Demonstration, ca. 1937. (State Library of Louisiana)

books to a population of 31,610 eligible borrowers, as compared with a school circulation of 14,355 books to 119,296 prospective readers. For the biennium, the Tri-Parish Library issued 604,770 books and magazines.[44] This significant achievement stemmed from several factors, including the availability of a much larger and more varied collection of books from which readers might choose, the greater likelihood of appealing titles readily at hand, the opportunity to base selections on browsing rather than a list in the newspaper, the presence of more highly trained personnel to provide assistance, and excellent organizational skills developed through the Library Commission's extensive experience.

Aside from the effort to bring together Concordia, Catahoula, and Tensas Parishes several years earlier, from which the last two had withdrawn because of adverse economic conditions, no multi-parish or multi-county library demonstration had previously been attempted in the United States, though a similar arrangement had succeeded in British Columbia. According to Culver, the tri-parish project demonstrated "the possibility of crossing parish lines and organizing a unit large enough to provide adequate support from taxation. It is a splendid example of cooperation on the part of three parish governing boards in order to provide the most economical and efficient library service possible." This also was to be the first Louisiana library demonstration financed entirely with state funds. As its first year ended, Governor Leche declared himself "heartily in accord with the library movement"—an affirmation the Citizens' Library Movement welcomed—but "against any new taxes." Library supporters feared that the severe economic depression in the area and the quantity of families on relief would make local tax support untenable and, despite Leche's resistance to taxes, viewed state funding as their only hope.[45]

The Louisiana Library Commission had requested an allocation of $350,000 for the biennium, of which $100,000 would support the commission, another $100,000 would fund new libraries, and the remaining $150,000 would aid the Tri-Parish Library and others already in operation, including the New Orleans Public Library. When the general appropriations bill went to the Legislature, however, it allocated just $50,000 to the Library Commission—a sum that Culver considered "pitiful." Members of the CLM hastened into action, plying the governor and legislators with entreaties. They turned out in force when a joint caucus of the House and Senate met, at Modisette's request, "to discuss and determine the best procedure for adequate state aid for library development." As a result of this meeting, funds were found to raise the library allotment to $100,000 per year. To fund the Tri-Parish Library's second and third years, $25,000 was earmarked annually, after which each parish held a tax election. Only Winn Parish—which enjoyed the advantage of having the extraordinarily personable and capable Sallie Farrell as its demonstration librarian—succeeded in passing the tax.[46]

Voters in both Grant and Jackson approved the tax in the popular vote but rejected it in property valuation, leaving "all the librarians 'most in tears." A delegation of leading citizens from Jackson Parish appealed to the commission "to carry on just long enough for another election to be called which they were sure would carry." It did, but some residents contested the election and demanded a recount. A district judge ruled that, although the tax carried in numbers, it lost by $5,000 in property valuation. In Grant Parish, certain politicians had spread the rumor that the library would remain, regardless of the election results. "One farmer in the parish," Culver reported, "went to a [library] board member and begged that the library be saved, saying there were 78 families in his district, only three took a newspaper, only one had a radio, and the only way they had to know what was going on in the world was from newspapers, magazines and books brought to them by the bookmobile." The librarians speculated that "the fact that this demonstration was financed by the State for three years may have been the reason for the failure. The people [may have] felt that the State should or would continue to support the library." But that wasn't how the program worked, and the parishes would wait two decades for another chance.[47]

Momentum

In the wake of the tri-parish experiment's success, other parishes began to queue up for demonstrations, and in 1938 the commission expanded its Extension Department to include a director and staff devoting full time to preparing, organizing, and supervising demonstrations. The next one combined Lincoln and Bienville Parishes in a bi-parish regional endeavor that included eighteen branches and a bookmobile with thirty-two weekly stops. Service began in Lincoln in February 1939 and in Bienville in June. Their collection of 8,321 books circulated 95,075 times in the first nine months. Two additional demonstrations opened in 1939, in Natchitoches Parish in June and in Terrebonne Parish in November. There resided in Terrebonne a large population of French speakers who read English with difficulty and sought out children's books, especially illustrated works of nonfiction, to improve their reading skills. To assist them, a staff member who spoke French rode the bookmobile into areas so isolated that some patrons traversed the bayous by boat to select books. Parish library service also began in East Baton Rouge, which skipped the demonstration phase because the police jury voted funds immediately. Thus, five Louisiana parishes acquired libraries in 1939. It was a tremendous step toward the Library Commission's goal of a library in every parish.[48]

A setback occurred in May 1940, when the Lincoln Parish library went down to a defeat attributed to unsettled political conditions in the parish. In popular vote, the measure passed by a slim margin but was firmly defeated in property valuation: 340 in favor (valuation: $553,748.83) and 332

The Louisiana Library Commission bookmobile makes a bayou-side stop in Terrebonne Parish just south of Houma, ca. 1940. The 1940-model vehicle weighed one ton. It had an all-steel body with outside shelving and a Ford cab truck and chassis, and cost $1,339. (Photo by Louisiana Works Progress Administration. State Library of Louisiana)

opposed (valuation: $642,683). Three months later the Bienville Parish library closed, as Culver explained it, "without a popular vote by common consent. The financial affairs of the parish were in a serious condition and it was felt that the expense of an election was inadvisable. A large number of people were in favor of the tax but it was felt the chances of reopening later would be greater than if an election were held and it failed to carry." More than twenty years passed before the libraries reopened, Lincoln in 1962 and Bienville in 1964.[49]

Still, the Great Depression exerted "a regressive effect on the state's economy, for it sustained a difficult way of life for its people," and their fear of increased taxes is understandable. High unemployment persisted,

agriculture remained depressed, and a shortage of capital curtailed industrial growth. Lumber, gas, petroleum, and sulfur prospered, but cotton, the
state's primary cash crop, declined dramatically in both acreage and price.
The New Deal helped cotton prices to rebound from the low of 1932–1933,
but the price of cotton in 1940 was thirty-five percent below its 1930 level.
Thousands of farm families could not sustain themselves, and many abandoned farming. "For those who remained," one historian observed, "the
1930s continued Louisiana's historic tradition of deprivation, coupled with
racial injustice for blacks. Dirt poor, with little education, most of the state's
farmers saw little change in their status as Louisiana's most oppressed
class of citizens."[50]

With Louisianians unable or unwilling to fund libraries, the Library
Commission's collaboration with two federal relief agencies, the Work
Projects Administration (WPA) and the National Youth Administration,
facilitated further progress. At first, the government intended the projects
to employ blue-collar workers to dig ditches, build bridges and roads, and
such, but more highly skilled citizens needed help, too. Some Tri-Parish
Demonstration Library personnel came from these agencies, which contributed managers for the branches and extra help at the central library in
Winnfield. Librarians trained and supervised the workers, who acquired
new skills; thus the program proved to be mutually beneficial. More extensive cooperation between the WPA and the commission soon evolved, with
emphasis on service. Under the latter's sponsorship, the WPA's Statewide
Library Service Project was set up in October 1938 and began operation the
following year. With the goal of stimulating permanent, locally supported
libraries, the project assisted the parish demonstrations by contributing 7,580 books and by furnishing nine "trained librarians [who worked]
as technical supervisors and [more than 250] WPA workers who serve as
branch library custodians, book repairers, bookmobile drivers, clerical assistants and even carpenters and painters when there is a need of renovat-
ing library quarters."[51]

Existing parish libraries received aid, as well. In Concordia, for example,
the WPA contributed five hundred books, as well as workers in the central
library, including a trained librarian who supervised other WPA workers
to ensure that they gave the utmost service, and in many branches. Thanks
at least in part to the boost given by the WPA project, "the library tax, in-

creased by a quarter of a mill, was repassed early in 1940, without a single dissenting vote in the entire parish—an achievement to be proud of." Two large units, to which at least one hundred workers were deployed, operated in New Orleans. At the New Orleans Public Library, WPA personnel worked in almost all departments of the main library and its branches, outnumbering library-paid personnel. The Howard Memorial Library at Tulane University assigned its WPA staff to help with weeding its extensive collection of Louisiana materials, arranging and labeling it, and putting protective covers on items that warranted careful handling and preservation. They also assisted with revamping the library's catalog.[52]

From the beginning of the WPA project through January 10, 1940, about $146,000 in federal funds poured into Louisiana libraries. The commission and local agencies contributed more than $105,000 to operate the demonstration libraries and five bookmobiles. Sarah Irwin Jones, who served as supervisor, reported that "the position of the project at the end of 1939 should be regarded as most fortunate. Among the 40-odd states having library projects, Louisiana has state aid for library development also. Library development here has a momentum, due to the fact that both state and government funds are available to carry on a planned program. The Statewide Library Project in Louisiana follows the leadership of the Commission, and is considered as an adjunct to the extension department of the Commission. Both have pooled resources to work for more and better libraries for Louisiana."[53]

During its second and third years (1940–41), the project continued its established activities and procedures, contributing another nineteen thousand books to Louisiana libraries. It employed seven librarians and between two hundred and three hundred workers with intermediate and skilled classifications. With emphasis on "books-to-the-people," these WPA workers served 130,000 readers who borrowed about 1.5 million books annually at distributing points and seventy-odd unit libraries in sixteen parishes, scattered from the north Louisiana hills to the bayou country in the south. The project provided its workers with systematic training, including bi-weekly classes for those assigned to parish libraries. This training blended the reading of twenty-four books on various subjects with instruction pertaining to Louisiana's statewide library plan and library techniques, such as application of the Dewey Decimal System. An emphasis of the 1941 course was aiding workers engaged as branch custodians to become better acquainted with the books they handled. After three successful years, the project closed in December 1941, to be superseded by a new one supportive of Louisiana libraries' war service program.[54]

In addition to the Statewide Library Service Project, the WPA funded the Louisiana branch of the Federal Writers' Project (FWP). Nationally, the FWP's best-remembered legacy is its American Guide series, a string of guidebooks that explored the history and travel attractions of the states, U.S. territories, and some cities. Under the sponsorship of Louisiana State University and the direction of writer Lyle Saxon, who had come to be regarded as "the recognized literary voice of Louisiana," the Louisiana Writers' Project went into action in 1935. Four years later, a funding shortfall jeopardized the project's future. Louisiana State University, the Louisiana Library Commission, and Governor Earl K. Long (Huey's brother) reached an agreement whereby the governor provided $2,000—supplemented a year later by $2,000 more—to ensure survival. In recognition of its role as financial administrator, the commission was named a joint sponsor. At the time, the Louisiana project had already published its *New Orleans City Guide* (Houghton Mifflin, 1938), but three other manuscripts had not yet been completed when the commission became associated with the project. Hastings House issued *Louisiana: A Guide to the State* in 1941, and four years later, Houghton Mifflin released *Gumbo Ya-Ya: A Collection of Louisiana Folk Tales,* both bearing the notation "Sponsored by the Louisiana Library Commission." The third manuscript, "A Black History of Louisiana," remains unpublished.[55]

These federal projects culminated a period of transition for the Louisiana Library Commission. Its efficacy proven by the tri-parish experiment, it moved beyond its initial stage of convincing Louisianians that they needed libraries, for a newly library-conscious public now widely agreed that they did. The commission began instead to concentrate on expanding and perfecting its ability to meet that need. "It is no longer a time for trying to convert people to books as a new experience, but of teaching them to make the most of the books which they have now," Culver declared. "The time is past where the library is for the bookish; and it is valuable today only in the number of times it can touch the daily life of the people among whom it is placed."[56]

CHAPTER 6

The Impact of World War II on Louisiana Libraries, 1941–1945

W ith parish demonstrations under way and Louisianians increasingly becoming library-conscious, the 1940s began auspiciously for the Louisiana Library Commission generally, which commemorated the fifteenth anniversary of its establishment, and for Essae Culver individually. In 1939 she had been elected first vice president of the American Library Association (ALA), a position that customarily led to the presidency—librarianship's highest professional honor—a year later. Holding this office focused national attention on Culver and her work in Louisiana to a greater extent than ever before, and the state basked in the reflection of her glory. The Louisiana Library Association hosted a reception in her honor, and the Baton Rouge Library Club held a dinner. "Since she first came to us some 15 years ago, to carry forward the library project in Louisiana," the editor of the Baton Rouge *State Times* applauded, "the service has vastly increased. From the offices here, thousands of books are sent out to readers in rural sections, or those living far from any library. She has guided the establishment of library units, and has helped create a love of reading, and a library concept. She and members of her staff have opened up a fascinating new world for hundreds of men and women, and have supplied them with the specific information they seek on numerous subjects." Unfailingly fashion-conscious, President-Elect Culver splurged on three new dresses and a coat to wear at the ALA's 1940 winter meetings in New York.[1]

The seventh woman to head the sixty-five-year-old ALA and the first female president elected from a southern state, Culver devoted her presidential year—July 1940 through June 1941—to two themes. One of these, eradicating booklessness, spread her ongoing campaign for rural libraries beyond Louisiana's borders to embrace all of the United States and Canada. This meshed with her second theme, mobilizing libraries for national defense. Although the United States had not yet entered the conflict in Europe that would become World War II, library leaders urged their colleagues, as Librarian of Congress Archibald MacLeish said, "to take up intellectual arms against fascism and 'educate the people of this country—ALL the people of this country—to the value of the democratic tradition.'"[2]

But to take up intellectual arms, the populace required both the ammunition of information and the ability to deploy it through reasoned thought. The ALA acclaimed the effectiveness of libraries to supply both information and adult education, and thus to cultivate support for democracy. As Culver accepted the organization's gavel in mid-1940, she concurred with the statement of Supreme Court Justice Louis Brandeis "that people who live away from contacts with the world—without newspapers, magazines, radios, books, and who see few people to give them new ideas, to give their minds food for thought—cannot uphold a democracy and they become easy prey of agitators; they believe anyone who speaks with assurance."[3]

According to ALA estimates, some 47 million North Americans lacked access to libraries, and perhaps as many as half of them dwelt beyond the reach of the intellectual and social contacts described by Justice Brandeis. Culver outlined a four-point program focused on intensifying efforts to obtain federal and state government aid by enlisting members of "professional, civic, service, and women's clubs in each community to make the objective known to state legislators and members of Congress," and on expanding and adapting demonstration programs, increasing the corps of national extension workers, and providing training for rural librarians. She anticipated accomplishing these last three through "mutual help among librarians of different states." Advocating the slogan "Deeds, Not Words," which expressed her professional and personal philosophy, she reminded the membership that "talkers are not doers" and encouraged librarians "to work together toward the goal of freedom and opportunity to read for all the people."[4]

Expanding upon that imperative when she delivered her presidential address a year later, Culver asserted, "There has never been a time when it was more important to have an informed citizenry; there has never been a time when people so needed to understand the meaning of events, or when the services of libraries in adapting individuals to life around them and to defense industries was so generally conceded to be of paramount importance to the democracies of the world, and to all parts of such democracies. . . . There are two courses of action open to us; we can ignore the larger opportunity of this crisis, or we can emerge, worn and tired perhaps, but infinitely strengthened in mind and spirit by our efforts to meet the challenge that is ours." Clearly, Culver advocated the latter. "The answer," she said, "is with us and our deeds. . . . Our battlefield as pointed out to us is all America wherever ignorance and superstition exist and wherever live those millions without an opportunity to advance through reading. We have an important part to play in the struggle, and by emerging and using our strength at this time of danger we can best make our libraries the fundamental guardians of popular liberty in the world today."[5]

"We Are Circulating Them with Greater Vigor"

By the fall of 1941, Louisiana libraries had offered "their resources to the 500,000 men in the state on maneuvers; to the defense industry workers who want books to improve their skills; to the man about town who wants to know the truth, in so far as it can be interpreted to him, about war events and changed social concepts of the world." Culver believed that "the greatest tribute that has ever been paid to libraries has been and is being paid today by Adolf Hitler. He is afraid of them—he is destroying some of them— he is carrying others off to Germany. He is afraid of the contribution they make to the mind and spirit of man. He is afraid of the truths they contain." Therefore, the librarian asserted, "not only must we try to make the soldier at home in Louisiana libraries, but we must try to make everyone understand that libraries play an important part in time of national emergency. Hitler is burning books, but we are circulating them with greater vigor." For the 1940–41 biennium, the Louisiana Library Commission reported a circulation of 1,384,204, an increase of 37 percent over any previous two-year period. Reflecting a national trend, however, borrowing decreased during the next biennium, to 1,044,060 volumes.[6]

Among their earliest contributions to the war effort, Louisiana libraries participated in the national Victory Book Campaign (VBC). Sponsored

During World War II, the federal government provided a small library at each camp that housed more than five thousand soldiers. Essae Culver visited as many Louisiana camps as she could. Here, she chats with servicemen at the Harding Field Base Library in Baton Rouge and with librarians Margaret Reed Gueymard (second from left), daughter of longtime Louisiana Library Commission member Margaret Reed and first head of the East Baton Rouge Parish Library; Edith Atkinson (fifth from left); and Ruth Ferguson (seventh from left), daughter of Milton Ferguson, ca. 1942. (Image courtesy of the East Baton Rouge Parish Library)

jointly by the American Library Association, the United States Red Cross, and the United Service Organizations (USO), the project gathered donated books for distribution to members of the armed forces, supplementing the publications available in collections maintained by the Army and Navy, and to base hospitals, USO clubhouses, and outposts wherever Americans were stationed. "Books," Culver asserted, "provide the only form of restful recreation in numbers of the camps and help our boys pass many otherwise homesick, lonely hours."[7]

The federal government provided a small library for each camp that housed more than five thousand soldiers. Culver visited as many Louisiana camps as she could, to ascertain what book services existed there and how libraries could cooperate. She reported that "in one camp in the first year there were not over 5,000 books to serve the 30,000 men, and although those books were chosen with care, the variety of subjects and the amount of technical material needed could not possibly have been anticipated. Army officials charged with building up these libraries stated that while in the last war recreational reading was most in demand in camp libraries, in this war practically all the users of the libraries wanted technical material, history, languages [of countries where they might see duty], etc." As the war continued, requests for technical publications, war information, and works on civilian defense further increased. Culver considered it "essential [also] that 'the wholesome recreational value' that only books can provide be made available to soldiers in the congested communities that have mushroomed around the camps."[8]

Books in greatest demand included those on current events, multiple branches of mathematics (needed in the study of ballistics), accounting, shorthand, business, salesmanship, lettering and mechanical drawing, photography, geography, and history, particularly of Europe and the Americas since 1900. Among works of fiction that held great appeal were historical novels, mysteries, westerns, and adventure, sports, and aviation stories. Patriotic, enthusiasm-building slogans such as "Books for the Boys," "Keep 'em Reading," and "Give Away the Book You Want Yourself" encouraged the public to contribute, while emphasizing the importance of quality content and good condition. A military official said that "this was a 'war of promotion examinations.' In camps and naval stations and forts all over the country and abroad, hundreds of thousands of American soldiers and sailors are studying in every spare moment to achieve higher rank. Many hundreds of thousands of text books have been made available to them through VBC, but the demand has always been more than the supply."[9]

Collection boxes stood ready in libraries of all types, as well as in schools, grocery and drug stores, hotels, movie theaters, office buildings, and bus and railroad stations (the same sort of highly trafficked locations where the Library Commission placed its demonstration collections); and Boy Scouts, Girl Scouts, Campfire Girls, and the Junior Red Cross collected books door-to-door. Culver served as state director for Louisiana and enlisted the commission staff as a whole to participate actively in all aspects of the work, from organizing it to distributing posters to sorting and packing books. Debora Abramson, assistant secretary of the Louisiana Library Commission, supervised activities in the rural parishes, and John Hall Jacobs, director of the New Orleans Public Library, headed efforts in the city. New Orleans, along with Shreveport, was designated as a regional collection center, and books were packed and stored in a borrowed warehouse while awaiting transport by the troop ships that sailed from the port. During the first six months of the campaign, Louisianians contributed fifty thousand volumes, leading all southern states. Some of the books went to nearby army camps, chiefly in Alexandria. Nationally, however, contributions reached just halfway to the goal of 10 million volumes, of which 2 million proved to be unusable because of outdated content or poor physical condition.[10]

Servicemen's ongoing need for books gave rise to a second Victory Book Campaign a year later. Culver again directed the Louisiana drive, requesting donations of the same sort of reading matter as before. This time she encouraged donors to write their names and addresses on each flyleaf "because the men will want to know who was thinking of them." Again, the national goal stood at 10 million volumes. Louisiana, with a quota of twenty thousand books, raised fifty thousand, ranking thirteenth in the nation and again leading all southern states. Although the number of books given by New Orleanians compared unfavorably to the quantity obtained from other cities of similar size, the percentage of usable donations was much higher.[11]

Meanwhile, parish libraries moved quickly to support national defense activities in their areas by extending services to military posts and defense plants, some of which employed thousands of workers. The plants intensified the clamor for books on technical subjects, such as automotive mechanics, electrical wiring, and reading blueprints, as men sought to refresh their skills or to cultivate new ones. In East Baton Rouge Parish, for example, the library reacted to an increase in requests for such information by establishing a branch for airmen at the Harding Army Air Field (today, the Baton Rouge Metropolitan Airport) and also adopted simplified registration procedures for servicemen. When gasoline and tire rationing began, the library doubled the number of books that could be checked out concurrently, from four to eight, and lengthened the loan period from two weeks to four, to lessen the frequency of visits.[12]

Soldiers from a training camp near Natchitoches all but took over the one-room Natchitoches Parish Library, August 1941. These soldiers were among those who used Louisiana Library Commission stationery for their correspondence, which carried the commission's name throughout the country. (Photo by Louisiana Works Progress Administration. State Library of Louisiana)

For the same reason, the Sabine Parish Library offered books by mail to all borrowers. It remained open until 11:00 p.m. when soldiers were on maneuvers and mailed packages and letters on behalf of servicemen unable to visit the post office. All of the libraries provided Louisiana Library Commission letterhead stationery for servicemen's correspondence, in hopes of publicizing the commission by spreading its name throughout the nation. When parish libraries could not fill requests at the local level, they forwarded the queries to headquarters. The policy was "to supply any information needed by anyone in Louisiana, if the information is obtainable, and this new demand has greatly increased the work of the reference and order departments." Meanwhile the staff shrank as personnel left for marriage or military service. "Every day brings word of more resignations," Culver complained in early 1943. One employee left to marry an Episcopal clergyman, and another "to go into WAACS or WAVES or somethin'!!"[13]

Throughout the state, "much of the librarians' time was given over to answering questions as to how such libraries happened to be in rural areas, how they were established and supported, etc. Other time-consuming questions were about Louisiana—and books on Louisiana history, topography, place-names, products, flowers, people, animals, and interesting places to visit. Material on New Orleans and on Huey Long were constantly in demand." In Winn and DeSoto Parishes and at Camp Claiborne in Rapides Parish, one of the most frequent queries was how to identify snakes, because draftees wanted to be able to recognize poisonous varieties indigenous to areas where they might be stationed. One soldier, however, brought to the library a coral snake in a jar, and a group inquired on behalf of a buddy who had already been bitten. Another Winn soldier, anticipating a ten-day furlough, asked in what state he and his girlfriend could get married most quickly. Among the men stationed at Fort Polk who used the Boyce Branch of the Rapides Parish Library were future generals George Patton and Dwight D. Eisenhower.[14]

Serving defense industries and military personnel stationed in the vicinity was just one aspect of Louisiana libraries' response, for the war involved and endangered civilians, too. Less than three weeks after Japan's attack on Pearl Harbor on December 7, 1941, drew the United States into the fight, President Franklin D. Roosevelt "urge[d] every library to make itself at once a War Information Center." This meant that it developed and maintained a comprehensive and up-to-date collection on all phases of the national war program, using those resources to answer questions and functioning as a clearinghouse for all kinds of information related to the conflict. Many Louisiana libraries responded to the president's call. Among other activities, they posted civil defense announcements, created patriotic exhibits, compiled a "Wartime Reading List," and disseminated informational pamphlets and other publications focused on current problems such as blackouts and what to do during an air raid, sent monthly by the Office of War Information. Culver considered all the resources of the library to constitute a War Information Center.[15]

Keeping people up-to-date about the goals of the war was thought to boost civilian morale, and libraries highlighted reading matter on the nature of the conflict and the backgrounds of the warring nations. Louisiana held the dubious distinction of being home to the nation's largest percentage (37.5) of persons over twenty-five years of age who did not go beyond fourth grade, almost 13 percent of whom had not completed a single year of formal schooling, as well as the lowest average grade completion (6.6). In the first ten months after the United States entered the war, the "Selective Service . . . found large numbers of [Louisiana] men unfit for army service because of low educational status." Adult education classes offered the best means of raising literacy rates and improving critical thinking skills, and parish libraries supplied the classes with material on democracy and citizenship. Red Cross units borrowed books on knitting and crocheting. "As more and more local boys were sent across, many parents came to the library for books about Australia, New Zealand, and the South Sea Islands. One man whose son was reported a prisoner of the Japanese asked that we send him all the pictures we could find of prisoners of war; just possibly he might see his son's face among them."[16]

"As Fast as Funds and Book Resources Would Allow"

"The war, of course, it is paramount," wrote the editor of the Alexandria *Town Talk* in 1941. "It touches every department of life. No subject is free from it. No conversation can long keep out of it." But the approach of war did nothing to hinder the progress of library demonstrations. Three of them—in the northern Louisiana parishes of Morehouse and Natchitoches and in coastal Terrebonne—ended in the fall of 1940, and all three parishes held successful tax elections. Natchitoches librarians, like their counterparts in other parishes, reported that "a constant stream of borrowers flows through the headquarters library and through each of the branches. And when the bookmobile reaches each bookmobile stop at its appointed hour, a group of eager readers are always there waiting for its arrival." In Terrebonne, where water covered more than 40 percent of the parish's area, "whole families row across the bayou when the bookmobile horn sounds." For five days a week, until gas and rubber rationing curtailed mileage everywhere, the vehicle traveled along the remotest waterways, forty to sixty miles daily, to "put books into the hands and homes of the people." As these demonstrations concluded, "new ones were being opened up as fast as funds and book resources would allow" in Bossier, Pointe Coupee, DeSoto, Rapides, and the second try in Vermilion.[17]

Demonstration libraries joined the win-the-war effort as soon as they opened. As the editor of the Pointe Coupee *Banner* wrote, "It seems a far cry from the battle fronts of the world to a small, Frenchly picturesque Louisiana parish, but rural America all over is awakening. Pointe Coupee may be a land of swaying cane and slender herons, of cool, breezy and abundant fishing on lovely False River, where there are green and white cottages set in gaudy flower gardens, and proud old pillared mansions greyed with age. But Pointe Coupee people read, and read books which link them in thinking with the outside world, crystallize for them American values, make each of them want to shoulder their part of the big war front." Just seven months into the year-long demonstration period, the police jury voted money to support the library after the demonstration ended. By that time, librarian Elizabeth Cammack had become convinced that the library had "entered into the lives of the readers whom it serves and is ready to help them meet their rigorous problems of today."[18]

The headquarters library in Baton Rouge had never been highly departmentalized, because, from the days when Essae Culver was the only employee, it had been necessary for every member of the comparatively small staff to take on any assigned task. But sometime during the 1940–41 biennium, perhaps impelled in part by the proliferation of demonstrations, headquarters services were separated functionally into three sections, although cooperation still took precedence over departmental lines. Administrative Services, headed by Culver, consisted of "direction and supervision of the entire staff and the activities of all departments; the carrying out of all functions as prescribed by law, such as giving advice and help to all communities wishing to establish libraries; planning campaigns of education leading up to establishment and directing publicity for all departments." Culver also lectured on various aspects of the commission's work at LSU and, when the instructor of the County and Regional Libraries course fell ill in 1941, delivered ten lectures, even while traveling extensively as ALA president.[19]

Experienced librarians under the direction of assistant secretary Debora Abramson staffed Reference and Circulation Services. They assisted legislators and visitors to commission offices; researched requests for information that could not be filled by the libraries or that came from residents of parishes where no libraries existed yet, usually shipping books the same day the requests arrived; administered the War Information Center; and compiled reading lists and assisted clubs with program planning. The kind of material clubwomen requested for their programs mirrored the tenor of the times: instead of topics such as interior decoration and gardening, they focused on public health, Pan-Americanism, and background information on the war.[20]

Mary Walton Harris headed Extension Services, previously known as the Parish and Regional Department, which oversaw all aspects of the demonstrations. Its personnel selected, purchased, and cataloged all books and prepared them for circulation and, during the demonstration period, provided general supervision. Because of a shortage of seasoned librarians to work in the parishes, Harris frequently visited the demonstrations and lent members of her staff to help out. Sallie Farrell, for example, assisted in parish libraries in Caddo, Winn, Rapides, and Calcasieu between 1939 and 1946, directing demonstrations in the last two. In remote areas without public lodging, she often found accommodations in the home of a library supporter, where she might reside for as long as two years while getting the parish library under way. In response to the great increase in field work, in mid-1941 Farrell was appointed to the position of "field worker," a title that appalled her mother by evoking images of "chop[ping] cotton or cut[ting] cane." After Mrs. Farrell complained to Essae Culver, the designation was changed to "field representative," later to "field consultant."[21]

In that capacity, Farrell visited existing libraries and campaigned successfully for the establishment of the Rapides Parish Library. A persuasive selling point for this particular demonstration was that it would benefit military personnel stationed in the area, as well as permanent residents. Influenced by the endorsements of Protestant, Catholic, and Jewish clergy, a former state superintendent of education who asserted that "next to preaching of the gospel, the next most elevating thing is giving our people plenty of clean literature to read," and the most diversified group that had ever appealed to it for the continuation of any project, the police jury acted quickly to appropriate $3,000 for its share of first-year expenses and to furnish facilities in the courthouse. Headquartered at Alexandria, the Rapides library opened in January 1942 as the largest single-parish demonstration to date, with an initial collection of twenty thousand volumes, a new type of bookmobile with its cab over the engine, and nine branches, including two for black residents. More than four thousand books circulated within the first two weeks. There being no other qualified librarian available to organize and administer the demonstration, Farrell agreed to direct it. "The job was some work and some play," she recalled. "I would go to the USO to dance with the soldiers and when they found out I had a car we would get invited to go to the Blue Moon [nightclub] in Bunkie. That was so much fun, and I was doing my patriotic duty."[22]

"Without Compensation or Hope of Reward"

After more than a decade of remarkable stability from 1926 through 1938, interrupted only by G. P. Wyckoff's resignation in 1930, the composition of the Louisiana Library Commission changed completely between the beginning of 1939 and the middle of 1942. Wyckoff, Katherine Hill, and Margaret Reed had been members since the commission's inception in 1920, and J. O. Modisette and Hugh M. Blain had joined them six years later. Blain died on December 30, 1938, and in November 1939 Governor Earl K. Long designated his sister, Clara Long (Mrs. W. M.) Knott of Many, to replace Blain. Knott was said to have "long been an enthusiastic supporter of libraries" who would bring "to the Commission first-hand knowledge of effective parish library operation." She never had the opportunity to do so, for her appointment was not presented to the Senate for approval and she did not become a commissioner.[23]

Soon after Governor Sam H. Jones took office in 1940, Katherine Hill sent him her resignation, after serving for the previous twenty of her eighty-three years. "It is with deep regret," Culver wrote, "that we lost [Miss Hill's] . . . valuable advice and help." She noted that for five years before Carnegie Corporation funds made possible her own employment as executive secretary, Hill had served as the commission's secretary and thenceforth as treasurer. When she died in 1949, the *State-Times* lauded her as a "civic leader and grand old lady of Baton Rouge" whose important contributions, in addition to her club activities and service to the Louisiana Library Commission, included working with the Red Cross during the First World War, teaching a Presbyterian bible class, financially helping many girls to attend college, and donating thousands of crepe myrtle trees to beautify Baton Rouge. Like "all members of the Louisiana Library Commission," Culver noted, she "serve[d] without compensation or hope of reward, except in the satisfaction that comes from seeing the educational advancement in the state as a result of their counsel and direction."[24]

Margaret Reed subsequently resigned from the commission, as well, their departures prompted, at least in part, by its impending reorganization—along with the entire executive branch of Louisiana government. Governor Jones had won election on a platform of "effect[ing] every possible economy in the state government," and he took the first step toward keeping his promise even before he had been sworn into office. To study the governmental structure and to devise a unified system of financial administration, he engaged Griffenhagen & Associates, an out-of-state firm specializing in public administration and finance, accounting, and management engineering. The outcome of the Griffenhagen study was doubly important, for, in addition to repositioning the commission in a new organizational hierarchy, it would impact budgets immediately and in the future. Culver spent the week of April 29 preparing reports required by the reorganization project, completing the most extensive one on Sunday, May 5. A week later, she and Modisette discussed the commission's work with a Griffenhagen representative for an hour and a half, but she had a headache that lasted all day.[25]

Despite early rumors that the Library Commission would be transferred to the Department of Education, its functions were assigned to Louisiana State University. The *Morning Advocate* reported, "As the arrangement of placing the state library agency under the State University is a rather unusual one, the new period which the Library commission will enter is expected to develop some important new phases of library extension work." Two years were allotted for the transition, and the governor asked Modisette to serve as "a one-man commission" until the reorganization had been accomplished. He agreed, for "he felt it was a trustee's job to interpret the library to governing bodies as well as to the people and to give encouragement to the staff, backing them on all undertakings. This he never failed to do" effectively, a contribution that the Library Commission needed during this transitional period, more, perhaps, than ever before.[26]

In addition to administrative restructuring, the reorganization plan involved physical shifting to bring regrouped departments together and to create space for the new Department of Finance. Shortly after the legislative session closed in July, Culver received word from the superintendent of buildings and grounds that, with the Library Commission now associated with LSU, its headquarters, located since 1932 on the eighteenth floor of the Capitol, would be moved to the former Hill Memorial Library on the old campus (which, coincidentally, had been donated to the university by Katherine Hill's father, in memory of his son and Katherine's brother). In an interview with Shirley Stephenson, however, Culver stated that she was told that "too many people used the elevators in the Capitol to visit the library. . . . Consequently the library was notified one day to be ready to move the next." For the first time in its fifteen years of operation, the commission suspended services while Hill Memorial, used in recent years to house the Highway Commission's legal department and to store its files and supplies, was repaired and the move, despite the Library Commission's objections, was accomplished. Limited services resumed after five weeks.[27]

A taxpaying citizen of East Baton Rouge Parish, O. Dolan Ricks, challenged the constitutionality of the reorganization plan, on the grounds that it barred all agencies except the Department of Finance from fiscal affairs. No action could be taken on the plan while the case crawled through the courts, and in May 1942, the Louisiana Supreme Court declared the entire reorganization to be unconstitutional. Though not administered by LSU, the Library Commission remained inconveniently in the Hill Memorial Library.[28]

"Louisiana Loses a Friend"

Prior to the 1942 session of the Legislature, the budget for the next biennium proposed a 30 percent cut in the Louisiana Library Commission's allocation, based on reasoning that no new libraries would be started in wartime. Culver argued that "greater demands for books and libraries appear in times of stress and strain than in prosperous peacetime," and the budget director assured her that if the demand for libraries continued at or above the previous level, an effort would be made to find additional funds. Without a commitment, however, the financial outlook seemed bleak.[29]

Modisette had been feeling unwell, and his physician in Jennings ordered him to New Orleans for a more extensive examination on June 3. Cul-

J. O. Modisette, chairman of the Louisiana Library Commission and of the Citizens' Library Movement (far right, partially obscured by fern), speaks at the dedication of the Lincoln Parish Library, February 1, 1939. Seated on the front row, left to right, are Ruston mayor Charles C. Goyne; Dr. E. S. Richardson, president of Louisiana Tech (former superintendent of Webster Parish schools); Shreveport mayor Sam Caldwell; Clarence E. Faulk, Jr., editor of the Ruston *Daily Leader* and local library chairman; Fred Williamson of Monroe; and Essae M. Culver, executive secretary of the Louisiana Library Commission, the only woman among the dignitaries. (State Library of Louisiana)

ver met him there on June 4 to confer about the commission's predicament. She "found him in great misery and very low spirited. Mrs. M. told me his condition is serious." Medical tests brought a devastating verdict: leukemia. Although only the family was to know, Mrs. Modisette confided the truth to Culver, who felt "sure the diagnosis is wrong." Clearly, however, he was "very, very ill and uncomfortable." When she saw him again the following weekend, he had been told what ailed him and prophetically "was afraid he would never leave the hospital." The Modisette children gathered at his bedside. Culver spent as much time as she could in New Orleans, and whenever her longtime friend felt well enough to see her, she sat with him while his family left the hospital for meals.[30]

Modisette's incapacitation could hardly have come at a worse time. Back at her office on June 15, Culver received a telephone call from the governor. "This is Sam Jones speaking," he said. "The State is in a very bad financial way and unless the sales tax [proposal] is carried [in the Legislature,] the Louisiana Library Commission budget will have to be *vetoed*. People can do without libraries in times like these but they cannot do without hospitals.'" Culver countered that "libraries [also] were needed in times like these" and promised to do what she could to convince legislators, but without Modisette's broad connections, she was unable to raise much support. Two days later, the sales tax failed. Without the monies it would have brought in, state revenues were inadequate to support the government, and Governor Jones announced that he would veto as many agencies as necessary to reduce expenditures to the level of revenues.[31]

The Library Commission was among those in danger of being axed from the budget completely. In a desperate effort to save it, Culver rallied the 350,000-member Citizens' Library Movement. As word spread that the commission and its services might be terminated, residents of every parish deluged the governor's office with supportive messages. "For God's sake," one citizen implored, "don't take books away from the people in the most illiterate state of the Union." Newspapers published supportive editorials, urging that every effort must be made to spare the library program. "Thousands of letters, telegrams and telephone messages convinced the Governor that the people wanted books and library service, and although some important institutions suffered loss of their entire budget, . . . the Louisiana Library Commission's appropriation was not vetoed." *Library Journal* editorialized, "It is indeed inspiring news to learn that Governor Jones of Louisiana saw fit to approve the Library Commission's budget while some other customary state services had to be abolished because of lack of funds. . . . It is our belief that governors, if they are fully informed, will take time from their busy day (supplemented by letters and telegrams from the constituents of the state) to do all in their power to aid public library service, if that service is being carried on as an integral part of community life throughout the state"—as it certainly was in Louisiana.[32]

Culver considered this success the Citizens' Library Movement's greatest achievement. Because of the foundation Modisette had built, it might also be considered his final contribution to the library cause that had long been so meaningful to him, for he died on Friday, June 19. The news reached Culver that afternoon as she arrived at a meeting in New Orleans about the WPA. She drove back to Baton Rouge and picked up Mary Mims and Debora Abramson, and they motored on to Jennings, where the funeral had been scheduled on June 21. En route, "the heavens simply opened up & poured for two days." At the Library Commission on Monday, a grieving Culver lamented, "Nothing seems [the] same."[33]

Recognizing Modisette's close association with the Library Commission, some of his friends sent condolences there as well as to his family. Tributes arrived from across the state and the nation, underscoring his dedication to libraries and the impact he had on their development. In Jennings, someone who knew him observed that the town "is not the same place without J. O.," and fresh flowers honoring Modisette's memory were placed in the library daily for several weeks. "In recognition of his years of devoted service and untiring efforts in behalf of public library development," the ALA honored him posthumously with a Citation of Merit, its highest honor for board members, and the Louisiana Library Association, which he had served for two terms as president, named an award in his honor.[34]

An editorial in the New Orleans *Times-Picayune* recalled that Modisette had "delivered many talks in advocacy of library extension in this and other states and worked in season and out to arouse interest in and active support for the cause . . . of more and better libraries and library services for Louisiana's people." The Baton Rouge *Morning Advocate*'s editorial, entitled "Louisiana Loses a Friend," summed it up: "He pioneered in advocating state and federal aid for libraries as a way of developing a library system which would reach beyond the confines of the city. . . . No country road deterred him when he went to speak to a community interested in establishing a library. Long hours of earnest talk and answering questions for the people at these meetings, he considered well spent. . . . Mr. Modisette never forgot the crossroads store view in all his 60 years as a lawyer and a booklover."[35]

Nor did Culver forget the library supporter who became her dear friend. Borrowing from a tribute that had been paid to Theodore Roosevelt, she wrote of Modisette, "we cannot approach him along the beaten paths of eulogy or satisfy ourselves with empty civilities of commonplace tributes, for he did not make his journey over main traveled roads, nor was he ever commonplace. Cold and pompous formalities would be unsuited to him who was devoid of affectation, who was never selfconscious. He had that entire simplicity of manner and mode of life which is the crowning result of the highest culture and finest literature. . . . [How] he truly wished to be remembered is [as] 'A Friend of Libraries.'" To commemorate the first anniversary of Modisette's death, she and Mary Mims visited his grave and left two vases of flowers.[36]

Modisette's demise deprived Louisiana's libraries of one of their most dedicated advocates and left the Louisiana Library Commission without a single member. Margaret Reed returned until Governor Jones replenished the commission. Culver wrote of Reed, "Such generosity of time, thought and effort in serving a public cause for over twenty years cannot be evaluated, but it is sincerely appreciated by the Commission staff." The new members, appointed in December 1942, were Judge Frank Voelker, chairman; Mary Mims, extension sociologist at LSU; General C. B. (Campbell Black) Hodges, president of Louisiana State University; Lois (Mrs. George) Lester, a longtime library supporter; and J. A. Ingram, mayor of Boyce. Probably recalling the difficulty of gathering the commissioners together for meetings during her early years in Louisiana, Culver wrote in her biennial report, "It is a pleasure here to record that for the first year of their service to the State there was not a single absence from a meeting of the Board. Their wholehearted interest and support have been a great encouragement to the whole staff."[37] Neither Voelker nor any future chairman would serve as long as Modisette, or be so closely associated with the Library Commission in the public mind.

"Reaching the Masses of Our People"

By the 1940s, the long-felt need for a book collection for black Louisianians had become acute, but there was no room for it at the crowded library headquarters. In her pioneering 1941 study of public libraries for black southerners, Eliza Gleason stated that "in Louisiana there was no service for Negroes from the state agency," which may have embarrassed the Louisiana Library Commission and spurred it to take steps toward correcting

Library patrons at the Negro Library Branch, sponsored by the State Library and housed at Southern University, Baton Rouge, ca. 1950s. (State Library of Louisiana)

the omission. Felton G. Clark, president of Southern University in Baton Rouge, a public university for black Louisianians, found space with an exterior door in Southern's administration building, and on June 17, 1943, the Louisiana Library Commission's Service for Colored People was opened. The service was intended to "supplement existing agencies, serve largely as an adult education agency, and provide a source of information on current activities of a world at war, and the part the citizen can take in formulating opinion now and after the war." Its name was selected to parallel that of the Colored Teachers' Association, but in 1946 it was changed to Negro Library Branch, also known as the Reference and Loan Branch Library.[38]

The book collection consisted of "non-fiction, volumes [that] contain materials of wide appeal for adult taste. Here are books of interest on all subjects—the War and the War effort, aviation, personal accounts of battle fronts; vocational books to aid the worker in all industries, educational books for the student and teacher; works on health, food and food production, nutrition, recreation, home-making, child care, handicraft; books on personal problems—religious, financial, and social. The collection is adapted to fit the needs of continuing education—both for the person who has lacked an opportunity, and for the person who wishes to continue his studies. No fiction is included as this is a Reference Library." Books were available upon request for loan to individuals, libraries, colleges, and schools anywhere in Louisiana. Borrowers paid return postage and assumed responsibility for loss or damage. With the inauguration of this service, the Library Commission could rightly state that it "extend[ed] books service to every adult individual in the state" and that its books and its service truly were free to *all*.[39]

Two years later, public library service to black citizens remained uncommon in the southern states. Louisiana's system was regarded—by partisan Louisianians, at least—as unique and by far the most extensive. Borrowers fell into three classes: those having access to public libraries; students enrolled in schools and other persons having access to school libraries, members of each group borrowing through their respective institutions; and persons having no library contact, who borrowed directly from commission headquarters. Patrons included housewives, ministers, teachers, students, nurses, businessmen, and others. For the first three years, they received assistance from Carrie C. Robinson, who held a master's degree in library science from the Hampton Institute Library School in Hampton, Virginia, established in 1925 for black students. One of the first members of her race employed in a professional capacity by a southern state, Robinson "firmly believed that the promoting of further reading interest among the masses of colored citizens of Louisiana is among the outstanding needs of the present." After the branch for black readers had operated for a year, she found that "encouraging progress is being made in reaching the masses of our people."[40]

In her report for 1944, the first full year of the reference library's operation, Robinson stated, "One observes readily from work in this type of library service that books and reading have been estranged rather than associated with life and living, generally. More and more one finds that the public feels that a book denotes laborious and unpleasant work. At

first most borrowers felt that only books of fiction were pleasure or helpful to read. That idea is gradually changing as not all borrowers know the
difference between fiction and non-fiction, and . . . the librarian has taken
advantage of this oversight by filling some requests with interesting and
easy-to-read non-fiction. It works."[41] The need for subterfuges such as this
underscores the inadequacy of education for black Louisianians during that
era and the extent to which reading books was unfamiliar to them.

A related problem was more deeply rooted. "Although at no time have
there been reasons for a marked degree of discouragement, this first year
has had a few bitters along with its sweets," Robinson related. "Perhaps second in importance to developing the service has been the necessity to act
as a promoter of better race relations. Not only have many people doubted
that there is a free library service for all, but some few have felt so keenly a
racial antipathy that they have been inclined to be antagonized even when
convinced that the service is theirs. On the contrary, more persons have
caught the significance of such an educational movement and want greatly
to see it developed—the many who do not realize that use and only use of
the service will bring about that end." Efforts to reach prospective readers in some parishes were thwarted because there the "plantation system"
still prevailed—a system that "of course does not advocate the promotion of
learning and reading." Robinson explained that groups of black residents in
those areas were led by "usually illiterate Negro preachers who do and say
only what they are told to do by their plantation owners. It was revealing to
note that we have not reached several such parishes."[42]

As the Library Commission had done in its early years, the Negro
Branch Library (later the Negro Services Department) attempted to contact its community through the press, but this proved to be difficult because
just a small percentage of black Louisianians read newspapers or joined
cultural organizations. Many were influenced most effectively through cler-
gymen and educators of their race. Like Essae Culver and members of the
commission almost twenty years before, Robinson traversed the state to
promote interest in libraries and reading, this time among the black population. She spoke and distributed printed information at racially segregated
conferences, workshops, schools, and universities from Shreveport to New
Orleans and many localities in between, describing available services and
encouraging listeners to use them.[43]

Among the universities, Grambling and especially Xavier were highly receptive; conversely, Southern University, which hosted the branch library, "seemingly has taken a callous attitude toward the service and is unable to envisage the role that the service might play in the program it attempts to promote." The librarian received no invitations to speak to students, nor did the university participate meaningfully in promotional efforts. Fearing that Southern University seemed to be trying "to silence the service to death," Robinson responded that "to ignore the attitude and work harder to make the service known in other parts of the state is perhaps the best way out." Her successor, Consuella B. Patty, noted that the branch owed its early survival in the face of opposition to Robinson's efforts, but by the end of 1945 it was leaving behind what Robinson diplomatically called its "bitters" and stood poised to "grow into an indispensable agency."[44]

"Where Do We Go from Here?"

Since 1925 Culver had personally carried out the field work that preceded parish library establishment. First came "surveys to determine the type of books best suited to the population and the percent of adult and children's books required. After the demonstration is opened, advice and help are given in the organization of the library and a continuing supervision given throughout the demonstration, and afterwards as requested." By 1942, however, she found it impossible to spend adequate time away from Baton Rouge because of the work engendered by reorganizing the commission's fiscal records for the Department of Finance and classifying personnel for the new civil service system. She relinquished the field work to Sarah Irwin Jones, who rejoined the staff after having worked at commission headquarters in its early years, and assigned an assistant to deal full-time with the vastly increased financial paperwork. Jones soon found that, with parishes beginning to queue up for libraries, she spent her time less in campaigning to establish new ones and more "with the setting up of demonstrations for operation, with assisting established libraries facing war-time emergencies of staff shortages, with advisory visits to many libraries, and with some publicity for general library promotion."[45]

Rapides Parish taxpayers passed the library tax by a comfortable margin in November 1942. The Citizens' Library Movement's speedy action had convinced Governor Jones that Louisianians wanted the Library Commission and needed its services, and the Board of Liquidation voted to restore the sum of $87,168.39 to its budget. But the funds, hamstrung by a pending court decision in a case brought against the board to test the validity of such actions, could not be reinstated expeditiously. The Supreme Court of Louisiana rendered a favorable decision in May 1943, and the money finally was deposited into the commission's account in the waning days of the year. All but $6,000 would revert to the State unless it was spent by the end of the fiscal year, six months away. With time so limited, Culver used most of it to buy books, which she stockpiled in anticipation of large-scale demonstrations. None opened in 1943, but in that year services for black Louisianians commenced, groundwork for libraries in state institutions began, and the police juries of Calcasieu and Tangipahoa Parishes passed resolutions of establishment.[46]

As the war continued, Culver found that "war-time difficulties ... [increasingly] affected the operation of the Extension Department. A large turn-over in staff has of necessity conditioned the activities and accomplishments of the department. Book prices increased and book stock of dealers decreased due to paper shortages. The department had difficulty in obtaining the titles wanted, particularly in reprint editions. Another restriction keenly felt in directing the operation of the demonstrations was the lack of bookmobiles to serve small communities and country sections. Too, there were difficulties in securing locations for parish headquarters in crowded towns, and for obtaining lumber for shelving and the necessary furniture such as heaters and electric fans." Travel restrictions curtailed bookmobile trips and visits to demonstrations by extension personnel.[47]

In her biennial report, Culver listed three noteworthy occurrences during 1944–45. The first of these was "the completion of twenty years of library service to the people of Louisiana by the Louisiana Library Commission" (she didn't count its five years of existence prior to her arrival). During those twenty years, the *Morning Advocate* noted, "she has driven an estimated 300,000 miles about the state—in sweltering summer heat or rainy winter cold, over good roads and bad, on an average of 800 to 1,000 miles a month. No section of Louisiana has been too far away or too inconvenient to reach in answer to the requests of hundreds of civic groups to 'come up and tell us how to get a library.'"[48]

Essae Martha Culver, ca. 1945.
(State Library of Louisiana)

The commission celebrated its two decades of progress with activities statewide, for Culver had friends everywhere. In the pages of the *Morning Advocate,* a perceptive journalist described her as "a busy little lady who has devoted her life to [the commission's] progress." The Baton Rouge *State-Times* noted that Culver "has helped to guide the destiny of practically all library work in Louisiana for the past 20 years while she has pushed the work of the commission to almost undreamed-of heights. Her way is one of intelligent leadership, of quietness in seeking a project, of untiring devotion to the cause of library service." Culver reminisced about her arrival in Baton Rouge after riding all day aboard a hot train that stopped at every station. "I thought I had come to the end of the world," she recalled. "And if I hadn't been taught, all my life, to stick to anything that I started, I would have gone right back on the next train."[49]

Milton Ferguson, then director of the Brooklyn Public Library, wrote to Culver on July 3, 1945, "The calendar says that you have been in Louisiana twenty years. Who am I to doubt the records? From one point of view it seems much longer than that but from another I can scarcely believe that time has run away so rapidly. Whatever one's feelings may be, the day is appropriate for congratulations and for all good wishes that you may continue year after year in the work you are doing so well.... Sometimes I have the feeling that if the effort of American librarians had been somewhat better directed, there might have been many Louisianas, instead of just one. Too many barren spots will remain throughout the country just as they did twenty years ago. I grant you that Essae M. Culvers do not come in dozens. Thus we have the answer to the problem."[50]

Harriet S. Daggett, who had been a commissioner in the early years and soon would return to the commission as its chairman, concurred: "The Library came first [for Culver], but not at the sacrifice of persons or principles. She had a great understanding of politics and forces—the need ... [never] to lose sight of her ultimate goal—to help people by seeing to it that they had books." Interviewers complained, "'I learned a lot about library development, but not a thing about Miss Culver herself.' Miss Culver talks so colorfully of the many personalities who figured in Louisiana library development that she distracts her biographers from her own forceful role. She talks, ... not about the course of her personal career, but about library progress, thinking always to actively inform the public, to mobilize public opinion. She has never wasted a word toward this end. A well-meaning friend once remarked that every well-rounded person ought to have a hobby. 'Well,' replied Miss Culver, 'I have one! Libraries!'" The demonstration system that she pioneered made possible the second significant accomplishment of the biennium: "the fact that greater progress in the development of public library service has been evident than in any previous two years."[51]

Third, Culver noted that "the radical change both in governmental and individual problems which came at the end of the war [in 1945] was reflected in new and greater demands upon our book resources and in re-direction of reading interests." She pointed out, "'The might of books in war-time was shown when the demand by the Army men was not for thousands of books but for millions, read on warships, in jungles and in foxholes.' Soldiers who read for pastime are anxious to read in peacetime." From veterans returning to civilian life came "requests for information on business and occupational enterprises of peacetime.... Establishment of small businesses seems particularly appealing to a large majority. Included in information desired are enterprises such as operation of filling stations, greenhouses, [and the] organization of advertising and real estate agencies."

One serviceman, seeking to capitalize on skills he acquired in the military, requested "information on vocations that would correspond to the work done by a Special Services Officer," a classification that included literary and artistic assignments. Another planned to construct a small stone cottage when he was discharged, and he needed elementary books on stone masonry, wiring, plumbing, carpentry, and roofing. Although the specifics differed, servicemen in general sought books that would help them answer the question, "Where do we go from here?"[52]

The Louisiana Library Commission, on the other hand, had a clear direction in the postwar world. "Its aim today, as in the beginning," Culver wrote at the end of 1945, "is parish-wide library service in every parish, and it is making every effort to reach that goal. In the meantime, however, through the Library Commission, every resident of Louisiana has access to library service."[53]

CHAPTER 7

Unprecedented Growth and Transition, 1945–1962

While war commanded the world's attention, the Louisiana Library Commission found that it had entered a new era. Since 1925 the commission had been teaching Louisianians the meaning of good library service—"a functioning parish library system with headquarters at the parish seat, as legally required, and branch libraries and stations in the towns and communities, with a bookmobile to serve rural sections, a collection of attractive books administered by a qualified parish librarian with direction and general supervision of the project given by the Library Commission." Executive secretary Essae M. Culver and members of her staff had presented talks to countless organizations and clubs in every part of the state, the late Board of Library Commissioners chairman J. O. Modisette had made radio broadcasts, articles in newspapers and magazines had disseminated information in print, satisfied borrowers had spread word of mouth, and residents of localities without libraries had observed what a difference they made in neighboring parishes. It became apparent in 1942 that the lesson had been learned, for in that year, "Louisiana people . . . sought library establishment as never before."[1]

With a mixture of delight and dismay, Culver reported that "parishes began applying for Commission-sponsored libraries more rapidly than it was possible to open the demonstrations. As soon as a police jury took the initial step of legally establishing a library by ordinance, the parish was placed on the Commission list to await its turn." As Sallie Farrell pointed out, "Not too many years ago in Louisiana the state library agency had to

Sallie Farrell assists Lafourche Parish children with books from the bookmobile, 1947. (State Library of Louisiana)

take the initiative in arousing the interest of the people in libraries. Today the people themselves are taking the lead. They are the aggressors." Libraries opened in Calcasieu and Tangipahoa Parishes in 1944 and in Madison and Acadia in 1945, the Louisiana Library Commission's twentieth anniversary year.[2]

Around this time—the mid-1940s—Culver began to receive public credit for advancing the demonstration system, adapting it in ways that made possible Louisiana's impressive progress and proved unarguably "what can be done over a relatively brief period of time by a forcefully administered state library commission" through "an active program of continuous field work." Throughout Louisiana, "almost everyone knows about libraries now. Those who have access to them have accepted them as an essential part of their daily lives and make good use of them. Those without them are either doing all they can to get a local library or are trying to find out just what steps to take." Sallie Farrell, who contributed directly to the establishment of forty-four parish libraries between 1936 and 1968, called the demonstration plan "an inspiration. It was a ready-made library all set up, with books and magazines on the shelf. It let people see what they were going to get. I would talk with people before to find out the interests of the area and stock books to match those interests. . . . Our program worked because we were able to start from nothing and show what advantages a library offered to people."[3]

As a natural consequence of increased applications during the early 1940s, demonstrations peaked during the postwar years, opening in Washington, Lafayette, and Livingston Parishes in 1946 and in Lafourche, Iberia, and Beauregard in 1947. More soon followed in Evangeline (1948); Avoyelles, Catahoula, and Jefferson (all in 1949); and St. Tammany (1950). Staff noted especially the contrasts among the parishes in this group, for Catahoula was among the smallest parishes and Jefferson, one of the largest. Avoyelles, in the center of the state, shared characteristics of the French-speaking parishes of Acadiana, farther south. By the commission's twenty-fifth anniversary on July 1 of that year, thirty-one parishes—nearly half—had libraries, twenty-six of which offered bookmobile service, and the waiting list numbered fourteen parishes. The demonstration that launched in Washington Parish on April 28, 1946, was the Louisiana Library Commission's last—not because it stopped staging them, but because, when the next one began operating in Lafayette Parish on August 6, the library agency had a new name. Future demonstrations opened under the auspices of the Louisiana State Library.[4]

As "the focal point of the total library resources" of Louisiana and with its statewide extension program, strong central collection, and reference services to state officials and departments and to the public, the agency had long since transcended the traditional functions of a library commission and taken on those of a state library. The name "Louisiana State Library," however, had been held by another agency, the Supreme Court law library in New Orleans, since its founding in 1833. On July 12, 1946, the Legislature approved Acts 102 and 103, designating the New Orleans institution as the Law Library of Louisiana so that the Louisiana Library Commission could become the Louisiana State Library. Effective at noon on July 31, the name change gave "each library the title correctly describing its functions. . . . An-

Essae M. Culver speaks at the opening of the Catahoula Parish Library in Harrisonburg, July 6, 1949. Seated to her left are Henry W. Bertrand, Jr., chairman of the Board of Library Commissioners, and Mayor W. E. Brown. (State Library of Louisiana)

other reason for the change in name was that many people wrote and referred to the commission as State library, causing frequently missent books and mail and necessitating repeated exchanges of such missent material between the two libraries," resulting in delays and possible losses. Concomitantly, Essae Culver, formerly executive secretary of the Louisiana Library Commission, became Louisiana's first state librarian.[5] In 1991 the agency received its current name, the State Library of Louisiana.

All services continued as before, with the addition of new functions and

A statewide Conference of Negro Librarians was held June 4–6, 1953, at Southern University in Baton Rouge, sponsored by the Negro Services Branch of the Louisiana State Library in cooperation with Southern University. Participants represented Southern University, the Louisiana State Library, and the State Department of Education. (State Library of Louisiana)

expansion of existing ones—without benefit of increased funds or staff—that included a more robust Legislative Reference Service. For years, many legislators had used the library's facilities, but during the Legislature's regular sessions in 1948, 1950, and 1952, the State Library augmented its reference support. From a desk in the Capitol, positioned near the legislative chambers, a staff member received requests for information and for background material on current legislation, which were answered with cooperation from the Louisiana State University Library and the university's Law Library. Culver reported that the legislators found this service both interesting and valuable, and that it "seemed to satisfy a real need." When Act 51 of 1952 established the Louisiana Legislative Council, the State Library's presence in the Capitol during sessions became superfluous, and its role changed to one of support for the council.[6]

As the state library agency established libraries in more parishes, the quantity of branches for black Louisianians grew, and the number of librarians staffing them increased proportionally. To permit them to experience the sort of conviviality and exchange of ideas that their white counterparts enjoyed at professional conferences, in 1949 the Negro Services Department sponsored the first statewide conference for librarians of color. From all over the state, they gathered at Southern University to hear President Clark call attention to the need for library service among members of their race. Other speakers included commissioners Mary Mims and Lois Lester, Essae Culver, and school library supervisor Sue Hefley, as well as other library advocates.[7]

The conferences continued through 1956, to be replaced in 1957 by a week-long program opened also to school librarians and co-sponsored by the State Department of Education. That format lasted just a year, supplanted in 1958 by a series of weekend classes for branch assistants whose formal education was limited. Librarians of color found further opportunity for professional interaction through the Library Section of the Louisiana Colored Teachers Association, reorganized in 1949 as the Library Department of the Louisiana Education Association. Since the Louisiana Library Association admitted its first black members in 1965, many have contributed significantly to that organization's work.[8]

"Decidedly a Forward Step"

Some Louisianians—the incarcerated, the mentally ill, the developmentally disabled—resided in state institutions and lacked access to the parish libraries that were proliferating throughout the state. Although the primary objective was to establish those libraries, in 1928 J. O. Modisette announced that Culver, "with her corps of assistants and helpers, is offering and rendering definite library service of the most skilled kind" to other types of libraries, as well. Together with public libraries, school libraries, colleges, clubs and community organizations, individuals, legislators and state officials, boards, and commissions, Modisette listed state institutions among those eligible to receive assistance, but they did not hasten to request it. "Institutions sometimes make use of our service," Culver commented in an interview five years later, citing a hospital's request for books on nutrition as an example of these infrequent queries.[9]

In about 1942, the chaplain at Louisiana State Penitentiary at Angola requested a collection of books that the prisoners could use to prepare themselves for defense jobs when they were released. The Library Commission lent technical books on subjects such as mechanical and diesel engines, automobile repair, carpentry, mathematics, bookkeeping, farming, and stenography, and the books enjoyed frequent circulation. Soon after, a relationship with the institutions began to develop. Some of them, notably the training schools, maintained their own small collections, and school personnel turned to the commission for help with selecting, buying, and cataloging books.[10]

Aware that "good reading material has a definite therapeutic value in mental cases . . . and is considered highly important in correctional institutions" to promote inmates' educational, recreational, cultural, and other interests, Culver took up the matter with the Department of Corrections, which had jurisdiction over the libraries but no experienced, trained personnel to administer them. On Culver's advice, in December 1943 the department employed Anna Johnson, a professional librarian who had worked in parish demonstrations and at the Veterans' Hospital in Pineville. Johnson's task was to develop library services, not only in the training schools but also in the nine charity hospitals, three mental hospitals, and various correctional institutions, including the penitentiary at Angola, under the commission's general supervision. Culver deemed this outcome "decidedly a forward step in library progress in Louisiana," but it did not develop as she probably anticipated. Less than two years later, Johnson had become discouraged because the Department of Corrections had not lived up to its promises. Her salary, $240 per month with $40 withheld for living expenses at Angola, had not increased. By 1948 she had moved to Michigan.[11]

After learning of Johnson's experiences, Culver conferred with the commission chairman, Judge Voelker, about withdrawing from the proposed demonstration at the penitentiary. The plans advanced, however, and on February 1, 1947, the Louisiana State Library initiated one of its most unusual demonstrations. Using an adaptation of the parish library plan, librarian Marvin Tanner established a central library at Angola with a branch in each of the seven farm camps, including camps for black prisoners and one for women. Inmate assistants, "selected on the basis of interest, education, ability to get along with other inmates, and knowledge of books," staffed each branch, with another assigned to headquarters. "Prisoners accept readily the responsibility required of them," Tanner reported, "and take pride in doing their work well. They are supplied with a manual of instructions and trained 'on the job' by the librarian." A bookmobile, consisting of an inmate-built trailer pulled by a jeep, visited the two most isolated camps.[12]

These libraries served the prison's personnel and its fluctuating population of convicts, some 2,200 in 1947. About 30 percent were illiterate; the reading ability of the others ranged "from the third-grade level to discriminating reading on the advanced level. As in any public library, fiction is most popular. The adventure story, the western, the love story or the historical novel, affords a means of relief from the monotony of penitentiary life and talk. The non-fiction reading interests are varied. Classified broadly they range in this order: useful arts and trades, literature, sports, religion, history, social sciences, travel, philosophy, languages, science, and biography." Like other prisons, Angola restricted publications that could have endangered others by, for example, inciting violence or instructing readers in the procurement of weapons or other contraband. Mystery and detective stories were omitted categorically. Although the restriction eliminated many books that would have been harmless, it circumvented the need for the librarian to separate the acceptable from the potentially inflammatory.[13]

During its first year, the library circulated 28,399 books and magazines, an average of 12.4 per capita and 47.3 per registered reader. As Culver anticipated, inmates used the library's resources not only for recreational and educational reading, but also for "settling disputes about some significant or insignificant fact, keeping up with current events through books and magazines, learning to play musical instruments for their own pleasure, various statistical information, to increase their knowledge of a trade or a future one, in general, to aid in making possible better adjustment on return to society." Younger men read about aviation, hobbies, travel, photography, and commercial art. Black inmates welcomed "any book to improve general knowledge, . . . abridged editions of the classics," and how-to books. The library supplied reference materials to inmates enrolled in correspondence courses and filled 430 special requests for information on a wide variety of subjects. Nonfiction accounted for an above-average 37 percent of the circulation.[14]

The Reference Department of the Louisiana State Library, crowded in its third home, the old Hill Memorial Library. Pictured in foreground are Edith Atkinson, Mattie Sue Mounce, and Vivian Cazayoux (the others are unidentified), 1947. (State Library of Louisiana)

As the demonstration period concluded, Tanner reported, "The reaction . . . has been very enthusiastic. Full cooperation was received from inmates and officials. Mr. C. D. Blalock, Superintendent, says, 'I consider the establishment of the library one of the best moves the penitentiary can make for education, recreation, and rehabilitation of the prisoners.' A good indication of inmate appreciation of library service is the care taken in returning and taking care of books. A remark heard frequently from the inmates is 'This library is what Angola needs most.'" One inmate found that "'the educational benefits derived from the library play a big part in rehabilitation,'" while another valued the library as a morale booster. Yet another considered "'reading . . . one of the outstanding pleasures on the farm,'" and a fourth noted that the library "'gives us an opportunity to read good literature as [we] never got around to reading before.'" The demonstration reportedly "was effective in 'rehabilitation work,' and prisoners obtained information on machinery, auto repairs, boiler construction, commercial photography and other subjects which helped fit them for making a livelihood following their release."[15]

The State Library expected the prison, like the parishes, to fund its library after the demonstration ended, but, despite the very positive responses from both the incarcerated and the administration, it closed on August 27, 1948. Rollo C. Lawrence, who had succeeded Blalock as Angola superintendent, declined to fund a trained librarian, preferring to initiate a program of vocational training in the building trades. He proposed to assign the chaplain, J. Duff Smith, to take charge of the library, a practice that had been nearly universal among nineteenth-century prisons and still lingered in some parts of the country. The library board questioned, however, whether the chaplain could devote adequate time to the project and "pointed out that without a trained librarian [to direct inmates' reading], the educational value of the project would be curtailed; books would be lost and misplaced, and . . . the library would inevitably deteriorate." Both the library board and Superintendent Lawrence expressed "deep regret" at the library's closure, but neither would yield. Tanner had obtained other employment and, on his last day at Angola, shipped the books back to the State Library for use elsewhere.[16] Nearly twenty years would pass before professional library services returned to Louisiana State Penitentiary.

"Dollars and Quarters"

While the library at Angola was born, flourished briefly, and died, parish library demonstrations forged ahead as quickly as the State Library could establish them—but it wasn't fast enough. Although two or three new demonstrations opened nearly every year, most parishes took four years or more to inch their way to the head of the line. Three obstacles impeded faster development. One difficulty was the shortage of trained librarians. Another was the need for "increased funds to carry on the accelerated program [of library establishment, which] would materially hasten fulfillment of Louisianians' ever-growing demands for books and information." Perhaps the greatest handicap, however, was the inadequacy of the facilities in which commission headquarters had been compelled to function since its relocation to the old Hill Memorial Library in 1940, in conjunction with Governor Sam Jones's reorganization of state government. Efforts to overcome all three obstacles occupied State Library personnel for almost twenty years, beginning in the early 1940s. As Culver would phrase it succinctly in 1952, "the statewide library program needs more 'dollars and quarters'"—dollars to fund additional demonstrations and quarters to house the State Library.[17]

When it moved, the Library Commission vacated modern facilities in the new Capitol, custom-designed just eight years before to suit its needs. Hill Memorial, however, had been built forty-one years previously for a comparatively small university. It reportedly offered the same amount of square footage that the commission had occupied in the Capitol, but Culver complained that the floor space was "not conveniently arranged for the administration of a modern state library service." More forcefully, she asserted that "the present quarters do not measure up in any respect to the minimum standards for library buildings."[18]

Of numerous drawbacks, perhaps the greatest was that Hill Memorial lacked any area large enough to accommodate the cataloging department, which handled book acquisitions for reference and circulating collections both at headquarters and for the demonstrations. Space constraints prevented purchasing books in quantity, resulting in the loss of discounts, and hampered efficiency by precluding an even flow of processes in logical sequence from one worker to the next. The commission set up two separate cataloging departments on different floors, which increased the expense of cataloging by necessitating duplication of effort and resources. At times, the basement, which housed cataloging for the demonstrations, "has been too crowded . . . with books and people to do the best and greatest amount of work possible," although both departments accomplished "a great volume of work" in spite of the limitations. Between July 1950 and June 1956, demonstrations commenced in Franklin (1950), Claiborne and Iberville (1951), Tensas and LaSalle (1952), Caldwell and St. Mary (1953), East Carroll (1954), St. Martin and St. Charles (1955), and Union (1956). In Franklin the police jury couldn't find enough money for the parish's share of the expenses. A member of the library board pleaded for permission to canvass house to house and thus raised $3,000.[19]

The location at the Capitol had "contributed largely to the effectiveness of the service to the state legislators, state officials and employees," and another shortcoming of Hill Memorial was that no parking area existed nearby. State officials and employees who had visited the library at the Capitol no longer came, which adversely affected services to state departments and to the Legislature when it was in session. To accommodate those users, a small branch operated from the basement of the Capitol. Remodeling Hill Memorial was not considered because federal engineers who had examined it while planning postwar projects had stated that the necessary alterations would cost more than constructing a new building. In the short term, commission staff did the best they could. With "all those hindrances," Culver recalled, "I don't know how we ever went ahead." In the long term, the library needed new facilities. By March of 1943, Culver had begun to negotiate the lengthy, hurdle-fraught process of obtaining a building of the library's own, located near the Capitol, but a decade would pass before meaningful progress occurred.[20]

Meanwhile, despite its cramped facilities, the State Library continued to implement new initiatives, including the acquisition of special collections. Culver had long been aware of the need to collect such materials; as early as 1928, she "appeal[ed] for the preservation of old Louisiana records," including books, newspapers, and manuscripts of inestimable value to historians. After Louisiana author Lyle Saxon died in 1946, the library began a memorial collection consisting of material relating to Saxon and to Louisiana history. Cammie G. Henry of Melrose Plantation, a close friend of Saxon and also acutely interested in Louisiana history, offered to donate her library of Louisiana-related books, manuscripts, and newspaper clippings whenever the library could accommodate it. Culver reported that "several other valuable collections have been tentatively offered to the commission when library space will permit housing and assembling them."[21]

To facilitate research on Louisiana, materials about the state always had been separated from the general collection. In 1949, growing demand for those materials required a librarian's full-time attention and led to the creation of the Louisiana Department, and Edith Atkinson was placed in charge of it. The department offered "books by native and resident Louisianians and books about Louisiana by other authors. It also includes state documents and publications of all the state departments, extensive files of newspapers and magazine clippings, as well as rare ephemera which will be of value to students of political and social history. . . . Of the 1320 requests answered by this department [during its first year and a half,] the majority were for information on the history of Louisiana and its natural resources and geological formations." The department assisted civic and study clubs throughout the state to plan programs and assisted with the State Library's commemorations of the sesquicentennial of the Louisiana Purchase (1953) and the Acadian Bicentennial (1955).[22]

After a survey revealed the need for a film service, in August 1949 the State Library initiated such a program under the direction of librarian Vivian Cazayoux. In the first five months, the thirty-seven 16mm films in the initial collection were shown 480 times to a total audience of 15,508. During the next two years, 191,418 viewers attended 4,572 showings of eighty-seven different films. Demand from home demonstration and civic clubs, parent-teacher associations, various youth groups, and other organizations soared beyond the library's capacity to satisfy it, and in 1951 approximately two hundred requests could not be filled. A grant of $5,000 from the Carnegie Corporation funded the compilation of a union catalog (not limited to the holdings of a single institution) of all 16mm films available free of charge for statewide circulation. The original compilation listed 1,001 films from sixty-five state, federal, commercial, and private agencies and helped to avoid unintentional duplication. Library personnel kept the catalog up-to-date and issued periodic supplements until videos supplanted films and online catalogs superseded lists on paper. In 1959 the library added recordings to the collection, renamed Films and Recordings. By the late 1980s, newer media had replaced vinyl recordings, and the department became known as the Audiovisual Resource Center.[23]

These growing collections exacerbated the shortage of space. Architectural plans for a new library building had been drawn up, and a bill to provide $2.5 million for its construction was introduced in 1948. Culver spent much of the first half of June waiting for hours at Appropriations Committee hearings, only to learn that the Building Bill would not be considered that day. When it finally went before the committee on June 16, Sallie Farrell won praise for her excellent presentation. But there was no money, and the bill died in committee. The following year, the State obtained permission from LSU to construct a Quonset hut adjacent to its present building, to use for storage. Culver soon learned, however, that the placement of the hut would have exacerbated the uncomfortable heat in the existing library

Vivian Cazayoux, first director of the Louisiana State Library's film service, and an unidentified library assistant inventory the small but rapidly growing collection of 16 mm films, ca. 1952. (State Library of Louisiana)

during the summer, and other Quonset huts in the vicinity had proven to be prone to invasions of rats. "Women and rats have never been compatible!" Culver observed tersely, and the library abandoned the idea. Library personnel continued to seek unsuccessfully to eke out more room by shifting materials and departments from one place to another within the building.[24]

By 1953 "the crowded condition of the Reference Department [had] reached such an acute stage . . . that in order to be able to shelve the book collection, part of the newspaper collection had to be stored in rented quarters and the entire book collection shifted into the space thus made available. Added shelving for reference books became a necessity at the expense of reducing space for readers, so that one notes with alarm the lack of space for patrons, and with regret that the available two reading tables are in a room in which as many as six staff members are working, and three typewriters in use." In April the Citizens' Library Movement identified two "urgently needed" projects: a new building and more money for library development. James L. Love of Hammond, president of the CLM, chairman of the Board of Library Commissioners, and son-in-law of the late J. O. Modisette, who had also held both positions in earlier years, "'want[ed] all Louisianians to realize . . . that the future of their library program is at stake. Louisiana has been widely recognized as a leader among all the states in developing rural libraries, but the program is almost at a standstill now because of very poor facilities, insufficient storage space and too little money.' . . . He added that offices are too crowded for efficient work, that the lighting and electric wiring are bad, and that the building is 'cold in the winter and hot in the summer.'"[25]

"A Dream of Many Years"

State officials eventually responded to the State Library's need for new facilities. Together with colleges, state institutions, and a few other projects, the library was included in a $30 million capital improvement program that the Legislature authorized in June 1954. William R. Burke of New Orleans was selected as structural architect and John J. Desmond of Hammond as designing architect. Desmond had pioneered a style of regional modernism that he innovatively adapted functionally and aesthetically to the American South. For the staff and especially for Culver, it would realize "a dream of many years." Selecting a location for the building, however, proved to be difficult, and some aspects of the project more nearly resembled a nightmare than a dream.[26]

"Three sites were chosen successively for the building and plans drawn up for those sites which were accepted by the Building Authority," Culver noted, "only to find for one reason or another [that] the land was not available." The third proposed site—on the east lawn of the Capitol, also known as the rose garden—drew especially vigorous protest, led by the Manchac Chapter of the Daughters of the American Revolution. DAR members objected because constructing the library on the east lawn would destroy existing plants and landscaping, cover the site of Fort Richmond and dislodge a marker placed thereon, and set an undesirable precedent for encroachment of state buildings on the Capitol grounds. Capitulating to the

Demolition of the old Hill Memorial Library, April 26, 1956. (State Library of Louisiana)

outcry, the Building Authority abandoned the possibility of erecting any building on the site and offered two alternatives: an area just north of the five-story Capitol annex or the library's current location on the Hill Memorial grounds. The latter ultimately was chosen, and on June 22, 1955, the Louisiana State Building Authority confirmed that the Library would be located there.[27]

On January 20, 1956, Culver and Desmond released detailed plans for a 94,000-square-foot, five-story contemporary structure that reflected "the classical qualities of order, simplicity and repose" and blended with other edifices in the State Capitol group. It would provide room enough for all library functions, including preparation of two demonstrations per year.

Plans called for the Negro Branch Library, then located at Southern University, and Braille and "talking" books for the blind and physically handicapped, housed at the New Orleans Public Library, to move to the State Library for the first time. Desmond had made "a conscious effort to make the entrance inviting, . . . [with a] broad expanse of glass across the front [that] shows the circulation desk within and . . . [behind it] the stacks of books, inviting one to read and browse." The main reading room and administrative offices would offer views of the Capitol and its grounds.[28]

Contracts for demolishing Hill Memorial and constructing the new building were awarded on April 5, 1956. As assistant state librarian Debora Abramson explained, "It was believed that if the façade was removed, the library could continue operating in the old building while the new one was under construction immediately in front of it." Razing the steps and front portion of the old Hill Memorial Library commenced promptly, and on April 26, much of the reference staff watched as the massive pillars came down. "However, on May 29, architects and city building inspectors declared it dangerous after several cracks developed" as a result of vibration of the heavy equipment being used to build the new library.[29]

Unaware that the structure was hazardous, personnel arrived for work, only to learn that the building had been condemned. Abramson telephoned the news to Culver at home as the state librarian was preparing to leave later that day for a trip to Austin. She arrived at the library fifteen minutes later "to find staff congregated on [the] sidewalk," sent them home for the day, canceled her plane reservations, and notified Desmond and Board of Commissioners chairman James Love of the situation. On the following day (Wednesday, May 30), Culver was given a deadline of Sunday evening to vacate the library. "Within a matter of days—and hectic ones they were—it was decided to tear down the old building," Abramson reported, "and the Building Authority requested Governor Earl Long to lease the second floor of the Commerce Building on Third Street for two years for the use of the library while the new building was under construction."[30]

Work on the new library ceased during "a dramatic and remarkably swift removal of some 90,000 books and all furniture and equipment from the Old Hill Memorial Building over the first week-end in June, in the face of a possible cave-in of the structure." During that weekend, Abramson continued, "the Readers' Services Department of the library was moved to the

Commerce Building. The Extension Department and books, furniture and equipment that could not be housed in the Commerce Building were moved to two buildings at the U.S. Engineering Depot at Sharp Station. The Library was closed from May 29 until August 6, 1956, while temporary shelving could be built and order restored following the crash move." Two moving firms were hired, and the staff spent twelve-hour days packing. "Most everything out of building by noon" on Sunday, June 3, Culver noted. "The impossible (or so we thot) had been accomplished with help of about 40 men & our staff." On "Monday all were tired but happy at out come." When library personnel attempted to organize their temporary facilities on July 5, however, they found the Commerce Building "not near[ly] ready. Shelves not placed, painting not done, etc.," and no telephone. Remodeling continued almost until August 6, the day the library reopened.[31]

Lois F. Shortess, head of the Extension Department, stated that her staff "has been even more inconvenienced than other departments of the State Library." Housed at the U.S. Air Force Station (popularly known as Sharp Station), separated from other library functions and personnel by a distance of ten miles, they were "handicapped not only by distance and cramped quarters but also by lack of running water and plumbing in the building, with no place to buy food or lunches. The Administrative Department of the library has been lenient and considerate by providing transportation for as many extension department employees as possible, and all those needing it, and by allowing transportation time during the workday. The members of the Extension Department staff have taken the inconveniences in good spirit, have been cooperative, and work has gone forward surprisingly well." During those years, the department prepared demonstrations for the parishes of Vernon (1956), Allen and St. Bernard (1957), and Cameron (1958), where the headquarters library was donated as a memorial to those who lost their lives in Hurricane Audrey the year before.[32]

On July 7, 1958, two years after the hasty departure from Hill Memorial, the staff began packing books for a happier move: to the library's own new building, "its fifth [home] and the only one which has been spacious enough to house all its departments and services." A source of particular satisfaction was the arrival of the Louisiana Union Catalog project, an effort spearheaded by the Louisiana Library Association to unite bibliographic data on thousands of Louisiana publications held by sixty libraries throughout the state and the Library of Congress. In 1956 the Legislature appropriated $13,000 per year to fund the Louisiana Union Catalog for two years. Although responsibility for the project rested with the State Library, which was therefore the logical headquarters, the Loyola University Library in New Orleans hosted the work until mid-1958, when the State Library could accept it. Intended to further Louisiana research by providing locations especially of scarce items and to facilitate shared cataloging in that pre-electronic era, the project collected 16,400 catalog cards, verified the information on them, and, in 1959, printed them in book form. Libraries continued to submit cards, and State Library personnel maintained the master file. Several supplements were published before the advent of online cataloging rendered the project obsolete. Service to black Louisianians moved to the new building in June 1958, the month of its fifteenth anniversary. In 1960, when the Louisiana Library Association engaged former LSU documents librarian Elizabeth Welker as its first paid secretary, the State Library had space to spare for an LLA office.[33]

Since June 1932, the New Orleans Public Library had distributed Braille and large-print books prepared by the federal government for sightless and visually impaired readers. As a regional depository for the materials and one of twenty public libraries offering the service, New Orleans Public supplied books via postage-free mail to qualified applicants in Arkansas and Mississippi, as well as Louisiana. By 1934 the collection had grown to three thousand, and library director Edward A. Parsons, who received accolades for his attention to services for the blind, announced the arrival of the library's first "talking book" machine, a phonograph-like device which permitted one or more sightless persons to "read by ear." After Parsons left the library in 1935, his successor asked the State Library to take over the service. Culver concurred that this statewide function belonged under the State Library's auspices, but she had no room for it. The new building made it possible at last, and 21,000 volumes were transferred to Baton Rouge. At the end of 1959, the Department for the Blind shipped an average of one-half ton of books and magazines per day. The expansion of services in 1966 to include people unable to handle books because of physical disabilities resulted in doubled circulation during the following year.[34]

Delays in the arrival of three floors of shelving and other equipment forced the suspension of library services for almost two months and post-

The new Louisiana State Library, with the State Capitol in the background, ca. 1958. (State Library of Louisiana)

poned the formal opening of the new building to November 9. On that day, the library invited the public to an open house, held instead of a formal dedication ceremony, and two thousand persons toured the new building. In the staff lounge, the wives of Governor Earl Long, Lieutenant Governor Lether Frazar, and other state officials poured coffee for visitors. Among them were state officials and legislators, delegations from all of the forty-seven parish libraries and from the parishes seeking demonstrations, and book-loving Louisianians. The building won awards from *Progressive Architecture Magazine* and the Gulf States Regional Competition of the American Institute of Architects in 1962 and, in 1963, received a merit award in the first Library Buildings Award program, sponsored by the American Institute of Architects, the American Library Association, and the National Book Committee.[35]

As a result of increased emphasis on book acquisitions during the 1960s, the collections surpassed the building's designed capacity by the end of the 1970s. The library turned to the stopgap measures of aggressively weeding little-used materials, extending stacks into areas formerly populated by staff and readers, and placing tens of thousands of volumes in off-site storage at LSU's Middleton Library, but again the State Library needed more space. In 1983 Thomas F. Jaques, Louisiana's third state librarian, began efforts to obtain funds for expansion, but again, the wheels of construction turned slowly. Money became available and an architect was selected in 1988, and ground finally was broken late in 1995. The three-year renovation and expansion added fifty thousand square feet and reoriented the building to face North Fourth Street, the avenue leading to the Capitol, at a cost of nearly $9 million.[36] Essae Culver would have been pleased that the library remained open throughout.

"A Necessity in an Unstable World"

The idea of federal aid to the states for the purpose of boosting both the quantity and quality of their public libraries, especially in the most inadequately served areas, began to emerge in the years after the First World War. Among its earliest proponents was J. O. Modisette, then chairman of the Board of Library Commissioners, who voiced the idea at a Southwestern Library Association meeting, likely the one held in Dallas in 1930, although Culver recalled it as having been in Oklahoma City. Modisette suggested an amount in the range of $3 million to $5 million, "and do you know," Culver reminisced in 1957, "the librarians were just simply stunned. One librarian, administrator of a large public library, got up and said, 'Why, I just simply can't think in such big terms as that much money.' Then it was proposed at a library meeting here in Louisiana at Lake Charles, . . . [but librarians] weren't ready for it. They didn't accept it at all and didn't endorse the idea." Modisette also advocated state aid and "prepared a brochure which was given to the legislature, proposing that 10% of all the funds dedicated to public education be appropriated for library development. That shocked members of the Legislature because so many of them thought the library was just an adjunct to a school or else it was just sort of a charitable proposition that the Women's Clubs were interested in."[37]

The economic depression of the 1930s, with the Second World War on its heels, consumed the attention of both the public and the American Library Association and delayed the quest for federal funds. As soon as the war ended, the ALA opened an office in Washington and began to devise a strategy for impressing members of Congress with the need for library development. Paul Howard, the first director of the Washington office, recalled a "consensus of opinion . . . 'that there should be a bill of some kind which would be specific enough in its objectives to be comprehensible, glamorous enough to stir the imagination, and limited enough in scope and time to avoid mass antagonism and competition with the National Education Association in its drive for federal aid to education.'" Library development in rural areas seemed to be at once the greatest need and the most politically appealing. A succession of Public Library Demonstration Bills, beginning in 1946, and the Library Services Act of 1956 resulted from these and subsequent discussions.[38]

When Emily Taft Douglas, a representative from Illinois, presented the first Public Library Demonstration Bill in the House of Representatives on March 12, 1946, she described it as "probably the cheapest means both of enriching existence to millions of Americans and of raising the quality of our citizens." The bill proposed allocating federal funds in the amount of $15 million for a four-year demonstration of library services to regions that lacked libraries—"largely rural, where handicaps of distance, poor roads, and low incomes have prevented the communities from having libraries." Describing Louisiana's demonstration program as a model, Douglas continued, "Experience has shown, however, that good rural service can be provided by using a large enough administrative area with a widespread system of branch libraries, service stations, and bookmobiles. Where the people have been offered such service, they have learned to value it and never want to be without it again. Books have become a necessity in an unstable world, and we cannot afford to deny large numbers of our people the chance for this basic means of education. . . . While rural library service is spreading, it is not doing so with enough speed to keep pace with the needs of the times." If enacted, the bill, and a companion measure introduced in the Senate by Lister Hill of Alabama, would hasten rural library development.[39]

The Hill-Douglas bill proposed that each participating state receive $25,000 annually for four years (later increased to five) to establish a basic demonstration using federal funds exclusively, and up to $75,000 more if the state raised matching funds for a more extensive project. State library agencies would submit plans, tailored to local conditions, to the U.S. Commissioner of Education. In addition, the bill provided for studying methods of delivering public library services, primarily in rural sections, and for examining the effect of planning on a wide-area basis. Culver testified on the bill's behalf before a U.S. Senate Sub-Committee on Education, along with the librarian of Congress, U.S. Commissioner of Education, and head of the ALA's Washington office. It won committee approval in both houses, but Congress adjourned without having acted upon it. Supporters introduced a new version during the next session of Congress. According to Culver, Louisiana's annual allotment of $100,000 would "accelerate the whole program of library development and would make library service available years sooner to the 832,000 people in 37 Louisiana parishes, now without service." Although the Senate passed the bill unanimously, it did not gain traction with the majority leadership in the House and was not brought to a final vote.[40]

A revised version that provided for increased funding, training for library personnel, and a strengthened role for state library agencies was introduced in the 1949 session of Congress, but it fell three votes short in the House because of efforts to balance the budget and a widespread conviction that the primary responsibility for library support should rest at the state level. "By now the proposed legislation was beginning to be something of a veteran in the halls of Congress, and no one was surprised" when it was presented for the fourth time during the following term—this time, by eight sponsors. Now somewhat revised again and renamed the Library Services Bill, it failed to move out of committee and was lost when Congress adjourned. The fifth attempt in 1953 met a similar fate.[41]

When the Eighty-Fourth Congress convened in January 1955, the legislation was reintroduced with endorsements from an impressive list of eighteen senators and twenty-seven representatives. The proposed law would authorize a total national expenditure of $7.5 million annually for five years; then it would expire. Sallie Farrell, who had worked actively for its passage from the beginning, testified before congressional committees, as she had in 1947 and 1952, describing the effectiveness of the plan. This time, both houses of Congress passed it, and President Dwight D. Eisenhower—who had used the resources of the Rapides Parish Library Demonstration while stationed in Louisiana during the war—signed the Library Services Act (LSA) into law on June 19, 1956, coinciding with the American Library Association conference which was in session in Miami. Culver remembered that "we were all quite excited when it was announced that the President had signed the Library Services Act. . . . We thought that the money was going to be available [to employ librarians] right after the first of July and that we could not waste any time at all in getting people because every other state was going to be recruiting people for this program. Now wasn't it fortunate that they weren't available immediately because the funds were not forthcoming until eight months later."[42]

The earliest plans submitted by the states won approval before the end of the year, and the Louisiana State Library received $40,000—the first federal funds in its history, aside from the value of benefits provided indirectly through Depression-era relief agencies—in March 1957. For fiscal 1958, the state's LSA allotment totaled $110,170, with a required match of $59,164 in state funds determined according to a formula based on per capita income and rural population. Since mid-1950, demonstrations had opened in thirteen parishes, an average of two per year. The money ostensibly permitted the State Library to accelerate its demonstration program, but the annual average number of demonstrations remained at two, with significantly reduced contributions by the local governments. In addition, an appropriation of $56,000 funded a successful demonstration of bookmobile service in Caddo Parish, where the locally supported Shreve Memorial Library had existed since 1923 but did not adequately serve a large area.[43]

Culver directed some of the LSA funds to various other projects that supported the State Library's demonstration program. Using $11,265 in federal funds and $1,142 from the state, for example, the library produced *Libraries for Louisiana,* a twenty-minute film intended for viewing by groups and by television audiences. Filmed at the State Library and at the demonstrations in Cameron and Plaquemines Parishes, where it starred local library users just being themselves, the documentary described the Louisiana demonstration program and the value of Louisiana's library service. It "personified the enthusiasm that the rural Louisianians have for their library service. . . . [Also, it introduced] the library to those ignorant of the many services available to them through this medium." Between its release

The documentary *Libraries for Louisiana,* filmed in part at the Cameron Parish Library, told the story of the spread of libraries across the state under the demonstration plan, 1960. (State Library of Louisiana)

in April 1960 and the end of 1961, it was broadcast on television three times and shown 110 times to groups in Louisiana, with a total attendance of 4,278. Another project aimed to recruit librarians to work in the parishes.[44]

"The Privilege of Bringing Knowledge to Others"

For forty years, the unfilled demand for librarians had been so great that in 1959 the Louisiana Library Association's State Planning Committee recognized "the need for a vigorous recruiting program to relieve the acute shortage of trained librarians." The committee recommended that the State Library plan and direct such a project if moneys could be found. Such an undertaking became possible with part of Louisiana's LSA funding, and in September 1959 the library engaged James Cookston, a former school librarian and an LSU Library School graduate and instructor, to conduct a one-year project (later extended for a second year) to interest young people in a career in librarianship. Cookston focused on four general areas for recruitment: high school students, college students, professional and service organizations, and library personnel. He contacted librarians, counselors, advisers, placement officers, and college deans, attended career days, appeared on television to publicize the need for librarians, and spoke before groups that included the Louisiana Teen-Age Librarians and the Louisiana Guidance Association. With help from a part-time assistant, he also began a publicity campaign.[45]

Newspaper articles touting the opportunities, requirements, responsibilities, and rewards of librarianship began to hit newsstands and subscribers' front porches in January 1960. A half-page spread in the *Morning Advocate* described the scope of positions in the library profession and the need for trained personnel to fill them: twelve thousand unfilled positions nationally, including seventy-six in Louisiana. According to a survey, recent graduates had a choice, on average, of twelve jobs. "With the certainty of federal aid for libraries," Essae Culver predicted, "and with 49 parish libraries already established in Louisiana, and the 50th (Jackson Parish) scheduled for mid-February, it is likely that there will be jobs for approximately 400 more trained librarians in all types of Louisiana libraries by 1964." The article declared the salary "comparable to [that of] other professions requiring a similar amount of training," outlined the necessary qualifications, and sought to dispel misconceptions, such as constantly working indoors surrounded by books, a lack of interaction with people, and having to be an intellectual. One of Cookston's emphases was the feasibility of relating library work to almost any subject area in which one might already have a background.[46]

Radio announcements, film showings, and exhibits and displays at parish fairs, festivals, and special events further publicized the library story and supported recruiting efforts. The State Library sought further to stimulate interest in the profession and to support recruitment efforts by offering two scholarships annually, each in the amount of $2,000, for graduate study leading to a master's degree in library science. Acceptance of the LSA-funded scholarships obligated the recipients to work in a Louisiana public library for two years.[47]

It soon became apparent that the recruiting project had succeeded. Enrollment grew in undergraduate and graduate programs throughout the state, and each semester the LSU Library School welcomed an increased number of better-qualified applicants. In the fall of 1962, the library enrolled an unusually large class of ninety-two students, placing it among the university's largest departments of graduate study. Some had just finished college, while others had graduated in the 1930s and had already held positions in a variety of fields. They came from ten states and from Formosa, Brazil, Cuba, the Canal Zone, and Czechoslovakia, possibly attracted by the Louisiana State Library's international reputation in the field of library extension and the popularity of its demonstration plan in smaller countries. The students cited many reasons for choosing a career in librarianship, including the inspiration of a librarian they knew, a love of books, and various aspects of the desire to help others. Eight enrollees attributed their decision to pursue library studies to publicity highlighting the demand for librarians. Cookston noted, "Among the intangibles that cannot be measured nor overlooked are increased public awareness of and interest in the importance of libraries and librarianship."[48]

In 1960 Congress extended the Library Services Act through June 1966, five years beyond its original expiration date. Two years after taking office in 1961, however, President John F. Kennedy recommended "'enactment of legislation to amend the Library Services Act by authorizing a three-year program of grants for urban as well as rural libraries and for construction as well as operation.' This recommendation was significant in that it planted the germ of the idea of what was to become the most influential library legislation in the nation's history—the 1964 Library Services and Construction Act," which President Lyndon B. Johnson signed on February 11, 1964. This legislation extended coverage to all parts of the country, regardless of population; provided a minimum allotment of $80,000 to each state for construction, including new construction, expansion, remodeling, and land acquisition; and greatly increased the amount of money authorized by the LSA.[49]

Despite steady infusions of federal funds, fiscal crises occurred with alarming regularity. According to a survey of Louisiana libraries in 1966–67, "The underlying philosophy in federal support of library development is that these funds are expected to generate interest and financial participation at the local and state levels. Such has not been the case in Louisiana as

far as the State itself is concerned." Money authorized by the Library Services and Construction Act was intended to supplement state funding for
libraries, not to replace it, but the State of Louisiana failed to maintain its
share of support. In the late 1960s, federal money accounted for 70 percent
of the State Library's funding.[50]

In her report for the 1966–67 biennium, Sallie Farrell affirmed that the
"reluctance of the State Legislature to meet its fiscal responsibilities for
library service is of grave concern. In 1966, the Legislature appropriated
$281,914 to the State Library, and in 1967 the appropriation was $289,599.
Without federal assistance, the Library would have been unable to continue
at its present level of services." These funds were intended "to promote the
further extension by the several states of public library services to areas
without such services or with inadequate services, but [in Louisiana,] only
a limited portion of the funds allotted have been used in improving existing
public libraries with inadequate service. The reason for this is, of course,
that these funds have had to be used to support the State Library. Although
use of these federal moneys to support State Library functions is legal and
beneficial in providing limited assistance to inadequately supported public
libraries, it is also a deprivation to these libraries. The inescapable conclusion is that the State is not assuming its fair share of support."[51]

The Louisiana State Library's program of library development continued smoothly in its permanent quarters. Culver was not surprised to find
that, "since for the first time since the library opened for service enough
space is available to house all departments under one roof, all the services
show a steady volume of increase.... The cost per unit demonstrations vary
with total population, number of distributing points, bookmobile routes,
number of books required, but the average for two medium-sized demonstrations [ca. 1957–58] was $53,768." Researcher Robert Charles Smith
concluded that grants from LSA and LSCA accelerated the demonstration
program and resulted in libraries that probably were superior to those that
would have been established with available state funds. Although numerous
libraries that antedated the federal programs obtained construction money
to replace or expand existing buildings or to erect new branches, the effect
of the funding on established libraries was negligible.[52]

During the remaining years of the Library Services Act, demonstrations
started in Plaquemines and Grant (1959); Jackson and Ascension (1960);

the Audubon Regional Library, comprised of St. Helena, West Feliciana, and East Feliciana Parishes (1961), the first regional demonstration since 1940 and the first to be established permanently, although West Feliciana later withdrew and now stands alone; and Red River (1962). For Grant and Jackson, these were successful second attempts to establish a parish library, after earlier efforts failed during the Great Depression.[53] The demonstration in Red River in the northwestern part of the state, one of Louisiana's smallest parishes in terms of both area and population, held special meaning: it was the last one that opened during Essae Culver's lengthy service as state librarian.

CHAPTER 8

A Statewide Legacy, 1962–1975

By the 1960s, social change was sweeping the United States. Although the Supreme Court's decision in *Brown v. Board of Education* (1954) had struck down segregation laws, resistance to integration continued to prevail. Libraries experienced less racial tension than did schools and public transit, for instance, in part because the impersonal task of selecting books shoulder-to-shoulder with other-race readers seemed less socially interactive than sitting side-by-side in classrooms or vehicles.[1]

Although some southern state librarians fought against desegregation, there is no evidence that Essae Culver, who had long advocated for library services for all, did so. In 1960, all fifty parish and public libraries then in existence in Louisiana offered some sort of service to black patrons, and five—in Calcasieu and East Baton Rouge Parishes and the cities of Lafayette, Lake Charles, and New Orleans—were fully integrated. Thirty-six libraries included at least one branch for black patrons, and eleven provided bookmobiles. The Negro Services Department began scaling back its activities in the early 1960s. When librarian Helen E. Britton resigned in August 1962, she was not replaced, and assistant librarians Billie Jean Hayes Roland and Gloria Spooner served successively as acting librarian. They handled circulation and reference services, but field work—including presentations to schools and organizations and training and workshops for branch and bookmobile assistants—halted. In 1964 the department closed, bringing an end to separate treatment of black citizens by the state library agency. Since that date, the State Library has offered "Books—Service—Free to All" on an equal

White youths board the Audubon Regional Library's red bookmobile in Jackson, East Feliciana Parish, 1962. East Feliciana and other parishes operated two racially segregated bookmobiles, red ones for white readers and blue ones for black readers. (State Library of Louisiana)

basis. However, because each parish library operates autonomously, each followed its own path to desegregation. Some warrant special mention.[2]

The desegregation of Louisiana parish libraries resembled that of other southern libraries, except that the Congress of Racial Equality (CORE), a national civil rights organization that challenged public segregation, focused on certain Louisiana libraries as part of testing compliance with the Civil Rights Act, passed on July 2, 1964. Just a week later, eighty-eight black youths in Ouachita Parish went in smaller groups to a movie theater, lunch counters, and other public places, and twelve of them visited the Anna Meyer Branch of the Ouachita Parish Library. No one challenged them while they sat down, read books, and consulted the card catalog, but when a young man sought to check out a book and requested an application for a borrower's card, he was referred to the Carver Branch for black readers. When he persisted, the police arrived and arrested seven youths who refused to leave; the other five left when asked. The seven were incarcerated

In the East Feliciana Parish town of Bains, black youngsters line up to visit the Audubon Regional Library's blue bookmobile for black readers on the day of its dedication, April 25, 1961. (State Library of Louisiana)

for three days. Similar scenarios played out at the parish library headquarters and other branches for white patrons, and in four other parishes: Jackson, St. Helena, and East and West Feliciana.[3]

Desegregation activity at the Clinton branch of the library in East Feliciana Parish was notable because it resulted in the only library desegregation case to be heard by the U.S. Supreme Court. On March 25, 1964, before the passage of the Civil Rights Act, Henry Brown and four other young black men went to the library and requested a book not available at that branch. The librarian arranged to obtain it from the State Library and offered Brown the options of having it mailed to him or picking it up from the bookmobile that served black residents, but the men were intent upon staging a sit-in and refused to leave. They were arrested and convicted in a "state court on charges of having violated a statute making it a criminal offense to congregate in a public building with intent to provoke, or under circumstances that may occasion, a breach of the peace, and to refuse to move on when so ordered by an authorized person."[4]

During oral arguments before the Supreme Court in 1965, Clinton district attorney Richard H. Kilbourne "argued that 'the issue is simply whether any person, or group of persons, have any right to use a facility such as a public library room as a place in which to loiter or create a nuisance, . . . to the extent that the employees . . . or those wishing to make a bona fide use of it, are embarrassed and disturbed.' He asserted that the library did not discriminate, that anyone could use the library, and that the defendants were treated courteously but that they had been arrested because they 'had no reason to loiter about the premises.'" Attorneys for the defense, pointing out that the Civil Rights Act ended racial segregation four months after the arrests, asserted that "the defendants' constitutional due process and equal protection rights" had been violated.[5]

In February 1966, the U.S. Supreme Court, finding "not . . . the slightest hint of either" intent to provoke or a breach of the peace, reversed the lower court's decision. "It is an unhappy circumstance," wrote Justice Abe Fortas in his majority opinion, "that the locus of these events was a public library—a place dedicated to quiet, to knowledge, and to beauty. It is a sad commentary that this hallowed place in the Parish of East Feliciana bore the ugly stamp of racism. It is sad, too, that it was a public library which, reasonably enough in the circumstances, was the stage for a confrontation between those discriminated against and the representatives of the offending parishes. . . . A State . . . may, of course, regulate the use of its libraries or other public facilities. But it must do so in a reasonable and nondiscriminatory manner, equally applicable to all and administered with equality to all." The convictions were reversed, and by the end of the year, the library in Clinton, along with all public libraries in Louisiana, had been desegregated.[6]

"Louisiana's First Lady of Libraries"

Early in 1962, the year in which Culver would reach her eightieth birthday, the *Morning Advocate* broke the front-page news that Louisiana's first—and, to that date, only—state librarian was retiring. Board of Library Commissioners chairman J. H. Henry announced on January 27,

> "It is with regret that we accede in Miss Culver's request and accept her resignation which we have had now for three years. . . . In all fair-

ness to her, and with appreciation for her outstanding contribution, we cannot again ask her to continue longer." Henry praised Miss Culver for her understanding of people and their desire for books; for the remarkable vision and foresight with which she planned and built a library program for Louisiana from nothing to its present enviable position of recognition at home and abroad; for the high standards of service she has always insisted upon, undaunted by difficulties and problems; for her refusal to compromise in matters affecting the quality of that service; and for her constant and unfailing devotion to the development and extension of that advice to even the most remote areas of the state.[7]

Some 350 well-wishers attended the dinner given in Culver's honor by the Baton Rouge Book Club on June 1, a month before she retired. One of the featured speakers, author and New Orleans *States-Item* columnist Charles L. "Pie" Dufour, described Culver as a "'phenomenon in public service,' an official who has outlasted dynasties and dictators." A concurrent resolution of the House of Representatives deemed her "one of the state's most outstanding citizens," and J. H. Henry presented a resolution naming her to the newly created position of state librarian emeritus. The American Library Association sent a letter of commendation. Notable among retirement gifts was a stereophonic phonograph from friends familiar with her love of music.[8]

Accolades were nothing new; they had been accumulating for years. Culver's alma mater, Pomona College in Claremont, California, had awarded her an honorary Doctor of Letters degree in 1954, in "public recognition of a distinguished career." Five years later, LSU had conferred an honorary doctorate upon a woman for the first time when it recognized Culver's years of library service to the state and country. The award presentation took place as part of the dedication of the university's new library, which "attracted nationwide attention not only in library circles but throughout the world of higher education." In 1964 the Louisiana Library Association instituted a meritorious service award to honor distinction in Louisiana librarianship and named it for Culver.[9]

Also in 1959, the American Library Association had bestowed upon Culver its highest honor, the Joseph W. Lippincott Award for distinguished librarianship. The accompanying citation read in part:

At a dinner honoring her as her retirement approached, Essae Martha Culver (right) chats with Florrinell F. Morton, director of the LSU Library School, and Emerson Greenaway, director of the Philadelphia Free Library, June 1, 1962. In his tribute to Culver, Greenaway pointed out that the effect of her work transcended the boundaries of Louisiana and influenced library development in other states. (State Library of Louisiana)

During a lifetime of service, Essae Martha Culver has provided the world of librarianship with a remarkable and inspired example of library leadership. Her profound influence on library development in the state of Louisiana clearly exhibits the work of a consummate librarian—one who has brought to the task administrative genius, political acumen, and a measureless capacity for sustained effort. Miss Culver's interest and leadership in all phases of library endeavor are attested by the breadth of her accomplishments. In the public library field, she organized a state-wide library service, originating for the task a demonstration method which has greatly influenced library development both in this country and abroad. She was instrumental in developing a strong school library program throughout the state and in establishing a library school at Louisiana State University. She built a poor and inadequate state commission library into the highly efficient, effective, and magnificently housed Louisiana State Library of today.[10]

Sallie Farrell described Culver as "a perfect boss, with complete confidence in her staff. Each one of us knew this and performed accordingly. Furthermore, it was fun and exciting—demanding perhaps, but never, never dull." Assistant state librarian Debora Abramson, who worked with Culver for thirty-two years, "'wish[ed] that all young librarians could have the privilege of working under Miss Essae's guidance.' Louisiana's first lady of libraries never assumed the lofty position of ivory tower leadership. Soon after a newcomer had been 'signed aboard,' Miss Culver would call him in for a personal conference. As one longtime co-worker remarked, 'Even if an employee had been hired to sweep the sidewalk in front of the library, Miss Culver thought he should know why the neat appearance of the library was important.'" That she also cared about her own appearance is suggested by recurring trips to the beauty parlor and by her penchant for fashionable clothes. During a visit to New Orleans, for example, she went to the Gus Mayer department store to pick up something for a friend, but "Alas! as usual it was my down fall—Got 2 dresses."[11]

"Each state library employee," said a staff member, "can recall countless incidents in which Miss Culver gave selflessly of her personal time and energy, and generously of her boundless capacity for friendship." Colleagues described her as a capable, sympathetic, and understanding administrator and a delightful friend. Culver held the annual Christmas parties in her living room until the number of guests outgrew the space. She genuinely cared about her co-workers and always welcomed them to her apartment to share her scarce leisure hours. A friend recalled, "She entertained often and delightfully. It was a joy to ring her doorbell and hear her pleasant greeting, 'Hi, there!' in a voice as young and fresh and vigorous as the day she arrived in Baton Rouge in 1925."[12]

Mary Walton Harris, the first employee Culver hired in 1925, wrote that "she had the ability to judge character and to draw others out while maintaining her own reserve. She has a great sense of humor ... it was never dull when Essae was in the group. She always had a tale or anecdote apropos, she read palms to bring warmth of feeling and good cheer that put even the youngest assistants at ease. Her tenacity of purpose through discouraging circumstances, her high mental capacity balanced by clear thinking, resulted, to sum up, in a well-rounded personality with the force to make itself felt." As Mississippi Library Commission director Lura Currier pointed out, Culver "has not had to reach her high place by putting other people in theirs.... She has achieved firmness without hardness, and if there is an iron fist in that velvet glove (which is very likely considering the scrimmages she has been through) it is never discernible." A Louisiana politician summed it up: "You just don't mess with Miss Essae," he said. "It ain't smart."[13]

In November 1961, when the Board of Library Commissioners contemplated the matter of Culver's successor, member Joel D. Fletcher, president of the University of Southwestern Louisiana (now the University of Louisiana at Lafayette) and a member also of the Lafayette Parish Library Board, "had in mind someone from Washington." He discussed the matter with Eugene Watson, director of the library at Northwestern State University in Natchitoches, who "told him it should be someone from this staff. If not D [Debora Abramson] whom he understood did not want it then it should be Sallie." Watson also talked with board chairman J. H. Henry and convinced him, as well. The board met on December 8, and in her journal Culver recorded unemotionally, "At this meet[ing] my resignation finally accepted and Sallie [appointed] State Libn effective July 1st 1962."[14]

"Million-Dollar Baby"

Born in Brookhaven, Mississippi, on December 29, 1909, Sallie Johnson Farrell earned degrees in English (Mississippi State College for Women, 1931) and in library science (University of Illinois, cum laude, 1932). She spent a year as librarian and part-time teacher at Picayune (Miss.) High School before setting off for the Big City. "I did what so many girls from southern small towns do," she recalled. "I headed for New York, with no job, no prospects of one, relying on my friends and relatives there to feed me!" She found work selling current fiction at Macy's, where she "spent so much time talking about books with customers" that her sales were low. The job didn't last long, and she obtained employment at the Queens Borough Public Library.[15]

Encouraged by her family to return closer to home, in 1936 she sought out Essae Culver at Columbia University, where she was teaching summer school, to discuss employment prospects at the Louisiana Library Commission. Farrell approached the redoubtable Culver "shaking like a leaf" but soon felt at ease, and the interview went well. When a reference position opened in the fall, Farrell accepted it. She later described that summer day in New York as "one of the most important days of my life."[16]

After a year at the reference desk, Farrell worked at the Shreve Memorial Library in Shreveport and then in the Tri-Parish and Winn Parish Library Demonstrations. In 1941 she moved to the position of field representative but spent most of the next five years assisting in the Rapides and Calcasieu demonstrations. She returned to work at headquarters in 1946 and, in 1954, was appointed director of field services. With smiles and enthusiasm, she assisted organizations, elected officials, and citizens interested in establishing libraries, shepherding them through the process from the initial step of cultivating local support to the police jury's passage of an ordinance of establishment to the final approval of a permanent library tax. Sometimes buttonholing police jurors in bars or barbershops, she was so successful at extracting parish funds from them that a juror remarked, "Sallie Farrell could sell an icebox to an Eskimo."[17]

Farrell headed the drive for funding to build a home of its own for the State Library. "'They called me the million dollar baby when I was trying to get the money to build the State Library,'" she recalled, although the structure actually cost $2 million. Farrell contacted seventy-five legislators "in their own bailiwicks" in 1948 alone. In the 1970s, "a library trustee was heard to say, 'If a legislator is not sold on libraries, Sallie Farrell hasn't gotten to him [yet].'"[18]

"A Dream . . . Becomes a Reality"

"I was never so scared as I was on the morning of July 1, 1962, the first day of my new job, when I arrived at the library and sat in Miss Culver's chair," Farrell recalled. "I had been around so long and I knew so many people—the trustees, librarians, officials, for example—so I didn't come into a strange environment. But it was having the responsibility and trying to do as well and striving to be as good an administrator as Miss Culver." She continued her predecessor's major initiative, the crusade to place libraries within easy reach of every Louisianian. When Culver retired, libraries existed in fifty-four parishes, and the waiting list had been nearly eradicated. In October 1962, the State Library launched its fifty-fifth demonstration, a second attempt in Lincoln Parish where the first, in 1939, had failed because of hard times.[19]

Farrell saw additional needs, however, and in 1963 the field consultants interrupted the push to complete the extension work, turning their attention primarily to broader matters. Emphasis shifted to cooperation and coordination among libraries to create strong regional programs, augmented by the State Library. Examples of the consultants' activities included easing new librarians into their jobs, escorting out-of-state visitors touring Louisiana libraries, and assisting to plan for new buildings. Much appreciated by parish librarians, this advisory service saved time and money for local libraries by avoiding mistakes that would have been costly financially and in terms of good community relations.[20]

A significant accomplishment was the formulation of standards for Louisiana's public libraries—"what is desirable in the structure and functioning of a public library, what services it is expected to offer, and what it must have as its resources (books, buildings and bookmobiles) and as staff, if it is to meet the needs of the people here and now." The Public Library Section of the Louisiana Library Association adopted the standards in 1965, and in their effort to achieve them, libraries entered into cooperative endeavors, such as sharing personnel to implement special projects, joint processing, reciprocal borrowing privileges for residents of different parishes, and bookmobiles crossing parish lines. In one of the more unusual collaborations, the Iberia and Vermilion Parish Libraries worked jointly to stock and administer the branch in the town of Delcambre, which straddles the boundary between the parishes.[21]

Demonstration libraries funded by the Library Services and Construction Act opened in 1964 in Bienville Parish, and the next year in St. Landry and West Baton Rouge Parishes. In St. Landry, a larger-than-average parish in central Louisiana, the police jury had rejected at least three prior appeals to request a demonstration library. Even super salesman Farrell found the police jury "'difficult. They thought they just didn't need a library and it was too expensive. They were so ornery, but I never let them think I thought they were ornery.'" A 1963 vote on a proposed parish-wide, one-cent sales tax for the library and road maintenance suffered a decisive defeat, attributable at least in part to active opposition by officials in Opelousas, Sunset, and Eunice, who believed that their towns would not receive a fair proportion of the revenues. Supporters asked for another chance, and Vivian Cazayoux directed the demonstration that started in February 1965. Investing $200,000 in the trial, the State Library set up branches in Opelousas and Eunice and sent four bookmobiles to cover the rest of the parish, along with 34,500 books and a staff of nineteen. Although the library enjoyed enthusiastic and extensive use, a 3 1/2-mill property tax to support it fell short by twenty-four votes, and it closed in March 1966. For the first time in twenty-six years, a parish failed to provide financial support to continue a Library Commission demonstration. Today, five towns in St. Landry maintain public libraries, but the parish remains without a unified library system.[22]

Just five parishes still lacked libraries, since St. Landry and Orleans offered services albeit not organized under State Library auspices. Successful demonstrations commenced in St. James and St. John the Baptist in 1966 and in West Carroll the following year. Also in 1967, Assumption Parish passed a resolution of establishment, and after launching its demonstration in May 1968, the State Library began preparing for "a very real milestone with the opening of public library service to the one parish remaining without it," for the police jury in Jefferson Davis Parish also had passed a resolution of establishment, despite the presence of the Jennings Public Library. In Jefferson Davis, unlike in St. Landry, a parish-wide library system would coexist with a city library. They have never merged, and, similarly, the St. Mary Parish Library did not fully incorporate Morgan City. Thomas F. Jaques, who succeeded Sallie Farrell as state librarian, said, "Those were compromises those ladies [Culver and Farrell] had to make." They were regrettable but preferable to leaving the parishes without rural libraries.[23]

With the grand opening of the Jefferson Davis Parish Library Demonstration less than a week away, the editor of the Baton Rouge *State Times* observed, "A dream which took nebulous form years ago, in the tenure of Miss Essae Martha Culver as Louisiana state librarian, becomes a reality October 20 [1968]. That it comes rather early in her own tenure as state

Both black and white library patrons attended the opening of the St. James Parish Demonstration Library on May 1, 1966 (shown here, the East Bank Branch in Lutcher). (State Library of Louisiana)

librarian must bring deep satisfaction to Miss Sally [*sic*] Farrell, who had shared the dream with her predecessor and sees it brought to full fruition as a tangible result of her own determination that the goal should be reached. That dream was that there would come a day when there would be public library service in every parish of Louisiana." The editorial also praised "the boards of directors of the State Library, [which,] from the first to the present one, have displayed a rare competence and much wisdom in charting courses and shaping policies and in the selection of those who were to steer the courses and effect the policies."[24]

At the age of eighty-six, Louisiana's first state librarian saw the entire state "Culverized." At the dedication, she watched and listened "with a great sense of reward" as her successor acknowledged the contributions made by library supporters during the preceding forty-three years. "It is

Upon the establishment of the Jefferson Davis Parish Library in 1968, the entire state was "Culverized." Louisiana's state librarian emeritus, Essae Martha Culver, and second state librarian, Sallie Farrell, are shown here at the dedication of the branch in Welsh, October 20, 1968. (State Library of Louisiana)

with . . . pride in accomplishment," Farrell said, "and deep appreciation for the vision and support of local and State officials, thousands of library trustees and other dedicated citizens throughout the State, and the press, radio and television that we announce the achievement of the long-sought goal of public library service in all of Louisiana's parishes," a landmark fully achieved in November 1969 when Jefferson Davis Parish assumed financial responsibility for the library and the Louisiana Library Commission's first failure became the Louisiana State Library's last success. Farrell pledged continued development, "which, it is hoped, will assure all Louisianians of strengthened and improved library service."[25]

Culver told the *State Times* that "Louisiana is now the only state which has a complete [library] service in every parish, . . . adding, 'Louisiana has made more progress in 25 years than any Northern state has made in 100. The enthusiasm of Louisiana people is what is responsible for this growth.'" Culver might have reiterated the sentence that closed her report on the Carnegie project in 1931: "In conclusion I wish to express my appreciation of the opportunity . . . for a most interesting and profitable experience and my thanks to the people of Louisiana who have so heartily cooperated."[26]

"Even If the Location Is a State Institution"

As the demonstration program for parish libraries ended, a new one began for institutional libraries. During the Culver years, the state library agency intermittently flirted with its moral and, since 1946, legal responsibility to provide library services to persons confined to Louisiana state institutions. Personnel at Louisiana State Penitentiary and at several other institutions sought and received professional advice from the State Library. In 1953, for example, "looking toward a planned program of improvement, the state director of institutions . . . requested that the State Library make a brief inventory and report on library resources in 16 institutions under his jurisdiction." Two field consultants completed the survey and subsequently compiled individualized lists of books suggested for addition to the institutions' collections. Around that time, also at the request of the director of institutions, the State Library made available for the use of Angola prisoners some five thousand adult books returned from former demonstrations. This program continued and, in about 1962, expanded to send discarded juvenile titles to the Louisiana Correctional and Industrial School (LCIS) at DeQuincy, but inadequate funding precluded meaningful library service. Also in 1962, Angola inmates lost the library's lending services because severe cuts to the budget meant that the prison could no longer spare a hundred dollars or so per year to return the books.[27]

In the late 1960s, the time was ripe for progress toward the goal "to provide high level library service to every resident of Louisiana regardless of location, even if the location is a State institution," largely because money became available in 1967 through the Library Services and Construction Act. Cooperative planning for joint financing with the Louisiana Department of Corrections and the State Department of Hospitals began in that year to establish two-year pilot library programs in correctional, health, and welfare facilities, much as demonstration libraries had been conducted in the parishes. The State Library contributed all of the materials, equipment, and furniture, and the institution provided space, any necessary renovations, and the essential personnel. At the end of the pilot program, the institution assumed administrative and financial responsibility, and the State Library continued to offer reference and interlibrary loan services, book processing, and consultation.[28]

The new initiative began with Louisiana State Penitentiary, where the library reopened in April 1968 with five thousand volumes. A bookmobile again carried publications to outlying work camps, and carts laden with them traveled through the corridors of Death Row. At the dedication, David Wade, director of the Louisiana State Department of Institutions, "praised the State Library for their assistance in getting the library started and said the library could never have been built without prison inmates who donated money received from the inmate blood plasma program to supplement state and federal funds." During the first year and a half, convicts verified their desire for a library by borrowing nearly 46,000 books. Librarian Jim Johnson explained the importance of reading at Angola: "The inmate is practically cut off from society, and he must have something to make him realize that the end of the world is not at hand. The suffering of the inmates is slight compared to that which some of history's famous, and sometimes tragic, figures have endured. By reading biographies of some of these men, the inmate can gain the knowledge that he has not sunk to the nadir of existence, that there is still something to be realized from life." Libraries at the state's other two correctional institutions for adults—LCIS and the Louisiana Correctional Institute for Women at St. Gabriel—followed in 1969.[29]

Next the pilot program moved on to hospitals and residential schools for Louisianians with developmental disabilities, beginning with the Central Louisiana State Hospital at Pineville in 1970 and Leesville State School in 1971. When Farrell retired in 1975, libraries had been dedicated also at Southeast Louisiana State Hospital and at Ruston, Hammond, and Belle Chasse State Schools, with those at East Louisiana State Hospital and Southwest State School getting under way. In all instances, library services were geared and programs developed to suit the needs of the population to be served. Marion Vedder, a consultant engaged in 1974 to assess the pilot programs, noted that they "would not be as well established, and might not

Inmates using the library at the Louisiana State Penitentiary at Angola, 1970s. (State Library of Louisiana)

even exist, without the services and support of the State Library." She found that some of the libraries needed larger or more advantageously positioned facilities, but the State Library had fulfilled its obligations and the program merited continuance.[30]

"Working Together Really Works"

During the same week of 1968 that the Jefferson Davis Parish Library Demonstration opened, in New Orleans a new Howard-Tilton Memorial Library and the New Orleans East Regional Library were dedicated in separate ceremonies. Farrell spoke at the latter ribbon-cutting, citing the facility as "an example of what can be achieved by local, state and federal cooperation." Throughout her tenure as state librarian, she believed so firmly that "working together really works" that she agreed to serve on the Louisiana Library Association's new Library Development Committee, which was charged with comprehensive planning for library development in Louisiana. In addition to librarians and educators, leaders in many fields, including politics, government, business, agriculture, communications, and the professions, served on the large committee. Further, she chaired the Survey Subcommittee appointed in 1965 to devise plans for a statewide study of public, school, college and university, and state-supported libraries and their services, and of undergraduate and graduate library education. The State Library financed the survey with Library Services and Construction Act funds.[31]

To conduct the study, LLA engaged John A. Humphry, director of the Brooklyn Public Library and soon to be named state librarian of New York, who had made similar surveys in Rhode Island and Delaware. Later, his brother James, chief librarian of the Metropolitan Museum of Art, assisted him. The information to be gathered by the Humphrys would enable them to "provide a state-wide view of libraries for librarians, library trustees and local and State officials; identify needs of libraries, measured against standards; recommend a direction for future cooperation and coordination; [and] determine funds needed for implementation of recommendations." Farrell anticipated that "the findings and recommendations ... should provide the basis for the development of a comprehensive plan for quality library services in Louisiana." The State Library served as liaison between LLA and the Humphrys.[32]

After nearly two years of work, the brothers submitted a draft report in December 1967 and a final version in time for the annual LLA conference in March. Their major recommendation was that Louisiana should establish seven multitype library systems, which they defined as "group[s] of libraries within a defined geographic area working together for the improvement of library service for all residents of the area." This, they explained, would facilitate such functions as interlibrary loan and reciprocal borrowing privileges for readers; centralized technical services (ordering, cataloging, and processing); and advice from specialists, such as children's librarians and bookmobile personnel. To implement the systems plan, the Humphrys recommended adding a new "bridge" between the existing two levels of resources and service provided by parish libraries and the State Library. This intermediate tier would be a comprehensive System Resource Center, offering materials and services beyond the scope of parish libraries but less advanced than the research collections and coordination that were the State Library's province. The report presented extensive detail as to how the reorganization should be accomplished.[33]

Seven library systems formed, initially named Southeast, Capital, South Central, Southwest, Central, Northeast, and Northwest, and the catchphrase became "cooperative effort." Upon LLA's recommendation, the State Library designated the Northeast system, comprised of the libraries of thirteen parishes and three academic institutions, as a prototype. Renamed the Trail Blazer Pilot Library System and directed by Frances Flanders, the pilot program began in April 1970 and concluded at the end of 1971 with "a solid base of accomplishments" that included most of the advantages predicted by the Humphry brothers. Funding diminished and plans had to be curtailed, but Flanders reported that throughout Northeast Louisiana, "the climate for support of all libraries has been developed. Public officials, as well as the general public, are more aware of the needs of libraries than they ever have been before."[34]

By 1979, four more systems had formed and either had died or served only as interlibrary loan centers "because of the uncertainty and irregularity of federal funding." As Tom Jaques explained in 2005, "When I put pencil to paper I could see that there was no way in the world that there was going to be enough federal money to develop the seven systems and continue them." Jaques also "had a philosophical disagreement about the need for regional library systems. That philosophical disagreement hinged on two factors: one, that Louisiana is a state that . . . [by that time had become] geographically conducive to quick travel from one end of the place to the other, so that you can get from New Orleans to Shreveport in five hours, and there are no hills or mountains or barriers to getting from one place to the other, so easy access and easy communication, physical communication between library systems was really much, much better than in many other states.[35]

"And secondly, I was concerned that the governance of . . . regional library systems was positioned so that they were not answerable to anybody particularly. . . . So I thought, 'You know, I'd better pull the plug on this and stop it while I can.' And I did so regretfully, but it was both a budgetary decision, a political decision, and what I felt then and truly feel now was in truly the best interest of library service in the state." The systems established some lasting relationships, and, said Jaques, "it's that cooperative relationship that I think was the essence of the idea, anyway. And it really didn't have to have the complex governance structure that was imposed on it. These folks

have managed to work together without attending to all that formal structure, and the State Library then was able to move forward with state-based
plans, for example, the Louisiana Library Network, without having to
deal with another—what I consider unnecessary—level of governance."[36]

With books within reach of every Louisianian (or about to be), the State
Library, under Farrell's leadership, engaged in "vigorous planning that
touches on many phases of library activity." As a result, the library "moved
in new directions initiating various types of programs designed to point up
clearly the benefits of regional and statewide cooperation and coordinated
services." Cooperation and collaboration would be the watchwords of Farrell's administration. Characteristically, however, fiscal crises hindered the
progress of ongoing programs and inhibited the implementation of new
ones. Increasingly, Farrell's reports referred to "services which had to be
discontinued, positions which had to be terminated, books and films which
could not be bought because of inadequate funding."[37]

One of the cooperative initiatives was the Louisiana State Library Processing Center, which began in 1968 as a three-year pilot project "to relieve parish libraries of cataloging work and expense" by acquiring books
and preparing them for circulation. Librarians at the State Library and at
each parish and institutional library selected books for that library, but
the Processing Center consolidated orders, thereby realizing substantial
discounts through quantity purchasing; eliminated duplication of effort
by uniformly cataloging a title once for all participating libraries that ordered it and producing catalog cards; and utilized mechanized equipment
and assembly-line techniques to prepare books for circulation, including
the creation of labels for spines, pockets, and check-out cards. By the end
of the pilot program, the Processing Center was shipping books within one
week of receiving them, and they arrived at the libraries almost shelf-ready.
Other cooperative endeavors included a rapid communications network,
regional in-service training, and the *LNR: Numerical Register of Books in
Louisiana Libraries,* a union catalog of holdings that facilitated locating
needed books for reference and interlibrary lending. Farrell considered
the *esprit de corps* demonstrated by this and other statewide collaborative
efforts to be "the greatest strength of Louisiana's library program."[38]

Epilogue

"Look About Louisiana"

I
f Essae Culver ever made a conscious decision not to use the return half of the round-trip ticket that rested in her pocket when she arrived from California, it probably was not until she retired. "The job is not done," she reminded Louisianians in 1962 as she prepared to step down after thirty-seven years at the head of the state library agency. "All the people in all the parishes—even in the most remote areas—must have library service. This is an obligation we owe to both present and future generations. And when this is accomplished, the goal must be to make the good better and the better best." When the last parish library was dedicated, she might have considered herself free of the obligation to stay, but in an interview with the *State Times* in conjunction with the event, she said, "I am perfectly content here [in Baton Rouge], . . . although I originally intended to return to California . . . but why go anywhere now."[1]

After years of residing in apartments, in about 1964 Culver bought a house, a bungalow in which she lived alone, as she always had, surrounded by memorabilia from family and friends. In 1965 Culver told the *State Times,* "'It's a joy not to be continually on the go, always meeting deadlines. . . . Staying at home is the greatest vacation of all. I thoroughly enjoy retirement, being able to catch up on my reading and listen to the music I've always enjoyed so much. . . . I don't miss my job because I keep in touch.'" When parishes opened demonstrations or dedicated new branches, she at-

Children from Bayou Boeuf School proudly holding "new books in shiny jackets," borrowed from the Lafourche Parish Library bookmobile, 1947. (State Library of Louisiana)

tended as an honored guest until vision problems forced her to curtail her social and professional activities.[2]

To celebrate her ninetieth birthday on November 15, 1972, "a small coterie of colleagues in former times and close friends all the time" initiated a campaign "among many whose professional and personal lives had been touched by hers" to shower Culver with birthday cards. The editor of the *Morning Advocate,* describing her as a "grand and pert lady" who is "so nice to be nice to," predicted that she would be deluged with hundreds of greetings mailed from every point of the compass. On December 3, Pie Dufour lauded her as "The Lady with the Book" and the "'Grande Dame of Louisiana Public Libraries' who . . . lit the torch that blazed the way to bring public libraries to every corner of the state." Dufour considered her "record of public service and cultural advancement in the state unmatched by anyone in the history of Louisiana."[3]

Exactly a month after Dufour's column appeared, Essae Martha Culver died of respiratory failure on January 3, 1973, after having been in Baton Rouge General Hospital since New Year's Eve. She was laid to rest at Rose-lawn Memorial Park and Mausoleum in Baton Rouge. "The pioneering under Miss Culver was hailed as a national model as parish libraries mush-roomed," wrote the editor of the New Orleans *Times-Picayune,* "but her largest satisfaction was to see libraries flourishing, rendering educational and recreational service, where none had been before." "Miss Culver held a unique place in the annals of state government and of the library world," eu-logized the editor of the Baton Rouge *State Times.* "It will be hers always."[4]

Culver touched the lives of generations of Louisianians who have never heard her name. As a perceptive journalist wrote in the *State Times* in 1969, she "was the right person, at the right time in the right place to spearhead a library development program of outstanding quality and national merit. Being in the right place, accepting the challenge, [was] attributed by Miss Culver to luck [but that] was only part of the picture. Miss Culver's modesty should not deceive as it was the vision, the leadership, the hard work and the devotion to a cause that brought the dream to fruition." As Dufour had written when Culver retired, "If you would see her monument, look about Louisiana."[5]

"Once upon a Time"

After almost thirty-nine years at the State Library, including thirteen as its head, Sallie Farrell stepped down in 1975 after a praiseworthy career that included a vice presidency of the American Library Association in 1954–55 and two terms on its council, selection as one of five librarians who toured the Soviet Union in 1961 as part of an exchange mission to study Soviet li-brary techniques, and receipt of LLA's Essae M. Culver Distinguished Ser-vice Award in 1971.

Taking part in establishing parish libraries was the most memorable as-pect of Farrell's career. She summed it up when she reminisced in 1993: "To think of all those little children coming to the bookmobile who never be-fore had the excitement of [handling] beautiful books. To remember all the openings of the libraries when people couldn't wait until the ribbon was cut to get in and check out books. . . . And we were providing very plain, simple

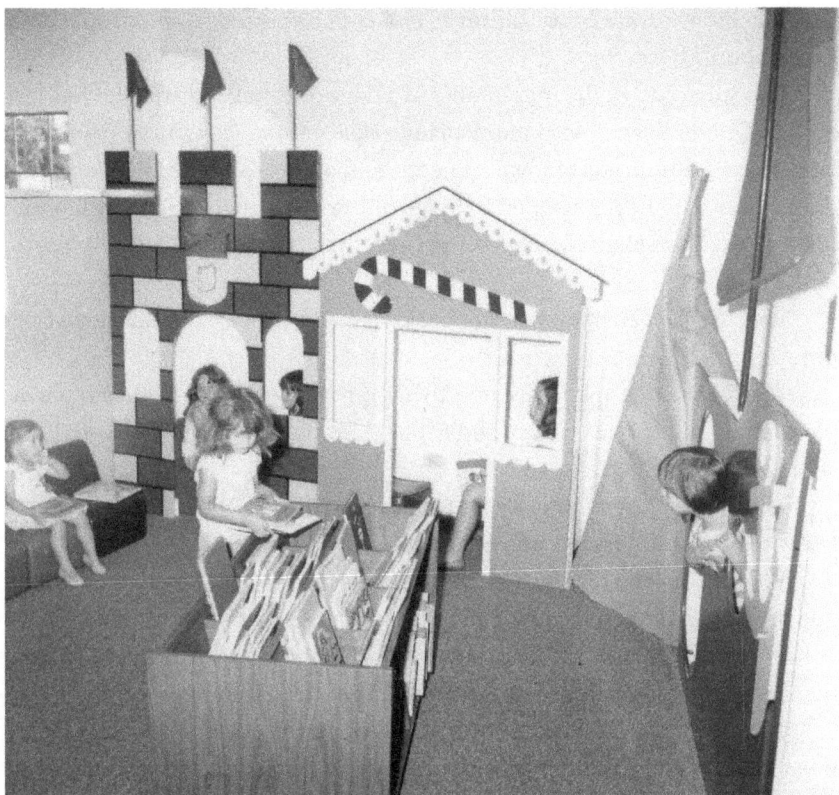

Storytelling area for children at the Assumption Parish Library in Napoleonville, 1960s. (State Library of Louisiana)

libraries, the bare essentials building-wise. I remember the headquarters library of Calcasieu Parish in an old store building, but oh, all the new books in shiny jackets! You can imagine what this was like; it was making books available to people who wanted them. That was wonderful."[6]

Farrell was invited to say a few words about the history and highlights of the Louisiana State Library at the LLA conference in 1976, the first since her retirement. Influenced by a collection of Persian tales she had been reading and perhaps recalling that some of Essae Culver's students and associates had secretly referred to her as "Queen Essae the First," she cast her presentation as a fairy tale.[7]

"The story of the State Library," she said, "could begin appropriately, 'Once upon a time.'

"The story has all the ingredients of a fairy tale—a beautiful and fearless queen (Queen Essae) with many princesses and princes (more princes in later years!), hundreds of loyal subjects, and a Lord High Chancellor of the Exchequer who never seemed to let go of the purse strings!" Farrell didn't identify the Lord High Chancellor, but surely she envisioned J. O. Modisette in the role.

"There was even a fairy godmother," she continued, "the Carnegie Corporation.

"The Queen dreamed a dream—to bring great treasures to all of her people to make their lives richer and fuller. And the dream came to pass—43 years later.

"The Queen who was very wise was aware of the needs of the people. She knew too that persuasion was more effective than coercion.

"The Queen who had great empathy and discernment attracted talented and dedicated persons to help her in her joyful and rewarding task.

"After many years of fruitful service the Queen stepped down. But all the princes and the princesses and the people continued their labors."[8]

More than half a century after the last parish library opened and almost as long since Sallie Farrell typed her fairy tale, the story continues. Although the specifics have changed, "all the princes and the princesses and the people [still] continue their labors." As fourth State Librarian Rebecca Hamilton says, "In good times and in times of natural disasters, economic downturns, and government downsizing, the State Library stands ready to go the extra mile to serve all of Louisiana's citizens by providing the most accurate, relevant and up to date information possible." And it all started with "the best [investment] the Carnegie Corporation made in an experiment of [this] kind" and an apprehensive librarian from California, feeding nickels into an electric fan on a hot Baton Rouge night in 1925.[9]

NOTES

Abbreviations of Frequently Cited Sources

Administrative Files ([Subject])	Administrative Files (Subject), State Library of Louisiana
Culver Papers	Essae M. Culver Papers, Louisiana Collection, State Library of Louisiana
Culver, [Journals], [date]	Essae M. Culver, [Journals], [date], in Essae M. Culver Papers, Louisiana Collection, State Library of Louisiana
LLC Scrapbook, [date]	Louisiana Library Commission Scrapbook, [date], Louisiana Collection, State Library of Louisiana
LLC Scrapbook-N, [date]	Louisiana Library Commission Scrapbook, Negro Library Branch, [date], Louisiana Collection, State Library of Louisiana
LLC, *Report*	Louisiana Library Commission, *Report on the Louisiana Library Demonstration, 1925–1930* (Baton Rouge: The Commission, 1931)
LJ	*Library Journal*
SCLA	Historical Archives of the Supreme Court of Louisiana, Earl K. Long Library, University of New Orleans
SF Scrapbook [#]	Sallie Farrell Scrapbook [#], Louisiana Collection, State Library of Louisiana
SLL Files	State Library of Louisiana Files

SLL Scrapbook, [title and/or date] State Library of Louisiana Scrapbook, [title and/or date], Louisiana Collection, State Library of Louisiana

VF ([Subject, if one is noted]) Vertical File ([Subject]), Louisiana Collection, State Library of Louisiana

Newspapers

Advocate	Baton Rouge *Advocate*
AP	Lake Charles *American Press*
BRI	Baton Rouge *Item*
BRIT	Baton Rouge *Item-Tribune*
BRMA	Baton Rouge *Morning Advocate*
BRST	Baton Rouge *State-Times*
DP	New Orleans *Daily Picayune*
DR	Jennings *Daily Record*
DW	Opelousas *Daily World*
Item	New Orleans *Item*
IT	New Orleans *Item-Tribune*
JDPN	*Jefferson Davis Parish News*
LR	*Louisiana Republican*
MCR	Morgan City *Review*
Meridional	Abbeville *Meridional*
News	Jennings *News*
Progress	Abbeville *Progress*
SJ	Shreveport *Journal*
ST	Shreveport *Times*
STA	Baton Rouge *State-Times Advocate*
States	New Orleans *States*
TP	New Orleans *Times-Picayune*
TT	Alexandria *Town Talk*

Prologue: From the Ladies of the Clubs to the Louisiana Library Commission, 1885–1925

1. "Library Society Organized in 1885 Disbands Charter after 45 Years of Service, Laid Foundations of Present Carnegie Structure," *JDPN*, Oct. 28, 1930 (first quotation); J. O. Modisette, "History of the Jennings Public Library" (unpublished paper, [1927?]), 3 (second quotation), in VF (Libraries—Jennings); Abigail A. Van Slyck, *Free to All: Carnegie Libraries & American Culture, 1890–1920* (Chicago: University of Chicago Press, 1995), 125–27; Walter D. Morse, *The Birth of Jennings and Jennings Firsts* ([S.l.: s.n., 1959?]), 38–40; Patricia Brady, "Literary Ladies of New Orleans in the Gilded Age," *Louisiana History* 33 (Spring 1992), 153–154.

2. Anne Firor Scott, *Natural Allies: Women's Associations in American History* (Urbana: University of Illinois Press, 1991), 112; Elizabeth Long, "Aflame with Culture: Reading and Social Mission in the Nineteenth-Century White Women's Literary Club Movement," in *The History of the Book in America*, Vol. 4: *Print in Motion: The Expansion of Publishing and Reading in the United States, 1880–1940*, ed. Carl F. Kaestle and Janice A. Radway (Chapel Hill: Published in association with the American Antiquarian Society by the University of North Carolina Press, 2009), 476; Paula D. Watson, "Founding Mothers: The Contribution of Women's Organizations to Public Library Development in the United States," *Library Quarterly* 64 (July 1994): 234–35; "Federated Activities," *TP*, Nov. 7, 1915; "Women Ask for Kindergartens in All Schools," *TP*, June 18, 1922; Van Slyck, *Free to All*, 132–35.

3. Bess Vaughan, "Shreve Memorial Library, Shreveport, La.," *Shreveport Magazine* (Apr. 1949), in VF (Libraries—Shreveport); Dolores B. Owen, "The Lafayette Public Library: Its Origin and Development," *LLA Bulletin* 56 (Fall 1993), 63–64; "The Story of Les Vingt-Quatre Library, Lafayette, Louisiana" (unpublished paper, [1934?]), 2–3 (quotation), in VF (Libraries—Lafayette); Gloria Spooner, "Establishment of African American Public Library Service in Louisiana," *Louisiana Libraries* 23.3 (Winter 2001), 23.

4. Watson, "Founding Mothers," 234–35; "Work of Women's Organizations Here and Elsewhere," *TP*, May 17, 1914 (quotations).

5. "The Growth of the Library Movement," *DP*, June 13, 1897 (quotation); untitled news item, *LJ* 42 (Jan. 1917), 65; Margaret McD. Reed, "Early History of the Library Movement in Louisiana," in Louisiana Library Commission, *Seventh Biennial Report of the Louisiana Library Commission, 1936–1937* (Baton Rouge: The Commission, 1933), 28; "History of the Louisiana Library Commission" (unpublished paper, 1928), 2, in VF (Libraries—Baton Rouge— LSL—History).

6. "The News with Orene Muse," transcript of broadcast over WJBO radio, July 9, 1945 (first and second quotations), in Culver Papers; "History of the Louisiana Library Commission," 2 (third quotation); Helen Wells Dodd, "What a State Library Commission Can Do for Louisiana," in *Louisiana State Library Association, 1911, Proceedings of the Meeting Held April 21–22, at Louisiana State University*, 6–10 (Baton Rouge: Louisiana State University, 1911), 6; Milton J. Ferguson, "The Trend toward County Libraries," *Proceedings of the Pacific Northwest Library Association* (1920), offprint, 4 (fourth quotation). *Statistical Abstract of the United States, 1920* (Washington, DC: Government Printing Office, 1921) reported that according to the 1910 census, 29 percent of Louisianians were illiterate. South Carolina, with 25.7 percent, came next. Nationwide, the illiteracy rate was 7.7 percent (p. 69).

7. "Need and Purpose of Library Commissions," *TP*, Dec. 3, 1916; League of Library Commissions, *Handbook* (Chicago: American Library Association, 1916), 14–15; Christine Pawley, "Advocate for Access: Lutie Stearns and the Traveling Libraries of the Wisconsin Free Library Commission, 1895–1914," *Libraries & Culture* 35 (Summer 2000), 434–35, 437, 440–43.

8. League of Library Commissions, *Handbook*, 14–15, [3]; "Need and Purpose of Library Commissions" (quotation).

9. Virginia Fairfax, [Untitled] (paper, annual meeting of the Louisiana Library Association, May 1, 1931), 2, in VF; Louisiana Legislature, *Acts Passed by the General Assembly of the State of Louisiana at the Regular Session, Begun and Held in the City of Baton Rouge on the Ninth*

Day of May, 1910 (Baton Rouge: New Advocate, 1910), 227–29 (first quotation); Reed, "Early History," 28–29; "Early History of the Louisiana Library Commission, 3 (second quotation); "State Library and Director Given Tribute," *BRST*, Apr. 1, 1950 (last quotation), in LSL Scrapbook, "Press Clippings for LSL, April 1948–January 21, 1951."

10. Louisiana Legislature, *Acts Passed by the General Assembly of the State of Louisiana at the Regular Session, Begun and Held in the City of Baton Rouge on the Tenth Day of May, 1920* (Baton Rouge: Ramires-Jones Printing Co., 1920), 372–75; Reed, "Early History," 29.

11. Reed, "Early History," 30; Katherine M. Hill to Rabbi David Fichman, July 27, 1922 (first quotation), in Administrative Files (Administration–Correspondence, LLC, 1920–1921); Margaret McD. Reed to Dr. A. W. Hayes, Feb. 20, 1922 (second quotation), in Administrative Files (Administration, LLC, 1925); "Report of Mrs. Owen W. Brown of work for the three months beginning March 1st and ending May 31st. 1923," in Administrative Files (Administration–Correspondence, LLC, 1922–1923); "Rural 'Travelling Libraries' Want of Federated Women," *Item*, Apr. 24, 1921, in LLC Scrapbook, 1925–1928. Sources differ as to whether the Legislature appropriated money for the commission in 1921 or 1922. A newspaper article confirms the earlier date. "Women Asked to Watch All Bills Clubs Sponsor," *TP*, June 11, 1922.

12. Reed, "Early History," 30; "History of the Louisiana Library Commission," 4 (quotation).

Chapter 1. Essae M. Culver Answers the Call, 1925

1. Carl F. Kaestle, "Seeing the Sites: Readers, Publishers, and Local Print Cultures in 1880," in *The History of the Book in America*, Vol. 4: *Print in Motion: The Expansion of Publishing and Reading in the United States, 1880–1940*, ed. Carl F. Kaestle and Janice A. Radway (Chapel Hill: Published in association with the American Antiquarian Society by the University of North Carolina Press, 2009), 24, 44.

2. Wayne A. Wiegand, *Part of Our Lives: A People's History of the American Public Library* (New York: Oxford University Press, 2015), 94; Milton J. Ferguson, "Why Louisiana?" in Louisiana Library Commission, *Report on the Louisiana Library Demonstration, 1925–1930* (Baton Rouge: The Commission, 1931; hereinafter LLC, *Report*), 7–8 (quotations); League of Library Commissions, *Handbook* (Chicago: American Library Association, 1922), 8. In 1942, the American Library Association incorporated the League of Library Commissions as an agency of the Library Extension Section of the Public Library Division (now Public Library Section). American Library Association, "League of Library Commissions File, 1904–1944," available at https://archives.library.illinois.edu/alaarchon/?p=collections/controlcard&id=7034 (accessed Aug. 20, 2017).

3. Ferguson, "Why Louisiana?" 8–9; "Papers and Proceedings of the Forty-Seventh Annual Meeting of the American Library Association (July 1925)," *Bulletin of the American Library Association* 19.4 (1925), 353 (quotation).

4. Ferguson, "Why Louisiana?" 8–9 (quotation); "Papers and Proceedings," 353–54.

5. Ferguson, "Why Louisiana?" 8–10; Louisiana Legislature, *Acts* (1920); Milton J. Fergu-

son, "A Quarter of a Century After," *Bulletin of the Louisiana Library Association* 13 (Spring 1950), 35–36 (quotation); Florence M. Jumonville, "Creating and Transmitting the Louisiana Memory: Teaching Louisiana History in the Schools" (Ph.D. dissertation, University of New Orleans, 1997), 24–27.

6. Milton J. Ferguson, "A Land of Romance," *Bulletin of the Louisiana Library Association* 2 (Dec. 1938), 3–4 (first quotation); [Untitled news item], *LJ* 50 (Apr. 15, 1925), 346 (second quotation); Ferguson, "Why Louisiana?" 9 (third quotation); Margaret McD. Reed to Mrs. Friend, Mar. 10, 1925, Administrative Files (State Library History) (fourth quotation).

7. Louisiana State Conference for Social Betterment, "League of Library Commissions Selects Louisiana for Library Demonstration Grant," press release, ca. Apr. 12, 1925, in Administrative Files (Administration, LLC, 1925).

8. Ibid. (quotation); "Plan Model Library Here before Long," [unidentified Baton Rouge newspaper], Aug. 2, 1925, in LLC Scrapbook, 1925–1928; [Untitled editorial], *LJ* 50 (Feb. 15, 1925), 176. Another letter in the Administration file cited above, from Milton Ferguson to G. P. Wyckoff on Mar. 23, 1925, suggests that Louisiana had been selected already, for Ferguson congratulated Wyckoff on his appointment and expressed confidence "that we shall work happily together." For additional information about the Louisiana State Library Association, see Florence M. Jumonville, "When We First Met: Conferences, Officers, and Activities of LSLA and LLA, 1909–1932," *Louisiana Libraries* 73.2 (Fall 2010), 7–16, and Alma Dawson and Florence M. Jumonville, eds., *A History of the Louisiana Library Association* (Baton Rouge: Louisiana Library Association, 2003).

9. Milton J. Ferguson to [G. P.] Wyckoff, Mar. 9, 1925 (quotation), and G. P. Wyckoff to Essae Culver, Apr. 9, 1925, both in Administrative Files (Administration—State Library History—75th Anniversary). For additional information about Essae M. Culver, see Florence M. Jumonville, "The Role of the State in the Organization of Statewide Library Service: Essae M. Culver, Louisiana's First State Librarian," *Library Trends* 52.4 (Spring 2004), 853–76.

10. Joseph Culver, a native of the area of Carlisle, Pennsylvania, graduated from Iron City Commercial College in Pittsburgh. He practiced law, pursued commercial interests that included insurance and banking, and worked as a teacher and as principal of a normal school in Burbank, Ohio. Probably enticed by opportunities in Pontiac, Illinois, he moved there in about 1859. He met Mary Murphy, like him a former teacher, and they married on December 12, 1861. In August 1862, Culver enlisted in the 129th Regiment of Illinois Volunteers because "I thought God & my country was calling upon me" to fight in the Civil War. He was mustered out on June 8, 1865, with the rank of captain. Culver became active in Republican politics, serving for two years as mayor of Pontiac and for four years as Livingston County judge. In 1879 he moved his family to Emporia, Kansas, where he continued to pursue interests in banking, law, and community affairs. Leslie W. Dunlap, "Introduction" in *"Your Affectionate Husband, J. F. Culver": Letters Written during the Civil War,* ed. Leslie W. Dunlap, notes by Edwin C. Bearss (Iowa City: Friends of the University of Iowa Libraries, 1978), ix–xi.

11. Ibid., 3; Pat Wilson, "Patter," *BRMA,* Mar. 8, 1946, in LLC Scrapbook, 1945–1947; Sue

Fontaine, "Talk of Many Things," *Bulletin of the Louisiana Library Association* 25 (Summer 1962), 62. Essae Culver's longtime colleague and friend Vivian Cazayoux verified the origin of her name in a conversation with the author, Sept. 25, 2003.

12. Essae M. Culver, "The Life and Times and Family of Essae M. Culver" (unpublished manuscript, [n.d.]), 1–2, photocopy from the Culver family in author's possession; Culver, [Journals], Oct. 15, 1954. According to notes copied from Culver's records by her nephew John C. Culver, her siblings were Franklin Allen Culver (1862–1863), Howard Dunmire Culver (1864–1896), Marion Allie Culver (1866–1953), Helen Newell Culver (1868–1872), Chester Murphy Culver (1870–1961), Harriett Margaret Culver (1872–1954), and Grace Culver (1877–1936).

13. Culver, "Life and Times," 1.

14. Ibid., 1; "Married Last Night," *Arizona Republican,* Dec. 24, 1896; Velma Taylor, "The Life of Essae M. Culver Is the Story of La. Libraries," *BRST,* May 16, 1962 (quotations); Phoenix Union High School, "Baccalaureate Service, 1901" (commencement program).

15. Essae M. Culver to Edna M. Sanderson, Associate Dean, Columbia University School of Library Service, Oct. 30, 1931; Edna M. Sanderson to Essae M. Culver, Nov. 9, 1931, both inserted in Culver, [Journals], 1937; Joanne E. Passet, *Cultural Crusaders: Women Librarians in the American West, 1900–1917* (Albuquerque: University of New Mexico Press, 1994), 25.

16. Taylor, "Life of Essae M. Culver"; Passet, *Cultural Crusaders,* 2–3, 51–52 (quotation, 2).

17. Taylor, "Life of Essae M. Culver" (first quotation); Sonja Sommerville, Community Relations/Volunteer Coordinator, Salem Public Library, e-mail message to author, July 12, 2005 (subsequent quotations).

18. "Presenting Essae M. Culver," *Bulletin of the Louisiana Library Association* 8 (March–June 1945), 5; Ray E. Held, *The Rise of the Public Library in California* (Chicago: American Library Association, 1973), 132–47. See also Debra Gold Hansen, "Depoliticizing the California State Library," *Information & Culture* 48.1 (2013), 68–90.

19. Passet, *Cultural Crusaders,* 90 (first quotation); Essae M. Culver, "A County Librarian at Work," *Bulletin of the American Library Association* 19.4 (1925), 355 (second quotation).

20. Culver, "County Librarian," 355 (first quotation), 356 (subsequent quotations).

21. *Current Biography: Who's News and Why, 1940* (New York: H. W. Wilson, 1940), s.v. Essae Martha Culver; Milton J. Ferguson to Essae M. Culver, Mar. 18, 1925, in VF (SLL, Correspondence, 1925–1926).

22. Essae M. Culver to Prof. G. P. Wyckoff, Tulane University, Apr. 29, 1925 (first quotation), in Administrative Files (State Library History—75th Anniversary); Essae M. Culver to Milton J. Ferguson, Apr. 30, 1925 (second quotation), and May 8, 1926, both in VF (SLL, Correspondence, 1925–1926).

23. Culver to Wyckoff, Apr. 29, 1925; Thomas Shuler Shaw, "Miss Essae Martha Culver: First Lady of Louisiana Librarians," *LLA Bulletin* 50 (Summer/Fall 1987), 12–13.

24. J. O. Modisette to Milton J. Ferguson, Nov. 8, 1927, in Administrative Files (Library History—J. O. Modisette, 1927) (quotation); Shaw, "Miss Essae Martha Culver," 12–13.

25. "Presenting Essae M. Culver," *Bulletin of the Louisiana Library Association* 8 (Mar.–June 1945), 5 (first and second quotations); G. P. Wyckoff to Essae M. Culver, May 17, 1925,

in Administrative Files (Correspondence, LLC—Administration); Culver, [Journals], July 21 (third quotation) and July 24, 1925.

26. Essae M. Culver, unpublished paper, County Librarians Luncheon, California Library Association, Oct. 12, 1954, 1 (first quotation); LLC, *Report*, 15, 26–27; Culver, [Journals], July 24–29, 1925; Essae M. Culver, "The Louisiana State Library," *Bulletin of the Louisiana Library Association* 16 (Spring 1953), 42; Essae M. Culver, interview by Becky and A. E. Schroeder, Mar. 15, 1972 (second quotation), cassette recording in Culver Papers (transcribed by the author).

27. Essae M. Culver to Milton J. Ferguson, Aug. 24, 1925 (quotation), in VF (SLL, Correspondence, 1925–1926); Culver, [Journals], Aug. 26, 1925; Culver, "Louisiana State Library," 42; Margaret Dixon and Nantelle Gittinger, *The First Twenty-Five Years of the Louisiana State Library, 1925–1950* (Baton Rouge: Louisiana State Library, 1950), 6.

28. LLC, *Report*, 16 (first quotation), 18; Louisiana Library Commission, *Second Biennial Report of the Louisiana Library Commission, 1926–1928* ([Baton Rouge: The Commission, 1928]), 5 (second quotation), 13.

29. LLC, *Report*, 20.

30. A. W. Hayes, undated notations (quotation); G. P. Wyckoff to Milton J. Ferguson, Mar. 16, 1925, both in Administrative Files (Administration—Correspondence, LLC); *A Dictionary of Louisiana Biography*, ed. Glenn R. Conrad (2 vols.; New Orleans: Louisiana Historical Association, 1988), s.v. Lucy Brown Foote.

31. Essae M. Culver to Milton J. Ferguson, Oct. 5, 1925 (first quotation), in VF (SLL, Correspondence, 1925–1926); Katherine Hill to Essae M. Culver, Oct. 5, 1925 (second quotation), in Administrative Files (Administration—Correspondence, LLC, 1925).

32. Milton J. Ferguson to Essae M. Culver, Oct. 9, 1925 (first quotation); Essae M. Culver to Mary Harris, Oct. 5, 1925 (second and third quotations); Milton J. Ferguson to Essae M. Culver, Oct. 6, 1925; Essae M. Culver to [Virginia] Fairfax, Dec. 15, 1925 (remaining quotations), all in VF (SLL, Correspondence, 1925–1926); Essae M. Culver to Louisiana Library Commission, Oct. 24, 1925, in Administrative Files (Administration—Correspondence, LLC, 1925); Culver, [Journals], Dec. 7, 1925.

33. Culver, [Journals], Sept. 21 and Oct. 26, 1925; Culver to Ferguson, Aug. 24, 1925; Ferguson to Culver, Oct. 6, 1925 (first quotation); Essae M. Culver to Milton J. Ferguson, Sept. 24, 1925 (second quotation), Nov. 24, 1925, and July 24, 1926, all in VF (SLL, Correspondence, 1925–1926).

34. Culver, [Journals], Oct. 26, 1925 (first quotation); LLC, *Report*, 24 (second and fourth quotations); Harriet Catherine Long, *County Library Service* (Chicago: American Library Association, 1925), 7 (third quotation).

35. LLC, *Report*, 24–25 (quotations); [Untitled news item], Apr. 15, 1925, 346; Orleans Territory, *Acts Passed at the First Session of the Legislative Council of the Territory of Orleans* (New Orleans: Printed by James M. Bradford, 1805), 322–35.

36. LLC, *Report*, 24.

37. Ibid.

38. Ibid., 27; Fontaine, "Talk of Many Things," 60 (quotation); Culver, [Journals], Feb. 7, 1926.

39. "Act No. 36 of 1926," in LLC, *Report*, 84–89; LLC, *Report*, 25 (first quotation); Culver,

unpublished paper, County Librarians Luncheon, 2; Fontaine, "Talk of Many Things," 15 (second quotation); Culver, [Journals], June 1-June 26, 1926 (third quotation, June 1, 1926).

40. "Library League Chief Awaited," *TP*, Sept. 22, 1926, in LLC Scrapbook, 1925–1928; "New Library Law Signed by Gov. Fuqua," *News*, July 2, 1926; "Act No. 36 of 1926," in LLC, *Report*, 84–89; Essae M. Culver to Milton J. Ferguson, June 29, 1926 (first quotation); Milton J. Ferguson to Essae M. Culver, July 14, 1926 (second quotation), both in VF (SLL, Correspondence, 1925–1926).

41. "Library Will Supply Information about Explosives, English Sparrows, Says Report on State Commission," Opelousas *News*, June 7, 1928; LLC, *Report*, 25 (first quotation), 31 (second quotation); Samuel Rothstein, "The Origins of Legislative Reference Services in the United States," *Legislative Studies Quarterly* 5 (Aug. 1990), 403; Paul D. Healey, "Go and Tell the World: Charles R. McCarthy and the Evolution of the Legislative Reference Movement, 1901–1917," *Law Library Journal* 99 (Winter 2007), 34–35, 40; Kenneth Cmiel, "Libraries, Books, and the Information Age," in *The History of the Book in America*, Vol. 5: *The Enduring Book: Print Culture in Post-War America*, ed. David Paul Nord, Joan Shelley Rubin, and Michael Schudson (Chapel Hill: Published in association with the American Antiquarian Society by the University of North Carolina Press, 2009), 325; "Government Libraries," in *Encyclopedia of Library History*, ed. Wayne A. Wiegand and Donald G. Davis, Jr. (New York: Garland, 1994), 246.

42. LLC, *Report*, 32 (first quotation); Louisiana Library Commission, *Second Biennial Report*, 5 (second quotation); "Library League Chief Awaited," *TP*, Sept. 22, 1926 (third quotation), in LLC Scrapbook, 1925–1928.

Chapter 2. Raising Funds for Parish Libraries, 1926

1. Louisiana Library Commission, *First Annual Report of the Louisiana Library Commission, 1925–1926* ([Baton Rouge: The Commission], 1926), 6; Culver, [Journals], Sept. 26, Oct. 5, and Oct. 9–10, 1925; Renee B. Stern, "Carrying Opportunity into the Parishes," *TP*, May 6, 1928, p. 2. For information about Mims's program of community organization, see Mary Mims with Georgia Williams Moritz, *The Awakening Community* (New York: Macmillan, 1932).

2. Culver, [Journals], Nov. 30–Dec. 4, 1925; Essae M. Culver to Milton J. Ferguson, Dec. 9, 1925 (quotation), in VF (SLL, Correspondence, 1915–1926).

3. New Orleans Public Library, "Records of the Orleans Parish Police Juries" (retrieved Oct. 28, 2018, from nutrias.org/~nopl/inv/neh/nehvj.htm) (quotation); Police Jury Association of Louisiana, *Parish Government Structure* [data file], 1999 (retrieved Nov. 12, 2018, from https://www.lpgov.org/page/ParishGovStructure).

4. Police Jury Association of Louisiana, *Parish Government Structure;* "Declares Public Library Is Poor Man's University," *BRMA*, Apr. 20, 1928, in LLC Scrapbook, 1925–1928.

5. Culver to Ferguson, Dec. 9, 1925.

6. Culver, [Journals], 1926, facing p. 1; Apr. 1, 1926 (first quotation); Apr. 12 (second quotation); Jan. 18, 1933 (third quotation); Apr. 13 (fifth quotation); "Librarian's Dream Comes True in La.," *BRST*, Oct. 23, 1968 (fourth quotation).

7. Culver, [Journals], Jan. 9, 1926 (first quotation); Essae M. Culver to Milton J. Ferguson, Feb. 2, 1926 (second quotation), in VF (SLL—Correspondence, 1925–1926).

8. Culver, [Journals], Nov. 26, 1926; Sue (Mrs. Henry A.) Fontaine, "Talk of Many Things," *Bulletin of the Louisiana Library Association* 25 (Summer 1962), 58–63+ (quotation).

9. Clara F. Baldwin, "League of Library Commissions," *Bulletin of the American Library Association* 21 (Oct. 1927), 428 (second quotation); Sue (Mrs. Henry) Fontaine, "Deeds—Not Words," also titled "The Essay on Essae," unpublished remarks presented at the meeting of the Library History Round Table, American Library Association conference, Chicago, July 15, 1963, 4–5 (other quotations), in VF (Librarians—Culver, Essae M.).

10. Culver, [Journals], Feb. 7–10, 1926 (short quotations); Essae M. Culver to Milton J. Ferguson, Feb. 15, 1926 (last quotation), in VF (SLL, Correspondence, 1925–1926).

11. LLC, *Report*, 27–29; Culver, [Journals], Mar. 2, 1926; Essae M. Culver to G. P. Wyckoff, Mar. 3, 1926, in Administrative Files (Administration—Correspondence, LLC); Essae M. Culver to Milton J. Ferguson, Mar. 4, 1926 (quotations), in VF (SLL, Correspondence, 1925–1926).

12. Essae M. Culver to Milton J. Ferguson, Dec. 14, 1926 (quotations), in VF (SLL, Correspondence, 1925–1926); LLC, *Report*, 32–33; "Richland Parish Free Library," [n.d. but ca. Mar. 1927], in VF (SLL, Correspondence, 1927–1928); Marguerite Young, "Don't Know? State Librarians Do—It's Part of Their Novel Job," *IT*, Dec. 26, 1926, in LLC Scrapbook, 1925–1928; "Even Floods Fail to Stop Drawing of Library Books," [Unidentified newspaper, n.d. but June 1927].

13. LLC, *Report*, 33–34 (first two quotations); "Even Floods Fail to Stop Drawing of Library Books" (third quotation).

14. "Memorial Book Collection Will Be Dedicated for Richland Library," *States*, Sept. 20, 1936, in LLC Scrapbook, 1925–1928.

15. "Simple Services for Captain Morris," *TP*, Sept. 26, 1918; New Orleans city directories, 1896–1947.

16. "Simple Services"; "Society," *TP*, Oct. 4, 1908; Nov. 26, 1911; May 30, 1913; Mar. 3, 1914; May 7, 1916; July 1, 1917; "Daughters of the Confederacy," *TP*, Sept. 21, 1910.

17. Carey Jay Ellis obituary, Franklin *Sun*, July 30, 1964; "Monroe Man Ends Life While Despondent," *STA*, May 24, 1926; Culver, [Journals], Feb. 9, Mar. 2, Dec. 7, 1926; Mar. 15, 1927.

18. Culver to Ferguson, Dec. 14, 1926 (first quotation); Essae M. Culver to Milton J. Ferguson, Mar. 26, 1927, in VF (SLL, Correspondence, 1927–1928); "Richland Parish Free Library."

19. Jim Bradshaw, "Great Flood of 1927," in *knowlouisiana.org, Encyclopedia of Louisiana*, http://www.knowlouisiana.org/entry/great-flood-of-1927. Accessed Sept. 11, 2017 (first quotation); Essae M. Culver to Milton J. Ferguson, May 16, 1927 (second quotation), in VF (SLL, Correspondence, 1927–1928).

20. Culver to Ferguson, May 6, 1927 (first quotation); Essae M. Culver to Milton J. Ferguson, May 16, 1927 (subsequent quotations), in VF (SLL, Correspondence, 1927–1928).

21. Bradshaw, "Great Flood of 1927"; LLC, *Report*, 34 (first quotation); Essae M. Culver to Milton J. Ferguson, May 16, 1927 (second quotation), in VF (SLL, Correspondence, 1927–1928).

22. LLC, *Report*, 34 (first quotation); Stern, "Carrying Opportunity into the Parishes" (second quotation); Culver to Ferguson, May 16, 1927.

23. "Memorial Book Collection" (quotation); Lillian Morris obituary, *TP,* Mar. 18, 1947.

24. Essie [*sic*] Martha Culver, "State Planning in Louisiana," *LJ* 60 (May 1, 1935).

25. Culver, [Journals], May 5, 1926; "Parish Library Is Plan for St. Mary," *MCR,* July 3, 1926; "St. Mary Parish Moves for Carnegie Library," *LR,* July 8, 1926; "To Pick Chairman of Library Drive," *MCR,* July 7, 1926, all in LLC Scrapbook, 1925–1928; Essae M. Culver to Milton J. Ferguson, July 8, 1926, in VF (SLL, Correspondence, 1925–1926).

26. Essae M. Culver to Milton J. Ferguson, May 8, 1926 in VF (SLL, Correspondence, 1925–1926).

27. Culver to Ferguson, July 8, 1926.

28. Essae M. Culver to Milton J. Ferguson, May 6, 1927 (first quotation), in VF (SLL, Correspondence, 1927–1928); Milton J. Ferguson to Essae M. Culver, July 14, 1926 (second quotation), in VF (SLL, Correspondence, 1925–1926); "Richland Parish Free Library" (third quotation).

29. Culver, [Journals], Jan. 27, 1926; "Five Libraries and 5 Stations for J. D. Parish," *AP,* Aug. 23, 1926; "Jefferson Davis Parish Votes to Have a Library," *BRST,* Sept. 3, 1926; "Neighbor Parish Takes Favorable Library Action," *AP,* Sept. 4. 1926; "Our Parish-Wide Library," *News,* Sept. 10, 1926 (quotation), all in LLC Scrapbook, 1925–1928.

30. Essae M. Culver to Milton J. Ferguson, Nov. 1, 1926 (quotation), in VF (SLL, Correspondence, 1925–1926); J. O. Modisette to C. P. Shaver, Nov. 24, 1926, in Administrative Files (State Library History—Modisette, 1927).

31. Essae M. Culver to J. O. Modisette, Nov. 3, 1926 (quotation), in Administrative Files (State Library History—Modisette, 1927); Culver, [Journals], Oct. 27–28, 1926; LLC, *Report,* 36.

32. Emma J. Sockrider, "Mrs. Sockrider Says Library Tax Unfair to Farmers," *News,* July 27, 1927, in LLC Scrapbook, 1925–1928; Essae M. Culver to Milton J. Ferguson, Nov. 23, 1926, in VF (SLL, Correspondence, 1925–1926); Modisette to Shaver, Nov. 24, 1926; LLC, *Report,* 36.

33. Culver to Ferguson, Nov. 23, 1926; Milton J. Ferguson to Essae M. Culver, Nov. 29, 1926 (quotation), in VF (SLL, Correspondence, 1925–1926); Modisette to Shaver, Nov. 24, 1926; LLC, *Report,* 36.

34. LLC, *Report,* 36–37; Ruth Rodgers, "Parish Library Very Popular," *News,* Feb. 22, 1927, in LLC Scrapbook, 1925–1928.

35. "Another View of the Free Library," Elton *Leader,* May 7, 1927, Ed Aguillard, "Ed Aguillard Strongly Urges Parish Library," *News,* July 19, 1927, "Let Us Reason Together," *News,* July 19, 1927, "Libraries in Jeff Davis," *States,* Aug. 16, 1927, and "Library Tax Defeated by Maj. 550 Votes," *News,* Aug. 26, 1927, all in LLC Scrapbook, 1925–1928; Essae M. Culver to Milton J. Ferguson, Sept. 6, 1927 (quotation), in VF (SLL, Correspondence, 1927–1928).

36. J. O. Modisette to Essae M. Culver, Aug. 23, 1927 (first quotation), in Administrative Files (State Library History—Modisette, 1927); Culver to Ferguson, Sept. 6, 1927 (subsequent quotations); Culver, [Journals], Aug. 29–Sept. 3, 1927.

37. LLC, *Report,* 37–38 (first quotation); "Parish Library Demonstration Is Far-Reaching,"

BRST, Aug. 20, 1927, in LLC Scrapbook, 1925–1928 (second quotation); Louisiana State Library, *New Directions in Library Service: Twenty-Third Report, 1968–1970* (Baton Rouge: [The Library, 1970]), 8.

Chapter 3. Developing the Louisiana Demonstration Plan, 1927–1929

1. LLC, *Report,* 38–39 (first quotation), 41; Milton J. Ferguson, "Why Louisiana?," in LLC, *Report,* 7–11, 11 (second quotation); Dick Wright, "Librarian Emeritus Dies at 90," *Advocate,* Jan. 4, 1973, p. 6-A (third quotation).

2. Essae M. Culver to Milton J. Ferguson, Sept. 6, 1926 (first quotation); Essae M. Culver to Milton J. Ferguson, July 24, 1926 (second quotation) and Oct. 15, 1926, all in VF (SLL, Correspondence, 1925–1926); J. O. Modisette to Frank A. Godchaux, Sr., Sept. 24, 1926, in Administrative File (State Library History—Modisette, 1926).

3. Culver to Ferguson, Sept. 6, 1926; Essae M. Culver to Milton J. Ferguson, July 24, 1926, and Oct. 15, 1926, both in VF (SLL, Correspondence, 1925–1926); "J. O. Modisette Appointed to La. Library Commission," *News,* Nov. 5, 1926; "Dr. H. M. Blain is Appointed on La. Library Com.," *BRST,* Dec. 2, 1926, both in LLC Scrapbook, 1925–1928.

4. Essae M. Culver to Milton J. Ferguson, Dec. 4, 1926 (quotation), in VF (SLL, Correspondence, 1925–1926); Culver, [Journals], July 2, 1927; Sue (Mrs. Henry A.) Fontaine, "Talk of Many Things," *Bulletin of the Louisiana Library Association* 25 (Summer 1962), 61.

5. J. O. Modisette to Milton J. Ferguson, Sept. 20, 1927 (quotation), in VF (SLL, Correspondence, 1927–1928).

6. LLC, *Report,* 39 (quotation), 41; Culver, [Journals], Mar. 14, 1928; Culver to Ferguson, Sept. 8, 1927.

7. "An Editorial: Louisiana Loses a Friend," *BRMA,* June 22, 1942; "Parent-Teacher Association News," [clipping from unidentified newspaper], Nov. 19, 1926 (first quotation), in LLC Scrapbook, 1925–1928; Alcée Fortier, ed., *Louisiana: Comprising Sketches of Parishes, Towns, Events, Institutions, and Persons, Arranged in Cyclopedic Form* (3 vols.; New York: Century Historical Association, 1914), III:303 (second quotation, III:304); Essae M. Culver, "The Modisette Award—1952," unpublished speech, Louisiana Library Association Convention (March 1952), in Administrative Files (Libraries—Modisette Awards—Historical LLA Information relating to); [Essae M Culver?], "James Oliver Modisette," *Bulletin of the Louisiana Library Association* 6 (Sept.-Dec. 1942), 3.

8. Fortier, *Louisiana,* III:303–4 (quotation, III:303); [Culver?], "James Oliver Modisette," 3; Charles J. Kappler, comp. and ed., *Indian Affairs: Laws and Treaties,* Vol. IV: *Laws* (Washington, DC: Government Printing Office, 1929), 48; SCLA, Minute Books, vol. 34, p. 358–59; "Parish Library Movement Lauded by Governor Long," *Journal,* [n.d. but late Sept. 1929], in LLC Scrapbook, 1929–1930.

9. J. O. Modisette to Milton J. Ferguson, Nov. 26, 1926, in Administrative Files (State Library History—Modisette, 1926).

10. [Essae M. Culver] to J. O. Modisette, Nov. 26, 1926 (first quotation), in Administrative Files (State Library History—Modisette, 1926); Milton J. Ferguson to Essae M. Culver, June 9, 1927 (second quotation), in VF (SLL, Correspondence, 1927–1928).

11. Milton J. Ferguson to Essae M. Culver, June 19, 1926 (first quotation); Essae M. Culver to Milton J. Ferguson, July 24, 1926 (subsequent quotations) and Dec. 4, 1926, all in VF (SLL, Correspondence, 1925–1926).

12. Essae M. Culver to Milton J. Ferguson, Sept. 6, 1926 (first quotation); Milton J. Ferguson to Essae M. Culver, May 19, 1926 (second quotation), both in VF (SLL, Correspondence, 1925–1926).

13. Essae M. Culver to J. O. Modisette, Oct. 27, 1927 (quotation); J. O. Modisette to Milton J. Ferguson, Nov. 8, 1927, both in Administrative Files (State Library History—Modisette, 1927).

14. Culver to Modisette, Oct. 27, 1927 (first quotation); Louisiana Library Commission, *Third Biennial Report,* 10 (second quotation); Louisiana Library Commission, *Fourth Biennial Report of the Louisiana Library Commission, 1930–1931* ([Baton Rouge: The Commission, 1931]), 6–7.

15. LLC, *Report,* 61–62; Mary Mims with Georgia Williams Moritz, *The Awakening Community* (New York: Macmillan, 1932), xxvi (quotation). In *The Awakening Community,* Mims explained that important problem solving must occur within a community of people who share common interests. As community organizer, she worked with residents of towns and rural areas to implement such projects as planting gardens, constructing churches, setting up branch libraries, and cooperatively determining the best variety of cotton to plant—and buying fertilizer for it in bulk, at a great saving (36, 45, 47).

16. LLC, *Report,* 51–56, 60; e.g., "Rapides Library Tax," in "Letters to the Editor," *TT,* Nov. 16, 1942, in LLC Scrapbook, 1942–1945; Louisiana Library Commission, *Second Biennial Report of the Louisiana Library Commission, 1926–1928* ([Baton Rouge: The Commission, 1928]), 6–7, 10.

17. Louisiana Library Commission, *Third Biennial Report of the Louisiana Library Commission, 1928–1930* ([Baton Rouge: The Commission, 1930]), 9; Wayne A. Wiegand, "The American Public Library: Construction of a Community Reading Institution," in *The History of the Book in America,* Vol. 4: *Print in Motion: The Expansion of Publishing and Reading in the United States, 1880–1940,* ed. Carl F. Kaestle and Janice A. Radway (Chapel Hill: Published in association with the American Antiquarian Society by the University of North Carolina Press, 2009), 433 (quotation).

18. LLC, *Report,* 67; "Miss Culver to Preside at Meeting," Minden *Signal-Tribune,* Mar. 30, 1929, in LLC Scrapbook, 1929–1930.

19. Findagrave.com, accessed Oct. 18, 2017; J. O. Modisette to E. M. Culver, Feb. 11 and Feb. 17, 1928, both in Administrative Files (State Library History—Modisette, 1928); Culver, [Journals], Aug. 24, 1929, July 24–Aug. 3, 1932 (first quotation, Aug. 1, 1932) and Memoranda page (second quotation), and June 4, 1935; "Library Changes Over Louisiana Are Announced," *BRST,* June 14, 1935; "Six States Are Represented in Library Science School at L. S. U.," *BRST,* Sept. 30, 1935.

20. Essae M. Culver to Milton J. Ferguson, Sept. 9, 1925, in VF (SLL, Correspondence,

1925–1926) (first quotation); Culver, "Louisiana State Library," 43 (second quotation); LLC, *Report*, 25 (third quotation).

21. Velma Taylor, "The Life of Essae M. Culver Is the Story of La. Libraries," *TP*, May 6, 1928, in LLC Scrapbook, 1925–1928; "Many Opportunities for Women Found in Librarianship, Avers Miss Culver, State's Executive," *TP*, Nov. 17, 1929 (quotation), in LLC Scrapbook, 1928–1929.

22. Culver, "Louisiana State Library," 43; LLC, *Report*, 25; Essae M. Culver to Milton J. Ferguson, Dec. 9, 1925, in VF (SLL, Correspondence, 1925–1926); "Librarian Profession Declared to Offer Fine Career in State Under System About to Start," [Unidentified newspaper], Jan. 6, 1926, in LLC Scrapbook, 1925–1928; Milton J. Ferguson to Essae M. Culver, June 19, 1926 (quotation), in VF (SLL, Correspondence, 1925–1926); "L.S.U. Offering Only Library Course in South This Summer Attracts Out-of-State Students," *BRST*, July 13, 1927.

23. LLC, *Report*, 61–62; Essae M. Culver, interview by Becky and A. E. Schroeder, Mar. 15, 1972 (quotation), cassette recording in Culver Papers (transcribed by the author).

24. Culver, Schroeder interview, Mar. 15, 1972.

25. Ibid.

26. Ibid.; Culver, [Journals], July 21, 1928.

27. [Gretta Smith], Memorandum to Essae M. Culver, [August 1928], in Administrative File (State Library History—Modisette, 1928).

28. J. O. Modisette to Milton J. Ferguson, May 23, 1928 (first and second quotations), Administrative Files (State Library History—Modisette, 1928); Huey P. Long to Louisiana Library Commission, Sept. 14, 1929 (last quotation), quoted in "Parish Library Movement Lauded by Governor Long," Shreveport *Journal*, [n.d. but late Sept. 1929], in LLC Scrapbook, 1928–1929.

29. LLC, *Report*, 40–41; Louisiana Library Commission, *Third Biennial Report*, 6; Culver, [Journals], 1928, passim; "Three Parishes Have United in Library Move," *BRST*, Mar. 14, 1928, in LLC Scrapbook, 1925–1928; J. O. Modisette to Essae M. Culver, May 3, 1928, in Administrative File (State Library History—Modisette, 1928).

30. "Concordia Parish Library Receives Heavy Patronage," *TP*, Mar. 17, 1929 (quotations), in LLC Scrapbook, 1928–1929; Louisiana Library Commission, *Third Biennial Report*, 8, 17.

31. Louisiana Library Commission, *Third Biennial Report*, 7 (first quotation); Louisiana Library Commission, *Fourth Biennial Report*, 16 (second quotation).

32. Louisiana Library Commission, *Third Biennial Report*, 7–8 (first quotation); "Concordia Votes Special Tax for Library Purposes," *BRST*, Sept. 18, 1929; "Concordia to Have Parish Library," *Advocate*, Sept. 19, 1929 (second quotation), both in LLC Scrapbook, 1928–1929; Gretchen K. Schenk, *County and Regional Library Development* (Chicago: American Library Association, 1954), 70 (third quotation).

33. R. L. Duffus, *Books, Their Place in a Democracy* (New York: Houghton Mifflin, 1930), 196 (first quotation); "Practical Services of Concordia Parish Library Told by President," *BRST*, Apr. 10, 1930 (subsequent quotations), in LLC Scrapbook, 1928–1929.

34. Rachel Violette, "The Value of a Public Library," *Louisiana* (Apr. 1929), 23–24; LLC, *Report*, 43 (quotation). For a thorough examination of *Plessy v. Ferguson*, see Steve Luxenberg, *Separate: The Story of* Plessy v. Ferguson, *and America's Journey from Slavery to Segregation* (New York: Norton, 2019).

35. Sarah Jones, "Library Demand Is Born in Louisiana," Memphis *Commercial Appeal,* Apr. 1928 (first quotation), in LLC Scrapbook, 1925–1928; Edna Holden, "The Cost of Book Truck Service—Is It Worth While?" *LJ* 55 (Feb. 1, 1930), 104 (second quotation); "'Bookmobile' Is Great Aid Supplying Reading Matter for Rural Residents," [Unidentified Monroe newspaper, n.d. but Mar. 1930] (third quotation), in LLC Scrapbook, 1928–1929.

36. "Bookmobiles Turn 100," *LJ* 130.16 (Oct. 2005), 24; Barbara Bader, "Treasure Island by the Roadside," *Horn Book Magazine* 75 (Jan./Feb. 1999), 4; Jennifer Cummings, "'How Can We Fail?': The Texas State Library's Traveling Libraries and Bookmobiles, 1916–1966," *Libraries & the Cultural Record* 44 (2009), 308–9; Holden, "Cost of Book Truck Service," 105 (quotation).

37. Cummings, "'How Can We Fail?,'" 309; "'Bookmobile' Is Great Aid" (quotation).

38. Michelle Hawk, "Bookmobile Services in Rural America: Past, Present, and Future," *Bookmobile and Outreach Services* 11.2 (2008), 59; "Knowledge Car from N.Y. Here on Tour of U.S.," *BRMA,* Jan. 24, 1930, in LLC Scrapbook, 1928–1929; "The Bookmobile as a Demonstration Book Truck," *LJ* 55 (Feb. 1, 1930), 110.

39. The costs expended by the Louisiana Library Commission on its first bookmobile compared favorably with those cited by Holden, which ranged from $860.25 to $1,850.00 for a 1½-ton model. "The Cost of Book Truck Service," 105; "The Bookmobile," *BRMA,* Oct. 5, 1929, in LLC Scrapbook, 1928–1929.

40. John W. Scott, "Highway Building in Louisiana: An Overdue Re-Appraisal," *Louisiana History* 44 (Winter 2003), 8, 11; Culver, [Journals], 1926, facing p. 1 (quotation); Bennett H. Wall, ed., *Louisiana: A History* (2nd ed.; Wheeling, IL: Forum Press, 1990), 274–75.

41. "The Bookmobile" (quotations); "Library-on-Wheels Exhibit Here 2 Days during Parish Fair," Winnfield *News American,* Oct. 11, 1929, in LLC Scrapbook, 1928–1929; LLC, *Report,* 56–57.

42. LLC, *Report,* 56–57 (quotation), 59.

43. Ibid., 58–59.

44. Ibid., 57 (quotation); Louisiana Library Commission, *Third Biennial Report,* 14.

45. LLC, *Report,* 57–58.

46. Ibid., 59.

47. "240 Requests for Information on Wide Variety of Subjects Answered by Library Commission in October," *BRST,* Nov. 1, 1929; Louisiana Library Commission, *Third Biennial Report,* 14.

48. "Bookmobile to Make Tour of Southwest La.," *BRST,* Feb. 18, 1930; "Bookmobile Will Go to Monroe for Library Meeting," *BRST,* Mar. 8, 1930; "Library Proposal Subject of Meet," Monroe *Post,* Mar. [15?], 1930; "Decide to Expand Service Available at Library Here," [Unidentified Monroe newspaper, Apr.? 1930] (quotation), all in LLC Scrapbook, 1928–1929; "Trainees at Camp Beauregard Have Access to Library," *TT,* July 18, 1930, in LLC Scrapbook, 1930–1935; Culver, [Journals], Jan. 10, 1930.

49. Agathine H. Goldstein, "Louisiana Libraries" (typescript, [1930]), 1, in LLC Scrapbook, 1930–1935.

50. Ibid. (first quotation); Winston De Ville, personal communication, July 19, 2008 (second quotation); Ferrel Guillory, "The Bookmobile That Opens up a World," *The Advocate,* Jan. 9, 2018 (subsequent quotations).

51. Essae M. Culver, "The Functions of State Supported Library Agencies," in Southeastern Library Association, *Addresses,* 12–14 ([S.1.: The Association, 1928]), 12; Taylor, "Life of Essae M. Culver"; Wyman W. Parker, "1959 ALA Awards, Citations, and Scholarships," *ALA Bulletin* 53 (Sept. 1959), 697 (first quotation); Lura Gibbons Currier, "The Lengthened Shadow: Essae M. Culver and the Louisiana State Library," *ALA Bulletin* 53 (Jan. 1959), 35 (second quotation); Annabelle Armstrong, "If You Have Library Problems, Just Ask Miss Essae M. Culver," *BRST,* Dec. 22, 1954; Kathryn Adams, "Bookmobile Service in Louisiana's Demonstration Libraries," in *The Bookmobile—A New Look,* ed. Lois G. Pennell (Chicago: American Library Association, 1969), 1.

52. Harris, "Louisiana Library Demonstration Plan," 89; Tommie Dora Barker, *Libraries of the South: A Report on Developments, 1930–1935* (Chicago: American Library Association, 1936), 155.

53. Louisiana State Library, "Plan Section 2.1 for Louisiana, Fiscal Year 1967, Library Services and Construction Act," 15 (first quotation), and Sallie Farrell, 59 (second quotation), both quoted by Julia King Avant, "Extending Library Service to Rural Areas in Louisiana" (Ph.D. dissertation, Indiana University, 1972).

54. "State-Sponsored Founding of Rural Libraries," *Christian Science Monitor,* Sept. 6, 1938.

55. Ibid. (quotation); Harris, "Louisiana Library Demonstration Plan," 89–90; Louisiana Library Commission, *Eleventh Annual Report of the Louisiana Library Commission, 1944–1945* (Baton Rouge: The Commission, [1946]), 20.

56. Harris, "Louisiana Library Demonstration Plan," 15 (quotations); "Wide Variety of Information Is Supplied by Library Commission," *BRST,* Feb. 25, 1928, in LLC Scrapbook, 1925–1928.

57. Harris, "Louisiana Library Demonstration Plan," 15; "Selected List of Children's Reading Given by La. Library," *BRST,* Nov. 8, 1926; "Picture Books Are Important as Means of Training Children," [Unidentified newspaper], Nov. 17, 1927, both in LLC Scrapbook, 1925–1928; "Delightful Books for Juvenile Readers Claim First Interest during Children's Book Week," *BRST,* Nov. 19, 1930, in LLC Scrapbook, 1930–1935.

58. Harris, "Louisiana Library Demonstration Plan," 15.

59. Ibid., 89–90; "Librarian Offers Program Matter for Use of Clubs," [Unidentified newspaper], Mar. 28, 1926, in LLC Scrapbook, 1925–1928; Louisiana State Library, *New Directions in Library Service, 1968–1970,* 19; Barker, *Libraries of the South,* 154 (quotation), 155; Avant, "Extending Library Service," 51.

60. Harris, "Louisiana Library Demonstration Plan," 89–90; Avant, "Extending Library Service," 50.

61. Parker, "1959 ALA Awards, 697 (quotation); "Librarian from Russia Impressed with System Here," *BRST,* Feb. 6, 1929, in LLC Scrapbook, 1929–1930; Louisiana State Library, *Twelfth Biennial Report of the Louisiana State Library, Formerly Louisiana Library Commission, 1946–1947* ([Baton Rouge]: The Library, 1948), 12; Louisiana State Library, *Fourteenth Biennial Report of the Louisiana State Library, Formerly Louisiana Library Commission, 1950–1951* (Baton Rouge: The Library, 1952), 2–3; Louisiana State Library, *Nineteenth Biennial*

Report of the Louisiana State Library, Formerly Louisiana Library Commission, 1960–1961 (Baton Rouge: [The Library], 1962), 1; "Foreign Visitor Praises Louisiana Library System," *Bulletin of the Louisiana Library Association* 24 (Fall 1961), 109–10; K. B. James, "Australian Librarian Commends Louisiana State Library's Demonstration Plan," *Bulletin of the Louisiana Library Association* 21 (Fall 1958), 111–17; Harris, "Louisiana Library Demonstration Plan," 89–91; Barker, *Libraries of the South*, 154–55.

62. Schenk, *County and Regional Library Development*, 75 (first quotation), 5 (third quotation); Culver, [Journals], Sept. 26, 1925; American Library Association, Office for Literacy and Outreach Services, *Different Voices, Common Quest: Adult Literacy & Outreach in Libraries!* ([Chicago: The Office], 2002), 2 (second quotation); American Library Association, "Interlibrary Loan Code for the United States" (2001), available at <http://www.ala.org/Content/NavigationMenu/RUSA/Professional_Tools4/Reference_Guidelines/Interlibrary_Loan_Code_for_the_United_States.htm>. Accessed Nov. 22, 2003.

63. Barker, *Libraries of the South*, 95 (first quotation); Essae M. Culver to J. O. Modisette, Feb. 9, 1928 (second quotation), in Administrative File (State Library History—Modisette, 1928); "Extension Expert Cites Advantages of Regional Library Organization," *BRST*, July 31, 1950 (third quotation), in LSL Scrapbook, 1950–1951.

64. Milton J. Ferguson to Essae M. Culver, July 3, 1945 (first quotation), in Culver Papers; Culver, quoted by Sue (Mrs. Henry) Fontaine, "Deeds—Not Words," also titled "The Essay on Essae," unpublished remarks presented at the meeting of the Library History Round Table, American Library Association conference, Chicago, July 15, 1963, 6 (second quotation), in LLC, VF—Librarians—Culver, Essae M.; Fontaine, "Talk of Many Things," 59–60; Culver, [Journals], Jan. 28, 1962 (third quotation); *Current Biography: Who's News and Why, 1940* (New York: H. W. Wilson, 1940), s.v. Essae Martha Culver (fourth quotation).

Chapter 4. Two Case Studies in Success: Webster and Vermilion Parishes

1. Carl F. Kaestle and Janice A. Radway, "Epilogue," in *The History of the Book in America*, Vol. 4: *Print in Motion: The Expansion of Publishing and Reading in the United States, 1880–1940*, ed. Carl F. Kaestle and Janice A. Radway (Chapel Hill: Published in association with the American Antiquarian Society by the University of North Carolina Press, 2009), 528; Cheryl Knott, *Not Free, Not for All: Public Libraries in the Age of Jim Crow* (Amherst: University of Massachusetts Press, 2015), 30; Ann Fabian, "Laboring Classes, New Readers, and Print Cultures," in *Perspectives on American Book History: Artifacts and Commentary*, ed. Scott E. Casper, Joanne D. Chaison, and Jeffrey D. Graves (Amherst: University of Massachusetts Press in Association with American Antiquarian Society and the Center for the Book, Library of Congress, 2002), 303–4 (quotations); Elizabeth McHenry, "Reading and Race Pride: The Literary Activism of Black Clubwomen," in *The History of the Book in America*, Vol. 4: *Print in Motion: The Expansion of Publishing and Reading in the United States, 1880–1940*, ed. Carl F. Kaestle and Janice A. Radway (Chapel Hill: Published in association with the American Antiquarian Society by the University of North Carolina Press, 2009), 492.

2. A. P. Tureaud to J. O. Modisette, Apr. 7, 1928; J. O. Modisette to A. P. Tureaud, Apr. 10, 1928; J. O. Modisette to Essae M. Culver, Apr. 10, 1928 (quotations), all in Administrative Files (State Library History—Modisette, 1928).

3. Tommie Dora Barker, *Libraries of the South: A Report on Developments, 1930–1935* (Chicago: American Library Association, 1936), 34 (quotation); "University and City Visited by Rosenwald Group," *BRMA*, Nov. 21, 1933, in LLC Scrapbook, 1930–1935.

4. LLC, *Report,* 44 (quotations); Louisiana Library Commission, *Third Biennial Report of the Louisiana Library Commission, 1928–1930* ([Baton Rouge: The Commission, 1930]), 11; Culver, [Journals], Oct. 1, 1929.

5. LLC, *Report,* 44–45 (quotations); Louis Round Wilson and Edward A. Wight, *County Library Service in the South: A Study of the Rosenwald County Library Demonstration* (Chicago: University of Chicago Press, 1935), 32; Barker, *Libraries of the South,* 34.

6. LLC, *Report,* 44–45; Kennon, quoted by Sue (Mrs. Henry) Fontaine, "Deeds—Not Words," also titled "The Essay on Essae," unpublished remarks presented at the meeting of the Library History Round Table, American Library Association conference, Chicago, July 15, 1963, 6, in VF (Librarians—Culver, Essae M.).

7. Wilson and Wight, *County Library Service,* 32; LLC, *Report,* 46–47; Louisiana Library Commission, *Fourth Biennial Report of the Louisiana Library Commission, 1930–1931* ([Baton Rouge: The Commission, 1932]), 13 (first quotation); Margaret R. Dixon, "The Webster Parish Library," *Louisiana Teachers Journal* (May 1930), in LLC Scrapbook, 1930–1935; Kari Butler, "Webster Parish Library," *LLA Bulletin* 61 (Fall 1998), 110; Gloria Spooner, "Establishment of African American Public Library Service in Louisiana," *Louisiana Libraries* 23.3 (Winter 2001), 23–24 (second quotation, 24).

8. Spooner, "African American Public Library Service," 23; "Library Commission Is Providing Book Service for Rural Communities," *BRMA*, May 16, 1932 (first quotation); Culver, quoted by Shirley Knowles Stephenson, "History of the Louisiana State Library, Formerly Louisiana Library Commission" (Ph.D. dissertation, Louisiana State University, 1957), 50; Wilson and Wight, *County Library Service,* 33 (third quotation); Barker, *Libraries of the South,* 36.

9. E. S. Richardson, "Book Service Free to All," *Bulletin of the American Library Association* 27.5 (May 1933), 213–15 (first quotation, 214; second and third quotations, 215).

10. Louisiana Library Commission, *Third Biennial Report,* 12; Louisiana Library Commission, *Fourth Biennial Report,* 12–13 (quotation, 12); Essae Martha Culver, "Webster Parish Library," *Louisiana Teachers' Association* (October 1929), 24.

11. E. S. Richardson, "'Ducks and Geese Are Flying South," *The Nation's Schools* 8.1 (July 1931), 49–51.

12. Ibid., 51–54 (quotation, 54).

13. Wilson and Wight, *County Library Service,* 34–35; Culver, [Journals], Oct. 3, 1929.

14. Wilson and Wight, *County Library Service,* 34–35.

15. LLC, *Report,* 47–48; Marion Humble, *Rural America Reads: A Study of Rural Library Service* (New York: American Association for Adult Education, 1938), 68 (first quotation); Barker, *Libraries of the South,* 52 (subsequent quotations); Louisiana Library Commission, *Fourth Biennial Report,* 12–13.

16. LLC, *Report,* 46, 49; Culver, [Journals], Mar. 31, 1933 and "Memoranda" page; Essae M.

Culver to Hugh M. Blain, Apr. 21, 1933, in VF (Correspondence, 1930–1933); Butler, "Webster Parish Library," 110 (quotation).

17. Louisiana Library Commission, *Fourth Biennial Report,* 12, 13 (quotation).

18. Wilson and Wight, *County Library Service,* 87, 212 (first quotation), 229 (second quotation).

19. Butler, "Webster Parish Library," 110–11; "History of Parish Library Is Told," Webster Parish *Review,* Nov. 14, 1939, in LLC Scrapbook, 1938–1940; Michael Fultz, "Black Public Libraries in the South in the Era of De Jure Segregation," *Libraries & the Cultural Record* 41.3 (Summer 2006), 345; Louisiana Library Commission, *Eighth Biennial Report of the Louisiana Library Commission, 1938–1939* (Baton Rouge: The Commission, [1940]), 23 (quotation).

20. Jackie Choate, "Vermilion Parish Library," *Louisiana Libraries* 62.3 (Winter 2000), 19; Christine Pawley, "Advocate for Access: Lutie Stearns and the Traveling Libraries of the Wisconsin Free Library Commission, 1895–1914," *Libraries & Culture* 35 (Summer 2000), 435–58 passim.

21. Culver, [Journals], Nov. 16–17, 1925; Mary W. Harris, "The Louisiana Library Demonstration Plan: Designed to Extend Public Library Service to the Entire Population of the State" (Baton Rouge: Louisiana State Library, Extension Department, 1952), 67–68 (quotation, 67); Annabelle Armstrong, "If You Have Library Problems, Just Ask Miss Essae M. Culver," *BRST,* Dec. 22, 1954.

22. "Acadians Found Nearly Illiterate," *New York Times,* Aug. 16, 1935, p. 17 (quotations); Harris, "Louisiana Library Demonstration Plan," 68, 74.

23. Harris, "Louisiana Library Demonstration Plan," 67–68; Armstrong, "If You Have Library Problems."

24. Armstrong, "If You Have Library Problems."

25. Ibid. (quotation); *History of Vermilion Parish, Louisiana* ([Abbeville, La.?]: Vermilion Historical Society, 1983), 35–36; "Parish Library Opening Dates," [n.d. but not before 1975], in SLL Files; "Parish Library in Vermilion to Open February 1," *BRST,* Jan. 19, 1931, in LLC Scrapbook, 1930–1935; Harriet Catherine Long, *County Library Service* (Chicago: American Library Association, 1925), 12.

26. Harris, "Louisiana Library Demonstration Plan," 8, 69; "Banquet Program Brought Library Meeting to Close," *AP,* May 2, 1931 (quotation), in LLC Scrapbook, 1931–1935.

27. "Banquet Program Brought Library Meeting to Close" (first quotation); "Library Commission Is Providing Book Service for Rural Communities," *MA,* May 16, 1932; and Essae M. Culver, "Library Extension," *Meridional,* Mar. 4, 1936 (second quotation), both in LLC Scrapbook, 1931–1935.

28. "Concerning Libraries," *Meridional,* Jan. 9, 1932, in LLC Scrapbook, 1931–1935.

29. Choate, "Vermilion Parish Library," 19; Harris, "Louisiana Library Demonstration Plan," 69 (quotation).

30. "Plan to Open Parish Library Next January," *Meridional,* Nov. 2, 1940; "New Vermilion Library to Open," *TP,* Feb. 25, 1941, both in LLC Scrapbook, 1940–1942; Harris, "Louisiana Library Demonstration Plan," 70.

31. Harris, "Louisiana Library Demonstration Plan," 70 (first quotation), 74 (last quota-

tion), 76; "Vermilion Library Establishes Record in Lending Books," *BRMA,* Mar. 22, 1941; [Untitled news item] and "Library Work Shows Progress in Two Months," both in *Progress,* May 17, 1941; "Libraries Help in National Defense," *Progress,* May 31, 1941 (second quotation), all in LLC Scrapbook, 1940–1942.

32. Harris, "Louisiana Library Demonstration Plan," 75–76; "Parish Circulates Total of 107,438 Books," *Progress,* Jan. 10, 1942, in LLC Scrapbook, 1940–1942; Douglas A. Galbi, "Book Circulation per U.S. Public Library User Since 1856," www.galbithink.org/libraries/circulation.htm, accessed Sept. 2, 2017.

33. "Vote on Library Tax Scheduled," *TP,* Jan. 7, 1942; "Vermilion Parish Library Tax Carries," [clipping from unidentified newspaper, Feb. 1942], both in LLC Scrapbook, 1940–1942; Harris, "Louisiana Library Demonstration Plan," 71; Essie [*sic*] Martha Culver, "State Planning in Louisiana," *LJ* 60 (May 1, 1935), 381.

34. Choate, "Vermilion Parish Library," 31.

35. Margaret Dixon, "Louisiana's 'Frontier' Libraries," *MA Magazine,* Aug. 3, 1952, in SLL Scrapbook, 1952–1953; *History of Vermilion Parish,* 36.

36. Dixon, "Frontier Libraries."

Chapter 5. The Depression Years, 1930–1941

1. Bennett H. Wall, ed., *Louisiana: A History,* 2nd ed. (Wheeling, IL: Forum Press, 1990), 306–8.

2. Louisiana Library Commission, *Seventh Biennial Report of the Louisiana Library Commission, 1936–1937* ([Baton Rouge: The Commission, 1938]), 12 (quotation), 36–37; Louisiana Library Commission, *Sixth Biennial Report of the Louisiana Library Commission, 1934–1935* ([Baton Rouge: The Commission, 1936]), 8, 18–19.

3. Essae M. Culver to Huey P. Long, Aug. 7, 1931; Essae M. Culver to Bertha L. Gunterman, Longmans, Green & Co., Apr. 15, 1933 (quotation); Essae M. Culver to Louise H. Seaman, The Macmillan Company, Apr. 17, 1933, all in VF (SLL, Correspondence, 1930–1933); Louisiana Library Commission, *Seventh Biennial Report,* 23–25.

4. Louisiana Library Commission, *Fifth Biennial Report of the Louisiana Library Commission, 1932–1933* ([Baton Rouge: The Commission, 1934]), 12–13 (first quotation, 13); Louisiana Library Commission, *Sixth Biennial Report,* 7–8; Louisiana Library Commission, *Eighth Biennial Report of the Louisiana Library Commission, 1938–1939* ([Baton Rouge: The Commission, 1940]), 13 (second quotation).

5. Essae M. Culver, interview by Becky and A. E. Schroeder, Mar. 15, 1972, cassette recording in Culver Papers (transcribed by the author).

6. J. H. McLaughlin, "Baton Rouge Has Advantages to Enable City to Continue to Grow as Business Center," *BRST,* May 16, 1932; Culver, [Journals], May 16–21, 1932; Louisiana Library Commission, *Fourth Biennial Report of the Louisiana Library Commission, 1930–1931* ([Baton Rouge: The Commission, 1932]), 11; "Library Commission Is Providing Book Service for Rural Communities," *BRMA,* May 16, 1932 (quotation).

7. "New Headquarters for Library Commission Are Very Desirable," *BRST,* June 2, 1932; "Rare Book Room," *BRMA,* June 3, 1932; "Library Work Being Extended to Many People," *BRST,* Aug. 10, 1932; "Authentic Prints of Paintings Are at Commission," *BRST,* Aug. 11, 1932, all in LLC Scrapbook, 1930–1935; Louisiana Library Commission, *Fourth Biennial Report,* 11.

8. While the commission served the entire state on $18,900, by comparison, the LSU Library served about three thousand on a budget of $45,000, and the New Orleans Public Library, with an appropriation of $100,000, fewer than half a million people. J. O. Modisette to George W. Delesdernier, June 10, 1932, in VF (SLL, Correspondence, 1930–1933); Louisiana Library Commission, *Fifth Biennial Report,* 6, 8, 15; Culver to Long, Aug. 7, 1931 (quotations); "Sabine Library Project Ready to Be Launched," *BRST,* Dec. 19, 1932; and "Nearly 7,000 Books Sent to Sabine Library," *BRST,* Jan. 10, 1933, both in LLC Scrapbook, 1930–1935.

9. Essae M. Culver to Huey P. Long, Nov. 25, 1932 (quotation), in VF (SLL, Correspondence, 1930–1933; Wall, ed., *Louisiana: A History,* 263–65.

10. Wall, ed., *Louisiana: A History,* 266, 275–76; John W. Scott, "Highway Building in Louisiana before Huey Long: An Overdue Re-Appraisal," *Louisiana History* 44 (Winter 2003), 15.

11. Culver, [Journals], Sept. 8–12, 1935 (quotations except next-to-last); William Ivy Hair, *The Kingfish and His Realm: The Life and Times of Huey P. Long* (Baton Rouge: Louisiana State University Press, 1991), 325 (next-to-last quotation).

12. "$250,000 Books Are Ordered for School Libraries," *BRST,* Mar. 10, 1937, in LLC Scrapbook, 1935–1937.

13. "Sabine Library Project Ready"; "Nearly 7,000 Books Sent to Sabine Library"; "Preparing for Sabine's Library," Many *Sabine Index,* Dec. 9, 1932; "Sabine Parish Library Has Hard Task Filling Many Book Requests," *BRST,* Feb. 4, 1933, all in LLC Scrapbook, 1930–1935.

14. "Sabine Parish Library Has Hard Task"; Agathine H. Goldstein, "Louisiana Libraries," (typescript, [1930]), 2 (first quotation); "Another Library Project," *BRST,* Dec. 15, 1932; "Two Substantial Gifts Are Given Library Service," *BRST,* Dec. 20, 1933; Michael F. Carrol, "Happiness Unfolded in Our Free Library," Many *Sabine Index,* Feb. 24, 1933 (second quotation), all in LLC Scrapbook, 1930–1935; "Parish Library Opening Dates" [n.d. but not before 1975], in State Library of Louisiana Files.

15. "Rural Women Reading Many Books Furnished by Library Commission," *BRST,* Feb. 5, 1934 (quotation); "Two Substantial Gifts Are Given Library Service," *BRST,* Dec. 20, 1933, both in LLC Scrapbook, 1930–1935.

16. "Another Library Project," *BRST,* Dec. 15, 1932 (first quotation); "Education Board Votes Financial Aid for New Library Experiments," [unidentified newspaper], Mar. 2, 1937, in LLC Scrapbook, 1935–1937; "Time for Reading Books," *BRMA,* May 7, 1933 (second quotation), in LLC Scrapbook, 1930–1935; "'Whys' of Reading Given in Lecture by Untermeyer," *TP,* Mar. 19, 1936 (third quotation).

17. "Parish Library Serves Refugees in Flooded Area," *TP,* Mar. 17, 1937 (quotation), in LLC Scrapbook, 1935–1937.

18. Ibid.

19. Shirley Knowles Stephenson, "History of the Louisiana State Library, Formerly Louisiana Library Commission" (Ph.D. dissertation, Louisiana State University, 1957), 62.

20. "Gill Dismissed as Library Head by Orleans Board," *TP,* Dec. 7, 1928; "Library Board Will Meet in Public Session Tonight to 'Positively' Fill Vacancy," *TP,* Apr. 2, 1936 (first quotation); Milton J. Ferguson, "Oh! Just Judge," *LJ* 61 (Mar. 15, 1936), 226 (second quotation); Culver, [Journals], Jan. 7, 1926 (other quotations).

21. "Trained Library Worker Is Urged for Gill's Place," *TP,* Dec. 13, 1928 (first quotation); "Moore Is Chosen to Succeed Gill as Library Head," *TP,* Mar. 14, 1929; Ferguson, "Oh! Just Judge," 226 (second quotation); "Walmsley Takes Over Control of Library System," *TP,* Feb. 24, 1932; "Directing Board Elects Attorney as Library Chief," *TP,* Mar. 5, 1932 (subsequent quotations); "Parsons Strikes Back at Critics in 61-Page Reply," *TP,* May 7, 1935.

22. Edward Alexander Parsons, *The Wonder and the Glory: Confessions of a Southern Bibliophile* (New York: Thistle Press, 1962), 275, 319–20; "Parsons Rites Set Wednesday," *TP,* Feb. 20, 1962; Clara Paletou (granddaughter of E. A. Parsons), conversation with the author, Mar. 23, 2018.

23. "'Reorganization' Comes High," *TP,* Mar. 9, 1932 (quotation); "Library to Save $7172 Per Year by Eliminating Jobs," *TP,* Jan. 3, 1935.

24. "Directors Defer Action on Public Library Position," *TP,* July 18, 1935; "Study of Library Conditions Here to Be Requested," *TP,* Jan. 17, 1935 (first quotation); "Librarian Plans 5-Day Operation of All Branches," *TP,* Jan. 19, 1935; "Hearing Ordered on Dismissal of Library Worker," *TP,* Feb. 16, 1935 (second quotation); "Naming of Trained Librarian Proposed," *TP,* Oct. 19, 1935; "Library Board Will Meet in Public Session Tonight to 'Positively' Fill Vacancy," *TP,* Apr. 2, 1936.

25. "Parsons' Ouster as Library Head Urged in Report," *TP,* May 3, 1935.

26. Edward A. Parsons, "An Inquiry into the Nature of a Certain 'Report of a Survey of the New Orleans Public Library'" ([New Orleans, 1935]), 2–3 (first and third quotations), 5 (second quotation); "Parsons Strikes Back at Critics in 61-Page Reply," *TP,* May 7, 1935; "Parsons Deposed as Librarian by Board Acting on Survey Findings," *TP,* May 11, 1935 (subsequent quotations); "Mildred Guthrie Is Appointed as Acting Librarian," *States,* June 2, 1935.

27. "Board to Select Public Librarian on Basis of Merit," *TP,* June 29, 1935; "Directors Defer Action"; "Civic Groups Plan Action in Library Snarl," *Morning Tribune,* Feb. 12, 1936 (first quotation); "Board of Library Proposes to Use Surveyors' Ideas," *TP,* Feb. 18, 1936 (second quotation); "Library Board Upheld," *TP,* Feb. 25, 1936, all in New Orleans city librarian scrapbook, SLL, Louisiana Collection.

28. "Quick Action on Librarian Urged," clipping from unidentified newspaper, undated but March 1936 (first quotation), in New Orleans city librarian scrapbook; "Naming Trained Librarian Urged upon Board Here," *TP,* Mar. 19, 1936 (Culver quotation); Milton J. Ferguson, "Second Battle of New Orleans," *LJ* 61 (Apr. 15, 1936), 314 (last quotation).

29. "Opposes Hiring Nonresident for Library Position," *TP,* Mar. 1, 1936; "Appointment of Librarian Delayed by Board's Action Amid Tumultuous Scene," *TP,* Mar. 21, 1936; "Buck to Decide on New Session of Library Body," *TP,* Mar. 23, 1936; "Librarian 'Positively' to Be Named on

April 2, States Head of Board," *TP,* Mar. 26, 1936; "M'Givaren Named Library Head in Stormy Session," *TP,* Apr. 3, 1936; "E. L. M'Givaren, Librarian, Dies in Vicksburg, Miss.," *TP,* Apr. 25, 1938; Ferguson, "Second Battle" (quotation).

30. "Appointment of MacLeish Brings Culver Protest," *BRMA,* June 10, 1939, in LLC Scrapbook, 1938–1940 (quotations); Frederick J. Stielow, "Librarian Warriors and Rapprochement: Carl Milam, Archibald MacLeish, and World War II," *Libraries & Culture* 25 (Fall 1990), 513–14.

31. Culver, [Journals], Oct. 12, 1928; Culver, Schroeder interview (quotations).

32. Marion A. Wright, "The Citizens Library Movement," *Bulletin of the American Library Association* 30 (July 1936), 533 (quotation; italics in original); Charles H. Stone, "Library Objectives in the Southeast," *Library Quarterly* 9.1 (Jan. 1939), 25.

33. Glenn H. Holloway, Holloway Saw Mill Co., Inc., to J. O. Modisette, Jan. 13, 1931, in Administrative Files (Modisette, 1931, State Library History); Essae M. Culver and Nantelle M. Gittinger, "A History of the Citizens' Library Movement," *Bulletin of the Louisiana Library Association* 17 (Winter 1954), 18–20 (quotation, 18); O. Max Gardner, "The Significance of the Citizens' Library Movement," *High School Journal* 12 (Dec. 1929), 301.

34. Culver and Gittinger, "Citizens' Library Movement," 18–19; "From a New Orleans Diary," *Bulletin of the American Library Association* 26.5 (May 1932), 339; "State Library Group Endorses Citizens Move: Many Requests Received by Library Commission, Is Report," *BRST,* Jan. 24, 1931; "Monroe Library Head Elected As State President," *TP,* Apr. 26, 1932, both in LLC Scrapbook, 1930–1935.

35. Culver and Gittinger, "Citizens' Library Movement," 19.

36. Glenn H. Holloway, "Trustees Section," *Bulletin of the American Library Association* 26, no. 8 (Aug. 1962), 662 (first quotation); "Move to Promote State's Library System Planned," *TP,* Apr. 4, 1937; "Citizens Library Group Organized," *SJ,* Apr. 26, 1937, both in LLC Scrapbook, 1935–1937; Culver and Gittinger, "Citizens' Library Movement," 20 (second quotation).

37. Culver and Gittinger, "Citizens' Library Movement," 20–21.

38. Louisiana Library Commission, *Third Biennial Report of the Louisiana Library Commission, 1928–1930* ([Baton Rouge: The Commission, 1930]), 16 (first quotation); Louisiana Library Commission, *Sixth Biennial Report,* 8, 9 (second quotation); Louisiana Library Commission, *Seventh Biennial Report of the Louisiana Library Commission, 1936–1937* ([Baton Rouge: The Commission, 1937]), 17.

39. Louisiana Library Commission, *Seventh Biennial Report,* 8.

40. "Education Board Votes Financial Aid."

41. "New Books Available at the School Library," Oakdale *Journal,* May 6, 1937; "Louisiana Ready to Conduct Test of Library Plans," *TP,* May 14, 1937, both in LLC Scrapbook, 1935–1937.

42. Louisiana Library Commission, *Seventh Biennial Report,* 8–9 (first quotation); "Library Service for Grant Parish," Colfax *Chronicle,* Mar. 12, 1937; "June 1 Is Date Planned for Library Opening," Winn *Enterprise,* Apr. 29, 1937; "8,000 Books Ready for Shipment to State's First Tri-Parish Library," *BRST,* May 21, 1937 (second quotation), all in LLC Scrapbook, 1935–1937.

43. "News from the State Capital," *BRI,* Mar. 5, 1937 (first quotation); "J. A. M'Millen Heads

State Library Body," *BRST,* Apr. 25, 1937 (second quotation), both in LLC Scrapbook, 1935–1937.

44. Harris, "Louisiana Library Demonstration Plan," 3. According to the Louisiana Library Commission's *Seventh Biennial Report* (p. 17), comparative statistics for the Tri-Parish Library and school libraries during the first six months of operation were:

	Tri-Parish Library	School Libraries
Total white population in area	31,610	119,296
Total registered borrowers	9,031	5,117
Total circulation	101,236	14,355
Number of distributing centers	19	56
Number of bookmobile routes	2	0
Percent of population registered	28.5	4.3
Average circulation per borrower	11.2	2.7

45. Harris, "Louisiana Library Demonstration Plan," 3 (first quotation); "Library Experiment," *BRST,* Mar. 2, 1937; "Leche Promises $100,000 Yearly to Aid Libraries," *TP,* May 26, 1937 (second quotation), both in LLC Scrapbook, 1935–1937; "Leche Favors Fund for Tri-Parish Library," *TT,* May 20, 1938 in LLC Scrapbook, 1938–1940; Culver and Gittinger, "Citizens' Library Movement," 21.

46. Culver and Gittinger, "Citizens' Library Movement," 21 (quotations); "Library Experiment," *BRST,* Mar. 2, 1937, in LLC Scrapbook, 1935–1937; "Leche Favors Fund for Tri-Parish Library," *TT,* May 20, 1938, in LLC Scrapbook, 1938–1940.

47. Culver, [Journals], Apr. 17, 1940 (first quotation); Louisiana Library Commission, *Ninth Biennial Report of the Louisiana Library Commission, 1940–1941* ([Baton Rouge: The Commission, 1942]), 30 (subsequent quotations)

48. Harris, "Louisiana Library Demonstration Plan," 3; "Regional Library Movement in La.," *Louisiana Tech Digest* (Dec. 15, 1939), in LLC Scrapbook; Louisiana Library Commission, *Eighth Biennial Report,* 17–19. For a novel based on the experiences of a bookmobile librarian in Terrebonne Parish, see Kimberly Willis Holt, *Part of Me: Stories of a Louisiana Family* (New York: Henry Holt & Co., 2006).

49. Louisiana Library Commission, *Ninth Biennial Report,* 30–31 (quotation, 31); "Parish Library Opening Dates."

50. Wall, ed., *Louisiana: A History,* 307–8.

51. David A. Taylor, *Soul of a People: The WPA Writers' Project Uncovers Depression America* (Hoboken, NJ: Wiley, 2009), 13; Louisiana Library Commission, *Eighth Biennial Report,* 30–31 (quotation), 32.

52. Louisiana Library Commission, *Eighth Biennial Report,* 31 (quotation), 32.

53. Ibid., 31–32 (quotation, 32).

54. Louisiana Library Commission, *Ninth Biennial Report,* 43–44 (quotation, 43).

55. Ibid., 45; Richard B. Megraw, *Confronting Modernity: Art and Society in Louisiana*

(Jackson: University Press of Mississippi, 2008), 155 (quotation). A copy of "A Black History of Louisiana" resides in the Marcus Christian Collection at the Earl K. Long Library, University of New Orleans. Christian headed the Louisiana project's "Negro unit," based at Dillard University, which compiled the history. See Joan Redding, "The Dillard Project: The Black Unit of the Louisiana Writers' Project," *Louisiana History* 32 (Winter 1992), 47–62, and Ronnie W. Clayton, "The Federal Writers' Project for Blacks in Louisiana," *Louisiana History* 19 (Summer 1978), 327–35.

56. Louisiana Library Commission, *Ninth Biennial Report,* 44–45 (quotation).

Chapter 6. The Impact of World War II on Louisiana Libraries, 1941–1945

1. "State Library Leader Will Leave Tomorrow for Convention; in Line for Election to Presidency in '40," *BRST,* June 13, 1939; "Miss Culver to Assume Presidency of American Library Association," *BRMA,* May 25, 1940; "Louisiana Shares Honor," *BRST,* May 27, 1940 (quotation); "Move Endorsed to Increase Sum for Libraries of the State," *Daily Advertiser,* Apr. 26, 1940; "Louisiana Librarians Open Annual Meeting," *AP,* May 1, 1941, all in LLC Scrapbook, 1938–1940; Culver, [Journals], Jan. 9, 1941.

2. Essae Martha Culver, "A Call to Action," *ALA Bulletin* 34.6 (June 1940), 377; Essae Martha Culver, "The Emergence of Libraries," *ALA Bulletin* 35.7 (July 1941), 410; Patti Clayton Becker, *Books and Libraries in American Society during World War II: Weapons in the War of Ideas* (New York: Routledge, 2005), 32–33 (MacLeish quotation, 32).

3. Culver, "Call to Action," 377–78.

4. Ibid., 379 (last quotation); "Public Library Seen as Vital to Democracy," *Christian Science Monitor,* June 3, 1940 (other quotations), in LLC Scrapbook, 1938–1940.

5. Culver, "Emergence of Libraries," 412 (first quotation), 413 (second quotation).

6. "How Your Library Serves You," Mansfield *Enterprise,* Sept. 18, 1941 (first and third quotations), in LLC Scrapbook, 1940–1942; Culver, "Emergence of Libraries," 410 (second quotation); Louisiana Library Commission, *Ninth Biennial Report of the Louisiana Library Commission, 1940–1941* (Baton Rouge: [The Commission, 1942]), 16; Louisiana Library Commission, *Tenth Biennial Report of the Louisiana Library Commission, 1942–1943* ([Baton Rouge: The Commission, 1944]), 10, 15.

7. "Manual for State and Local Directors, Victory Book Campaign," *ALA Bulletin* 36.1, pt. 2 (Jan. 1942), 3; "Plea Made for Soldiers Books," *BRMA,* Feb. 12, 1942 (quotation), in LLC Scrapbook, 1940–1942.

8. Louisiana Library Commission, *Ninth Biennial Report,* 20–22 (first quotation); Louisiana Library Commission, *Tenth Biennial Report,* 15; "Libraries at Army Camps Will Be Provided, Miss Culver Says," *SJ,* Mar. 26, 1941 (second quotation), in LLC Scrapbook, 1940–1942.

9. "Manual for State and Local Directors," 7–8; "Oversubscribed, But Victory Book Drive to Go On," *BRMA,* Sept. 15, 1942 (quotation), in LLC Scrapbook, 1940–1942.

10. Louisiana Library Commission, *Ninth Biennial Report,* 22–23; Louisiana Library Commission, *Tenth Biennial Report,* 16; John M. Connor, "The Victory Book Campaign," *ALA*

Bulletin 36.6 (June 1942), 377; Virginia Rogers Smith, "'Give Good Books, Give More Books': The Victory Book Campaign," *LLA Bulletin* 56.3 (Winter 1994), 133; Becker, *Books and Libraries*, 133.

11. "Victory Book Campaign to Open Here and Over Nation on Monday," *BRMA*, Jan. 11, 1942; "1,000 More Books Needed in Drive," *BRMA*, Jan. 29, 1942 (quotation); "Still Need More Books in Victory Campaign," *BRST*, Feb. 13, 1942; "Louisiana Leads in Victory Book Drive," *TP*, Mar. 15, 1942; "Mrs. Moore Is Named to Head Library Group," Monroe *News Star*, Apr. 17, 1942, all in LLC Scrapbook, 1940–1942.

12. "Camp Claiborne Librarian Praises State Commission," *BRMA*, Sept. 12, 1941, in LLC Scrapbook, 1940–1942; Connie Phelps, "Louisiana Parish Libraries and World War II: A Survey," *LLA Bulletin* 56.3 (Winter 1994), 137–40.

13. Phelps, "Louisiana Parish Libraries," 137–40; Louisiana Library Commission, *Ninth Biennial Report*, 20, 22 (first quotation); Culver, [Journals], Feb. 26, 1943 (subsequent quotations).

14. Louisiana Library Commission, *Ninth Biennial Report*, 20 (quotation); Phelps, "Louisiana Parish Libraries," 140–42; Sharin McMonagle, "Rapides Parish Library," *LLA Bulletin* 61. 2 (Fall 1998), 107.

15. "Suggested Activities for Wartime Library Service," *ALA Bulletin* 36.1, pt. 1 (Jan. 1942), 6 (quotation); Louisiana Library Commission, *Ninth Biennial Report*, 26, 28; Phelps, "Louisiana Parish Libraries," 137; "Louisiana Libraries Aid in National Defense Program," *BRMA*, July 2, 1941, in LLC Scrapbook, 1940–1942; Culver, [Journals], Sept. 3, 1940.

16. Louisiana Library Commission, *Ninth Biennial Report*, 28; Phelps, "Louisiana Parish Libraries," 137; Louisiana Department of Education, "Illiteracy and War Information," ([Baton Rouge: The Department], October 1941), [1] (first quotation), in Culver Papers; "Louisiana Libraries Aid in National Defense Program," *BRMA*, July 2, 1941, in LLC Scrapbook, 1940–1942; "Report on Vermilion Parish's Library and 'What They Read' Prove Need for Unit for Acadia, Commission Secretary Points Out," [Unidentified newspaper, 1944?] (second quotation), in LLC Scrapbook, 1942–1945.

17. Also, residents of several other, longer-organized parishes voted to renew their library taxes. "Local Issues," *TT*, Sept. 4, 1941 (first quotation); "Library-Tax," Natchitoches *Times*, Nov. 1, 1940 (second quotation); "Terrebonne Library Nears Birthday," *TP*, Oct. 27, 1940 (third and fourth quotations), all in LLC Scrapbook, 1940–1942; Louisiana Library Commission, *Ninth Biennial Report*, 31–32 (last quotation).

18. "Library Made Official Information Center for Defense Council," Pointe Coupee *Banner*, May 21, 1942, in LLC Scrapbook, 1940–1942.

19. Louisiana State Library, *Thirteenth Biennial Report of the Louisiana State Library, Formerly Louisiana Library Commission, 1948–1949* (Baton Rouge: [The Library], 1950]), [6]; Louisiana Library Commission, *Ninth Biennial Report*, 19 (quotation), 23–28.

20. Louisiana Library Commission, *Ninth Biennial Report*, 25–28; Nantelle Gittinger, "Reading Tastes of Louisiana Residents Change as Result of War, Librarians Report," *BRMA*, Apr. 19, 1942, in LLC Scrapbook, 1940–1942.

21. Louisiana Library Commission, *Ninth Biennial Report*, 24, 28–29; Shirley Benton, "Re-

tiring Is 'Going to Be Fun,'" Baton Rouge *Sunday Advocate,* June 22, 1975, 1-D (quotation), in Sallie Farrell Scrapbook [#2], Farrell Papers.

22. "Parish May Get State Library Demonstration," *TT,* Sept. 2, 1941; "Rapides Jury Calls Election on Tax for Nov. 5," *TT,* Sept. 29, 1942; (first quotation) "Police Jury Acts to Establish Rapides Library," *TT,* Sept. 9, 1941; "Library Commission Will Open Unit in Rapides Parish," *BRMA,* Dec. 5, 1941; "Rapides Library Circulates 4,086 Books in 2 Weeks," *TT,* Feb. 6, 1942, all in LLC Scrapbook, 1940–1942; Louisiana Library Commission, *Ninth Biennial Report,* 24; Anne Price, "Louisiana's Librarian: Sallie Farrell's Political Savvy and Winning Smile Helped Build a Statewide Network of Libraries," *Sunday Advocate Magazine,* July 16, 2000 (second quotation).

23. Louisiana Library Commission, *Eighth Biennial Report of the Louisiana Library Commission, 1938–1939* ([Baton Rouge: The Commission, 1939]), [4]; Louisiana Library Commission, *Ninth Biennial Report,* [5] (quotation); Louisiana Library Commission, *Tenth Biennial Report,* [4]; Find a Grave database, https://www.findagrave.com/memorial/27981204/clara-knott, accessed May 28, 2018.

24. Louisiana Library Commission, *Ninth Biennial Report,* [4] (first quotation), [5] (last quotation); "Miss Kate Hill Dies at Home," *BRST,* Feb. 25, 1949 (second quotation).

25. Louisiana Library Commission, *Ninth Biennial Report,* [5]; "Consolidation of State Departments Studied," *BRMA,* May 1, 1940 (quotation), in LLC Scrapbook, 1938–1940; Culver, [Journals], Apr. 29-May 12, 1940.

26. Nantelle Mitchiner, "Louisiana Library Commission Completes 15th Year of Work," *BRMA,* Dec. 29, 1940 (first quotation), in LLC Scrapbook, 1940–1942; Essae M. Culver, "The Louisiana State Library," *Bulletin of the Louisiana Library Association* 16.4 (Spring 1953), 45; Louisiana Library Commission, *Ninth Biennial Report,* [11]-[12] (second quotation).

27. "Library Commission Services to Be Discontinued Tomorrow," *BRMA,* Sept. 15, 1940; "Circulation Department of Commission Library Open in New Quarters," *BRST,* Oct. 15, 1940, both in LLC Scrapbook, 1938–1940; Essae M. Culver, interviewed by Shirley Knowles Stephenson, Oct. 15, 1956 and Nov. 16, 1956, "History of the Louisiana State Library, Formerly Louisiana Library Commission" (Ph.D. dissertation, Louisiana State University, 1957), 152–53 (quotation); Louisiana Library Commission, *Ninth Biennial Report,* 17–18.

28. Ricks v. Close, Director of Finance, et al., 201 La. 242, 9 So. 2d 534, 1942 (May 25, 1942).

29. Louisiana Library Commission, *Tenth Biennial Report,* 13.

30. Culver, [Journals], June 4–7 (first quotation, June 4; second quotation, June 6) and 13 (last quotation), 1942.

31. Culver, [Journals], June 15 (quotations), June 17, 1942.

32. Culver and Gittinger, "History of the Citizens' Library Movement," 22 (first quotation); "Libraries Endangered," *SJ,* July 4, 1942, in LLC Scrapbook, 1940–1942; Louisiana Library Commission, *Ninth Biennial Report,* [10]-[11] (second quotation); "Governors Approve Library Service," *LJ* (Oct. 1, 1942), in LLC Scrapbook, 1942–1945 (third quotation).

33. Culver, [Journals], June 19–22, 1942 (quotations, June 19 and June 22).

34. For example, W. B. MacMillan, Louisiana State Rice Milling Company, Inc., to Essae M. Culver, June 23, 1942, in Administrative File (State Library History—Culver); [Essae M. Cul-

ver?], "James Oliver Modisette," *Bulletin of the Louisiana Library Association* 6 (Sept.–Dec. 1942), 4 (first quotation); Essae Martha Culver, "James Oliver Modisette: Friend of Libraries," *American Library Association Bulletin* 36.14, pt. 1 (Dec. 1, 1942), 817 (second quotation).

35. "Library Champion Passes," *TP,* June 22, 1942 (first quotation); "An Editorial: Louisiana Loses a Friend," *BRMA,* June 22, 1942 (second quotation), both in LLC Scrapbook, 1940–1942.

36. Louisiana Library Commission, *Ninth Biennial Report,* [7]-[8] (quotation); Culver, [Journals], June 18, 1943.

37. Louisiana Library Commission, *Ninth Biennial Report,* [5]; "Louisiana Loses a Friend"; Louisiana Library Commission, *Tenth Biennial Report,* 10 (quotation).

38. Louisiana Library Commission, Reference Service for Colored People, "Brief Report on the First Seven Months Service. June through December 1943," in VF (Libraries—Baton Rouge—LSL—Negro Services Department Reports—Annual—1943-1949); [Invitation to library opening, 1943]; [Flyer #1, Louisiana Library Commission Service for Colored People, n.d. but 1943] (second quotation); Consuella B. Patty, "Negro Library News," Pittsburg *Courier,* Feb. 16, 1946, all in LLC Scrapbook, Negro Library Branch, 1943–1954; Eliza Gleason, *The Southern Negro and the Public Library: A Study of the Government and Administration of Public Library Service to Negroes in the South* (Chicago: University of Chicago Press, 1941), 72 (first quotation); Louisiana Library Commission, *Tenth Biennial Report,* 20; "Parish Library Opening Dates" [n.d. but not before 1975], in State Library of Louisiana Files.

39. [Flyer #1, Louisiana Library Commission Service for Colored People] (first quotation); [Flyer #2, Louisiana Library Commission Service for Colored People, n.d. but 1943] (second quotation), both in LLC Scrapbook, Negro Library Branch, 1943–1954.

40. "Louisianan, Librarian Takes Post at Mississippi School," Pittsburg *Courier,* Sept. 22, 1945; "Librarian Visits Shreveport, North La.," Shreveport *Sun,* July 22, 1944 (quotations), in LLC Scrapbook, Negro Library Branch, 1943–1954; Gloria Spooner, "Establishment of African American Public Library Service in Louisiana," *Louisiana Libraries* 23.3 (Winter 2001), 24; "Multicultural Societies and Ethnic Minorities, Services to," in *Encyclopedia of Library History,* ed. Wayne A. Wiegand and Donald G. Davis, Jr. (New York: Garland, 1994), 441.

41. "Annual Narrative Report for the Year 1944," in VF (Libraries—Baton Rouge—LSL—Negro Services Department Reports—Annual—1943-1949).

42. Ibid.

43. Ibid.

44. Ibid. (quotations except last); "Annual Narrative Report for the Year 1945" (last quotation), in VF (Libraries—Baton Rouge—LSL—Negro Services Department Reports—Annual—1943-1949); Louisiana Library Commission, *Eleventh Annual Report of the Louisiana Library Commission, 1944-1945* (Baton Rouge: The Commission, [1946]), 13.

45. Louisiana Library Commission, *Tenth Biennial Report,* 11, 17 (first quotation); Louisiana Library Commission, *Eleventh Biennial Report,* 13 (second quotation).

46. Louisiana Library Commission, *Tenth Biennial Report,* 13–14, 18; Culver, [Journals], Oct. 13, 1943; Wall v. Gremillion, 203 La. 444, 14 So. 2d 52, 1943 (May 17, 1943); Louisiana Library Commission, *Eleventh Biennial Report,* [11]. Parish libraries operating in 1943 were

Richland (opened 1926); Concordia (1928); Webster (1929); Sabine (1933); Winn (1937); Bienville, Natchitoches, East Baton Rouge, and Terrebonne (1939); Morehouse, Ouachita, and Bossier (1940); Vermilion, Pointe Coupee, and DeSoto (1941); and Rapides (1942). "Parish Library Opening Dates."

47. Louisiana Library Commission, *Eleventh Biennial Report,* 18.

48. Ibid., [9] (first quotation); "Popularizing Libraries Is Her Forte," *BRMA,* Aug. 4, 1946 (second quotation), in LLC Scrapbook, 1945–1947.

49. James J. Corbett, "Library Commission to Mark 20th Anniversary on July 7," *BRMA,* June 26, 1945 (first quotation); Orene Muse, "Miss Culver Will Be Honored," *BRST,* July 5, 1945 (second and third quotations), both in LLC Scrapbook, 1945–1947.

50. Milton J. Ferguson to Essae M. Culver, July 3, 1945, in Administrative Files (Administration—Correspondence, LLC).

51. Sue (Mrs. Henry) Fontaine, "Deeds—Not Words," also titled "The Essay on Essae," unpublished remarks presented at the meeting of the Library History Round Table, American Library Association conference, Chicago, July 15, 1963, 9 (first and second quotations), in LLC, VF (Librarians—Culver, Essae M.); Louisiana Library Commission, *Eleventh Biennial Report,* [9] (last quotation).

52. Louisiana Library Commission, *Eleventh Biennial Report,* [9] (first quotation); Alice Hebert, "Servicemen Turning to Books for Information on Postwar Problems," *BRST,* Sept. 10, 1945 (subsequent quotations), in LLC Scrapbook, 1945–1947.

53. Louisiana Library Commission, *Eleventh Biennial Report,* 26.

Chapter 7. Unprecedented Growth and Transition, 1945–1962

1. Mary W. Harris, "The Louisiana Library Demonstration Plan: Designed to Extend Public Library Service to the Entire Population of the State" (Baton Rouge: Louisiana State Library, Extension Department, 1952), 2 (first quotation); Louisiana Library Commission, *Tenth Biennial Report of the Louisiana Library Commission, 1942–1943* ([Baton Rouge: The Commission, 1944]), 13 (second quotation).

2. Louisiana Library Commission, *Eleventh Biennial Report of the Louisiana Library Commission, 1944–1945* (Baton Rouge: The Commission, [1946]), 11; Margaret Dixon and Nantelle Gittinger, *The First Twenty-Five Years of the Louisiana State Library, 1925–1950* (Baton Rouge: Louisiana State Library, 1950), 21–22 (first quotation); Louisiana Library Commission, *Twelfth Biennial Report of the Louisiana State Library, 1946–1947* ([Baton Rouge: The Commission, 1948]), 13 (second quotation); "Parish Library Opening Dates" [n.d. but not before 1975], in State Library of Louisiana Files.

3. Tommie Dora Barker, *Libraries of the South: A Report on Developments, 1930–1935* (Chicago: American Library Association, 1936), 93 (first two quotations); Dixon and Gittinger, *First Twenty-Five Years,* 24, 27 (third quotation); Anne Price, "Louisiana's Librarian: Sallie Farrell's Political Savvy and Winning Smile Helped Build a Statewide Network of Libraries," *Sunday Advocate Magazine,* July 16, 2000 (fourth quotation).

4. "Parish Library Opening Dates"; Louisiana Library Commission, *Twelfth Biennial Report*, 37; Louisiana State Library, *Fourteenth Biennial Report of the Louisiana State Library, Formerly Louisiana Library Commission, 1950–1951* (Baton Rouge: [The Library, 1952]), 15; Dixon and Gittinger, *First Twenty-Five Years*, 24.

5. National Association of State Libraries, "The Role of the State Library," [unpublished typescript, n.d. but ca. 1950], [1] (first quotation), in Culver Papers; Louisiana Library Commission, *Twelfth Biennial Report*, [9]; Louisiana Library Commission, *Ninth Biennial Report*, 25; Ethel E. Himmel and William J. Wilson, comps., *The Functions and Roles of State Library Agencies* (Chicago: American Library Association, 2000), vii; Helen Maestri, "The New Orleans Public Library in the Nineteenth Century," *Bulletin of the Louisiana Library Association* 15.2 (Spring 1952), 37; "Davis Signs," *BRMA*, July 13, 1946; "Library Bookmobile to Travel Twice Weekly; Comm. Changes Name," Houma *Courier*, July 25, 1946 (second quotation); "Library Changes Title Wednesday," *TP*, July 26, 1946, and similar articles in other newspapers, all in LLC Scrapbook, 1945–1947. For more about the first state library, see Faye Phillips, "'To Build upon the Foundation': Charles Gayarré's Vision for the Louisiana State Library," *Libraries & the Cultural Record* 43 (2008), 56–76.

6. Louisiana State Library, *Thirteenth Biennial Report of the Louisiana State Library, Formerly Louisiana Library Commission, 1948–1949* (Baton Rouge: [The Library, 1950]), 9; Louisiana State Library, *Fourteenth Biennial Report*, 12 (quotation); "State Library Sets Up Service for Lawmakers," *BRST*, May 17, 1950; Louisiana State Library, *Fifteenth Biennial Report of the Louisiana State Library, Formerly Louisiana Library Commission, 1952–1953* (Baton Rouge: [The Library, 1954]), 4–5.

7. "Negro Librarians Hold Conference," *BRMA*, Aug. 3, 1949, in LLC Scrapbook, Negro Library Branch, 1943–1954, SLL, Louisiana Collection.

8. Gloria Spooner, "Establishment of African American Public Library Service in Louisiana," *Louisiana Libraries* 23.3 (Winter 2001), 25; Alma Dawson, "The Participation of African Americans in the Louisiana Library Association," in *A History of the Louisiana Library Association, 1925–2000*, ed. Alma Dawson and Florence M. Jumonville, 101–120 (Baton Rouge: Louisiana Library Association, 2003), 114–15, 117.

9. J. O. Modisette, "Rural Libraries and the Schools," *Louisiana Club Woman* ([Sept.?] 1928), 14 (first quotation), in LLC Scrapbook, 1925–1928; "Rural Women Reading Many Books Furnished by Library Commission," *BRST*, Feb. 5, 1934 (second quotation), in LLC Scrapbook, 1930–1935.

10. "Judge Voelker Named Head of State Library Commission," *BRMA*, Jan. 13, 1943, in LLC Scrapbook, 1942–1945; Louisiana Library Commission, *Tenth Biennial Report*, 12–13.

11. "Book Service to Institutions Set by Commission," *BRMA*, July 23, 1943 (first quotation); "Plan Library Services for All Institutions under State Department," *BRMA*, May 20, 1944, both in LLC Scrapbook, 1942–1945; Louisiana Library Commission, *Tenth Biennial Report*, 12–13 (second quotation, 13); Culver, [Journals], Jan. 26, 1945, Aug. 12, 1945, Memorandum page, 1948.

12. Culver, [Journals], Aug. 13, 1945; "Library Progress Is Reported at Board Meeting"; *BRMA*, July 25, 1947, in LLC/LSL Scrapbook, 1945–1947; "Close Library Demonstration at

State Penal Farm at Angola," *BRST,* Aug. 27, 1948, in LSL Scrapbook, 1947–1949; Louisiana State Library, *Twelfth Biennial Report of the Louisiana State Library, formerly Louisiana Library Commission, 1946–1947* ([Baton Rouge: The Library, 1948]), 29 (quotation).

13. Louisiana State Library, *Twelfth Biennial Report,* 31–32 (quotation, 32); Andrew Hart, "Librarians Despise Censorship. How Can Prison Librarians Handle That? It's Complicated," *Washington Post,* Jan. 16, 2018.

14. Louisiana State Library, *Twelfth Biennial Report,* 29–32 (first quotation, 32; second quotation, 29); Edward W. Stagg, "Rehabilitation Program Major Need at Angola," *Item,* May 2, 1950, in LSL Scrapbook, 1950.

15. Louisiana State Library, *Twelfth Biennial Report,* 31–32 (quotations except last); "Close Library Demonstration" (last quotation).

16. "Close Library Demonstration"; Tammi Arford, "Captive Knowledge: Censorship and Control in Prison Libraries" (Ph.D. dissertation, Northeastern University, 2013), 23; Kathrina Sarah Litchfield, "A Critical Impasse: Literacy Practice in American Prisons and the Future of Transformative Reading" (M.A. thesis, University of Iowa, 2014), 25, 28; "New Library at DeQuincy Correctional and Industrial School," *LLA Bulletin* 32 (Spring 1969), 46; Louisiana State Library, *Sixteenth Biennial Report of the Louisiana State Library, formerly Louisiana Library Commission, 1954–1955* (Baton Rouge: [The Library, 1956]), 8.

17. "Parish Library Opening Dates"; Dixon and Gittinger, *First Twenty-Five Years,* 27 (first quotation); "Added Money for Libraries Needed, Says State Unit," *BRMA,* Apr. 16, 1952 (second quotation).

18. Louisiana Library Commission, *Ninth Biennial Report of the Louisiana Library Commission, 1940–1941* ([Baton Rouge: The Commission, 1942]), 18 (first quotation), 16 (second quotation).

19. Ibid., 17–19 (first quotation, 19; second quotation, 18); "State Library in Need of Dollars, 'Quarters,'" *BRST,* Apr. 20, 1952; Wilbur C. Holtman, *The Second Twenty-Five Years of the Louisiana State Library, 1950–1975* (Baton Rouge, 1975), 10.

20. Louisiana Library Commission, *Ninth Biennial Report,* 18 (first quotation); Culver, [Journals], May 4–13, 1943; Essae M. Culver, interview by Becky and A. E. Schroeder, Mar. 15, 1972 (second quotation), cassette recording in Culver Papers (transcribed by the author).

21. "Library Commission, Sponsored by Clubs, Now Serves Many," *TP,* Mar. 18, 1928 (first quotation), in LLC Scrapbook, 1925–1928; "Mrs. Cammie G. Henry Offers Rare Collection to Library Commission," *BRST,* May 15, 1946, in LSL Scrapbook, 1945–1947 (second quotation).

22. Louisiana State Library, *Thirteenth Biennial Report,* 12–13 (quotation); Louisiana State Library, *Fifteenth Biennial Report,* 5–6; Wanda Horn, "After 30 Years in Library—Retirement," Baton Rouge *Sunday Advocate,* Sept. 9, 1973.

23. Louisiana State Library, *Thirteenth Biennial Report,* 10; Louisiana State Library, *Fourteenth Biennial Report,* 14–15; Louisiana State Library, *Eighteenth Biennial Report of the Louisiana State Library, formerly Louisiana Library Commission, 1958–1959* (Baton Rouge: [The Library, 1960]), 18; Sharilynn Aucoin, "State Library of Louisiana: Special Services Branch," *Louisiana Libraries* 62.1 (Summer 1999), 9.

24. Culver, [Journals], May 26–June 25, 1948, May 3–4, 1949; "LSU Board Authorizes New Salary Schedule for Faculty Members," *BRMA,* Feb. 6, 1949; "State Library in Need of More

Money or Room," *BRMA,* Mar. 26, 1949; "State Library to Get Hut for Book Storage," *BRST,* Apr. 28, 1949; "State Library Has Spring Cleaning, Needs More Space," *BRST,* May 23, 1951; Essae M. Culver, quoted by Thomas Shuler Shaw, "Miss Essae Martha Culver: First Lady of Louisiana Librarians," *LLA Bulletin* 50 (Summer/Fall 1987), 15 (quotation).

25. Louisiana State Library, *Fifteenth Biennial Report,* 5 (first quotation); "New Library Building and More Funds Aims of Group," *BRMA,* Aug. 14, 1953 (second quotation).

26. Margaret Dixon, "$30 Million Bond Issue Is Likely to Be Proposed by Kennon to Legislature," *BRST,* Nov. 29, 1953; "East Lawn Site for New Library Protested Anew," *BRMA,* Jan. 27, 1955; "Set Protest on Site for New Library," *BRST,* Feb. 2, 1955; "Building Authority to Abandon East Lawn as Future Building Site," *BRST,* Feb. 17, 1955, all in LSL Buildings Scrapbook; "Act 13," *STA,* June 22, 1954; J. Michael Desmond, "John Jacob Desmond," in *knowlouisiana. org Encyclopedia of Louisiana,* http://www.knowlouisiana.org/entry/john-jacob-desmond, accessed July 14, 2018; Margaret Dixon, "Slate Dedication of New State Library," *BRMA,* Oct. 2, 1958 (quotation).

27. Louisiana State Library, *Sixteenth Biennial Report,* 2 (quotation); "East Lawn Site for New Library Protested Anew," *BRMA,* Jan. 27, 1955; "Set Protest on Site for New Library," *BRST,* Feb. 2, 1955; "Building Authority to Abandon East Lawn as Future Building Site," *BRST,* Feb. 17, 1955; "Site for Library Given Approval," *TP,* Mar. 4, 1955; "Minutes of Louisiana State Building Authority Meeting of June 22, 1955," all in LSL Buildings Scrapbook.

28. "Award of AIA Presented to State Library," *BRST,* Oct. 11, 1958 (first quotation); "Plans for La. State Library Are Outlined," *BRMA,* Jan. 20, 1956; Dixon, "Dedication of New State Library" (second quotation); "Library, Church among Winners," *TP,* Jan. 27, 1956; "Award Contract for State Library," *BRST,* Apr. 5, 1956, all in LSL Buildings Scrapbook.

29. Louisiana State Library, *Seventeenth Biennial Report of the Louisiana State Library, formerly Louisiana Library Commission, 1956–1957* (Baton Rouge: [The Library, 1958]), 25 (quotations); Culver, [Journals], Apr. 26, 1956.

30. Culver, [Journals], May 29–June 3, 1956 (first quotation, May 29); Louisiana State Library, *Seventeenth Biennial Report,* 25 (second quotation); "May Demolish State Library or Repair It," *BRST,* May 30, 1956.

31. "State Library to Reopen Monday in Temporary Downtown Offices," *BRST,* Aug. 4, 1956 (first quotation), in LSL Buildings Scrapbook; Louisiana State Library, *Seventeenth Biennial Report,* 25 (second quotation); Culver, [Journals], May 29–June 4, 1956 (third and fourth quotations, June 3), July 5–August 6 (fifth quotation, July 5).

32. Louisiana State Library, *Seventeenth Biennial Report,* 15–16 (quotation); Louisiana State Library, *Twentieth Biennial Report of the Louisiana State Library, formerly Louisiana Library Commission, 1962–1963* (Baton Rouge: [The Library, 1964]), 16.

33. Dixon, "Dedication of New State Library" (quotation); Louisiana State Library, *Eighteenth Biennial Report,* 25–26; Eva L. Porter, "The Louisiana Union Catalog," *Bulletin of the Louisiana Library Association* 22.4 (Winter 1959), 117–18, 132; Louisiana State Library, *Twentieth Biennial Report,* 3; Spooner, "African American Public Library Service," 25.

34. "Books for Blind," *TP,* June 11, 1932; "Books for Blind Added by Library," *TP,* Sept. 25, 1932; "Demand for Braille Books on Increase," *TP,* July 21, 1933; "Library Acquires 'Talking Book' to Aid Sightless," *TP,* June 21, 1934; Louisiana State Library, *Fourteenth Biennial Re-*

port, 10; Louisiana State Library, *Eighteenth Biennial Report,* 18–19; Aucoin, "Special Services Branch," 10; Louisiana State Library, *Library Service for a Changing Louisiana: Louisiana State Library Twenty-Second Biennial Report, 1966–67* (Baton Rouge: [The Library, 1968]), 3–4 (quotation, 4).

35. Louisiana State Library, *Eighteenth Biennial Report,* [1]; Louisiana State Library, *Twentieth Biennial Report,* 3.

36. Michael R. McKann, "The Same Building, But a New Look: State Library of Louisiana," *Louisiana Libraries* 62.1 (Summer 1999), 4–5; Thomas F. Jaques, "State Library of Louisiana: The Purpose and Focus," *Louisiana Libraries* 62.1 (Summer 1999), 3.

37. Hawthorne Daniel, *Public Libraries for Everyone: The Growth and Development of Library Services in the United States, Especially since the Passage of the Library Services Act* (Garden City, NY: Doubleday, 1961), 35; "Lois Shortess Given Position at Library Meet," *BRMA,* Oct. 31, 1930; Essae M. Culver, "Federal Aid to Libraries," *Bulletin of the Louisiana Library Association* 20.4 (Fall 1957), 177 (quotations).

38. James W. Fry, "LSA and LSCA, 1956–1973: A Legislative History," *Library Trends* 24.1 (July 1975), 8; Daniel, *Public Libraries for Everyone,* 38–41 (quotation, 39).

39. Emily Taft Douglas, "Library Demonstration Bill Introduced," *ALA Bulletin* 40.4 (Apr. 1946), 122.

40. Ibid., 123; "Rural Public Library Service," *Bulletin of the Louisiana Library Association* 9.3 (Mar. 1946), 89; Emily Taft Douglas, "Rural Libraries in America," *ALA Bulletin* 40.8 (Sept. 1, 1946), 269; Carl H. Milam, "Executive Secretary's Report," *ALA Bulletin* 40.11 (Oct. 15, 1946), 325; "Library Demonstration Bill, S. 48—H.R. 2465," *ALA Bulletin* 41.5 (May 1947), 134; "Extension of Library Services," *ALA Bulletin* 42.11 (Oct. 15, 1948), 417; "Louisiana Library Program Expands," Delhi *Dispatch,* June 5, 1946, and "Fed'l Funds for Libraries Okayed by U.S. Senate," *BRMA,* Feb. 27, 1948 (quotation), both in LSL Scrapbook, 1947–1949. For the complete text of the bill, see "The Library Demonstration Bill," *ALA Bulletin* 40.5 (May 1946), 158–59.

41. Clara Fielder, "Library Demonstration Bill Introduced," *ALA Bulletin* 43.2 (Feb. 1949), 76; Daniel, *Public Libraries,* 42–47 (quotation, 42).

42. Daniel, *Public Libraries,* 42–47; Louisiana's Second State Librarian Is Appointed," [unidentified news clipping], Feb. 8, 1962, in Sallie Farrell Scrapbook [#1]; Culver, "Federal Aid," 177 (quotation); Robert Charles Smith, "A Historical Study of Selected Effects of Federal Funding upon Public Libraries in Louisiana, 1956–1973" (Ed.D. dissertation, Louisiana State University, 1975), 63.

43. "Parish Library Opening Dates"; Louisiana State Library, *Seventeenth Biennial Report,* 9; Louisiana State Library, *Eighteenth Biennial* Report, 3, 8–9; Avant, "Extending Library Service," 49; John G. Lorenz, "Library Services Act—The First Three Years," *ALA Bulletin* 54.1 (Jan. 1960), 23.

44. Louisiana State Library, *Nineteenth Biennial Report of the Louisiana State Library, formerly Louisiana Library Commission, 1960–1961* (Baton Rouge: [The Library, 1962]), 11–12; Louisiana State Library, *Eighteenth Biennial Report,* 25; "Libraries for Louisiana," *Bulletin of the Louisiana Library Association* 23.3 (Fall 1960), 90 (quotation). "Libraries for Louisiana" can be viewed through the Louisiana Digital Library (http://louisianadigitallibrary.org).

45. Louisiana State Library, *Eighteenth Biennial Report,* 9–10 (quotation, 9).

46. Sue Fontaine, "Libraries—A Changing Scene," *BRMA,* Jan. 17, 1960.

47. Louisiana State Library, *Twentieth Biennial Report of the Louisiana State Library, formerly Louisiana Library Commission, 1962–1963* (Baton Rouge: [The Library, 1964]), 34; Velma J. Taylor, "The Louisiana State Recruitment Project," *ALA Bulletin* 56.4 (Apr. 1962), 354.

48. Louisiana State Library, *Nineteenth Biennial Report,* 24–25 (quotation, 25); "Students from Varied Fields Find New World in Libraries," *BRMA,* Dec. 9, 1962.

49. Fry, "LSA and LSCA," 13–15 (quotation, 15).

50. Louisiana State Library, *New Directions in Library Service: Twenty-Third Report, 1968–1970* (Baton Rouge: [The Library, 1970]), [1]; John A. Humphry and James Humphry III, *Library Service in Louisiana: Keeping Pace with Progress in the State* (New York: [s.n.], 1968), 90 (quotation), hereinafter cited as *Humphry Report;* Louisiana State Library, *Library Service for a Changing Louisiana: Twenty-Second Biennial Report* (Baton Rouge: [The Library, 1968]), 13–14.

51. Louisiana State Library, *Twenty-Second Biennial Report,* 13–14.

52. [Untitled typescript, ca. 1958] (quotation), in Culver Papers—Buildings; Smith, "Historical Study," 218–19.

53. "Parish Library Opening Dates"; Louisiana State Library, *Twentieth Biennial Report,* 10; "Miss Culver to Retire from La. Library Post; Miss Farrell Successor," *Sunday Advocate,* Jan. 28, 1962; Thomas F. Jaques, interview with the author, June 23, 2005.

Chapter 8. A Statewide Legacy, 1962–1975

1. Michael Fultz, "Black Public Libraries in the South in the Era of De Jure Segregation," *Libraries & the Cultural Record* 41.3 (Summer 2006), 337–59, 348–49.

2. James V. Carmichael, Jr., "Southern Librarianship and the Culture of Resentment," *Libraries & Culture* 40.3 (Summer 2005), 327; Gloria Spooner, "Establishment of African American Public Library Service in Louisiana," *Louisiana Libraries* 23.3 (Winter 2001), 25; Louisiana State Library, *Twentieth Biennial Report of the Louisiana State Library, Formerly Louisiana Library Commission, 1962–1963* (Baton Rouge: The Library, 1964), 32.

3. Wayne A. Wiegand and Shirley A. Wiegand, *The Desegregation of Public Libraries in the Jim Crow South: Civil Rights and Local Activism* (Baton Rouge: Louisiana State University Press, 2018), 168–75, passim.

4. Ibid., 179–84; *Brown v. Louisiana,* 383 U.S. 131 (quotations).

5. Wiegand and Wiegand, *Desegregation of Public Libraries,* 182.

6. Ibid., 184; *Brown v. Louisiana,* 383 U.S. 131 (quotations).

7. "Miss Culver to Retire from La. Library Post; Miss Farrell Successor," *BRST,* Jan. 28, 1962.

8. "Miss Culver Is Honored by Hundreds at Banquet," *BRST,* June 2, 1962.

9. Cary J. Richardson, "Pomona College Honors Essae M. Culver," *Bulletin of the Louisiana Library Association* 17.4 (Fall 1954), 131–32 (first quotation, 131); "Citation for University Honors Essae Martha Culver," *Bulletin of the Louisiana Library Association* 22.4 (Winter 1959),

106; Margaret Dixon, "LSU Library Dedication," *Bulletin of the Louisiana Library Association* 22.4 (Winter 1959), 107 (second quotation); Alma Dawson, "Awards," in *A History of the Louisiana Library Association, 1925–2000,* ed. Alma Dawson and Florence M. Jumonville, 55–82 (Baton Rouge: Louisiana Library Association, 2003), 61.

10. Wyman W. Parker, "1959 ALA Awards, Citations, and Scholarships," *ALA Bulletin* 53.8 (Sept. 1959), 697–98.

11. Sallie Farrell, [Untitled address], Baton Rouge Book Club, Mar. 19, 1975 (first quotation), in Administrative Files (Farrell—Talks and Notes); Sue (Mrs. Henry) Fontaine, "Deeds—Not Words," also titled "The Essay on Essae," unpublished remarks presented at the meeting of the Library History Round Table, American Library Association conference, Chicago, July 15, 1963, 8 (second quotation), in VF (Librarians—Culver, Essae M.); Culver, [Journals], Mar. 3, 1933 (third quotation).

12. Fontaine, "Essay on Essae," 9 (first quotation); Thomas Shuler Shaw, "Miss Essae Martha Culver: First Lady of Louisiana Librarians," *LLA Bulletin* 50 (Summer/Fall 1987), 11–17 (second quotation, 17).

13. Fontaine, "Essay on Essae," 9–10 (all quotations except last); Lura Gibbons Currier, "The Lengthened Shadow: Essae M. Culver and the Louisiana State Library," *ALA Bulletin* 53.1 (Jan. 1959), 37 (last quotation).

14. Culver, [Journals], Nov. 14, 1961 (first quotation); Nov. 17, 1961 (second quotation); Dec. 8, 1961 (third quotation).

15. Beth Michel, "39 Years of Library Service," Baton Rouge *Enterprise,* Apr. 20–26, 1978 (quotations); Anne Price, "Louisiana's Librarian: Sallie Farrell's Political Savvy and Winning Smile Helped Build a Statewide Network of Libraries," *Sunday Advocate Magazine,* July 16, 2000.

16. Michel, "39 Years of Library Service" (quotations); Price, "Louisiana's Librarian."

17. Price, "Louisiana's Librarian"; Benton, "Retiring Is 'Going to Be Fun'" (quotation).

18. Sallie Farrell, speech to Baton Rouge Book Club, Mar. 19, 1975 (first and second quotations), in Administrative Files (Farrell—Talks and Notes); "'Super Salesman' of Louisiana Libraries Retires," article from unidentified magazine, [1975] (last quotation), in Administrative Files (State Library History).

19. Ada D. Jarred and Thurlow Mayeux, "An Interview with Sallie Farrell," *LLA Bulletin* 56 (Fall 1993), 91 (quotation); Louisiana State Library, *Twentieth Biennial Report,* 7–8.

20. Louisiana State Library, *Twentieth Biennial Report,* 7, 18; Louisiana State Library, *Twenty-First Biennial Report of the Louisiana State Library, Formerly Louisiana Library Commission, 1964–1965* (Baton Rouge: [The Library, 1966]), 15.

21. Louisiana State Library, *Twenty-First Biennial Report,* 6–7.

22. Ibid., [1], 11; Price, "Louisiana's Librarian" (quotation); "Trial Library for St. Landry Is Requested," *BRMA,* Jan. 9, 1963; "Voters Defeat Tax Proposal in St. Landry," *BRMA,* June 16, 1963; "Miss Cazayoux to Head Area Trial Library," *BRMA,* Mar. 3, 1964; "Library Service Report Is Made in St. Landry," *BRMA,* June 19, 1964; "Library Is Dedicated in St. Landry," *BRMA,* Mar. 3, 1965; "St. Landry Library Board Mulls Second Service Vote," *BRMA,* Nov. 4, 1965; "Library Will Halt Service in St. Landry," *BRMA,* Mar. 8, 1966; Louisiana State Library, *Library Service for a Changing Louisiana: Twenty-Second Biennial Report* (Baton Rouge: [The Library,

1968]), 2; "'Public Movement' Needed for St. Landry Library Changes," Lafayette *Daily Adver-tiser,* Apr. 11, 2017.

23. Louisiana State Library, *Twenty-Second Biennial Report,* 2 (first quotation); *Humphry Report,* 23; Thomas F. Jaques, interview with the author, June 23, 2005 (second quotation).

24. Louisiana State Library, *Twenty-Second Biennial Report,* 2; "A Dream Becomes Real-ity," *BRST,* Oct. 14, 1968 (quotations).

25. Dick Wright, "Librarian Emeritus Dies at 90," *BRMA,* Jan. 4, 1973 (first quotation), in Lou-isiana State Library files; "Librarian's Dream Comes True in La.," *BRST,* Oct. 23, 1968 (second and fourth quotations); "All Louisianians Now Have Library," *BRST,* Oct. 21, 1968 (third quotation).

26. "Librarian's Dream Comes True in La." (first quotation); "State Librarian Came Here on Loan; Stayed 37 Years," *BRMA,* May 17, 1962 (second quotation); LLC, *Report,* 69 (third quotation).

27. Louisiana State Library, *New Directions in Library Service: Twenty-Third Report, 1968–1970* (Baton Rouge: [The Library, 1970]), 9; Louisiana State Library, *Fifteenth Biennial Report,* 15 (quotation), 17; Louisiana State Library, *Twenty-First Biennial Report,* 32; Vivian Cazayoux et al., "Inside Louisiana's Correctional Institution Libraries," *LLA Bulletin* 32.4 (Winter 1970), 156; Martha Wilson, "State Prison Education Program Being Curtailed," *BRST,* Aug. 1, 1962.

28. Marion Vedder, "Louisiana State Library, Institutional Library Pilot Program, an Eval-uation: November 5–27, 1974" (Schenectady, NY, 1975), 1–2 (quotation, 2), hereinafter cited as Vedder Report; Louisiana State Library, *Clear Purpose—Complete Commitment: A Long-Range Program to Provide Louisianians with Library and Information Services Adequate to Their Needs, 1973–1977* (Baton Rouge: Louisiana State Library, 1972), 34.

29. "Ceremonies Open New Library at La. Penitentiary," [Unidentified, undated newspa-per] (first quotation), in SF Scrapbook [#]2; C. M. Hargroder, "Dedication Is Conducted for New Angola Library," *TP,* Apr. 3, 1968; Louisiana State Library, *Twenty-Third Report,* 9–10; Cazayoux, "Inside Louisiana's Correctional Institution Libraries," 156–59 (second quotation, 159); Wilbur C. Holtman, *The Second Twenty-Five Years of the Louisiana State Library, 1950–1975* (Baton Rouge, 1975), 27–28.

30. "New Hospital Library Opens," *LLA Bulletin* 33.2 (Summer 1970), 59; *Vedder Report,* 5, 18–19 (quotation, 19).

31. "East Regional Library Opened," *TP,* Oct. 24, 1968 (first quotation); Louisiana State Library, *Twenty-Third Report,* [1] (second quotation); *Humphry Report,* 7–8.

32. Louisiana State Library, *Twenty-First Biennial Report,* 2 (first quotation); Louisiana State Library, *Twenty-Second Biennial Report,* 3 (second quotation).

33. *Humphry Report,* 67–71.

34. Holtman, *Second Twenty-Five Years,* [8] (first quotation); "Trail Blazer System Is Un-derway," *LLA Bulletin* 33.2 (Summer 1970), 60; "A Look at the Trail Blazer Library System," *LLA Bulletin* 35.3 (Fall 1973), 115 (second quotation).

35. "Where Have All the Systems Gone?," *LLA Bulletin* 44.3 (Winter 1981), 129 (first quo-tation); Thomas F. Jaques, interview with the author, June 23, 2005 (second quotation).

36. Jaques interview.

37. Louisiana State Library, *Twenty-Third Report,* [1] (first quotation); Louisiana State

Library, *Limited Funds = Limited Services: Twenty-Fourth Report, 1971–1973* (Baton Rouge: [The Library, 1974]), 1 (second quotation).

38. Louisiana State Library, *Twenty-Third Report,* 4–7; Gary Phillips, "The LSL Processing Center in Action," *LLA Bulletin* 42.3 (Winter 1980), 64 (first quotation); Louisiana State Library, *Twenty-Fourth Report,* 1 (second quotation), 5.

Epilogue: "Look About Louisiana"

1. Velma Taylor, "The Life of Essae M. Culver Is the Story of La. Libraries," *TP,* May 6, 1928, in LLC Scrapbook, 1925–1928 (first quotation); Cynthia Woody, "Essae Martha Culver's Name Suggests Libraries; A Gentle Lady Remembers," *BRST,* June 27, 1969 (subsequent quotations).

2. Woody, "Essae Martha Culver's Name"; Marilyn Smallwood, "Preparation Is Key to Making Retirement a Time of Enjoyment," *BRST,* May 5, 1965 (quotation); e.g., "Mid-City Library Ground-Breaking Slated Tomorrow," *BRST,* Jan. 11, 1966.

3. "So Nice to Be Nice To," *BRMA,* Nov. 14, 1972 (first three quotations); Charles L. Dufour, "Essae M. Culver Deservedly Praised," *TP,* Dec. 3, 1972 (subsequent quotations).

4. Published reports state that Culver died on Tuesday evening, which was January 2. On an annotated copy of the death notice in State Library files, the date is changed, in what appears to be Sallie Farrell's handwriting, to "Wednesday morning," which was January 3. Dick Wright, "Librarian Emeritus Dies at 90," *BRMA,* Jan. 4, 1973; "Dr. Culver, Ex-Library Chief, Dies," *BRST,* Jan. 3, 1973; "Miss Essae Culver," *TP,* Jan. 5, 1973 (first quotation); "Miss Culver," *BRST,* Jan. 5, 1973 (second quotation).

5. Woody, "Essae Martha Culver's Name" (first quotation); Charles L. Dufour, "Honors Set for Miss Culver, State Librarian for 37 Years," New Orleans *States-Item,* June 1, 1962, in Culver files (second quotation)

6. Ada D. Jarred and Thurlow Mayeux, "An Interview with Sallie Farrell," *LLA Bulletin* 56.2 (Fall 1993), 91–92.

7. "Retiring State Librarian Honored at Banquet Here," *BRMA,* June 2, 1962 (first quotation); Sallie Farrell, [Untitled address], Louisiana Library Association Convention, Lafayette, Mar. 31, 1976, 1 (second quotation), in Administrative Files (Farrell—Talks and Notes).

8. Farrell, [Untitled address], 1–2.

9. Farrell, [Untitled address], 2 (first quotation); Rebecca Hamilton, "Message from the State Librarian," State Library of Louisiana web site, http://www.state.lib.la.us/about-the-state-library/message-from-the-state-librarian (second quotation), accessed Aug. 1, 2018; Milton J. Ferguson to Essae M. Culver, July 3, 1945 (third quotation), in Culver Papers.

SOURCES CONSULTED

Special Collections

State Library of Louisiana
    Louisiana Collection
        Essae M. Culver Papers
        Sallie Farrell Papers
        Scrapbooks
        Vertical Files
    Office of the State Librarian Files

The Historic New Orleans Collection
    Edward A. Parsons Papers

Notarial Archives of New Orleans
    Notarial Acts of Hugues Lavergne

Earl K. Long Library, University of New Orleans
    Marcus Christian Collection
    Historical Archives of the Supreme Court of Louisiana

Salem (Oregon) Public Library

Dissertations and Reports

Arford, Tammi. "Captive Knowledge: Censorship and Control in Prison Libraries." Ph.D. dissertation, Northeastern University, 2013.

Avant, Julia King. "Extending Library Service to Rural Areas in Louisiana, 1956–1969." Ph.D. dissertation, Indiana University, 1972.

Harris, Mary W. "The Louisiana Library Demonstration Plan: Designed to Extend Public Library Service to the Entire Population of the State." Baton Rouge: Louisiana State Library, Extension Department, 1952.

Jumonville, Florence M. "Creating and Transmitting the Louisiana Memory: Teaching Louisiana History in the Schools." Ph.D. dissertation, University of New Orleans, 1997.

Litchfield, Kathrina Sarah. "A Critical Impasse: Literacy Practice in American Prisons and the Future of Transformative Reading." M.A. thesis, University of Iowa, 2014.

"Parish Library Opening Dates," [n.d. but not before 1975], in State Library of Louisiana Files.

Parsons, Edward A. "An Inquiry into the Nature of a Certain 'Report of a Survey of the New Orleans Public Library.'" [New Orleans, 1935].

Smith, Robert Charles. "A Historical Study of Selected Effects of Federal Funding upon Public Libraries in Louisiana, 1956–1973." Ed.D. dissertation, Louisiana State University, 1975.

Stephenson, Shirley Knowles. "History of the Louisiana State Library, Formerly Louisiana Library Commission." Ph.D. dissertation, Louisiana State University, 1957.

Vedder, Marion. "Louisiana State Library, Institutional Library Pilot Program, an Evaluation: November 5–27, 1974." Schenectady, NY: [s.n.], 1975.

Serials

Acts of the Legislature of Louisiana

League of Library Commissions. *Handbook*. Chicago: American Library Association, 1916–1922.

Louisiana Library Commission / Louisiana State Library / State Library of Louisiana
Annual/biennial reports.
Clear Purpose—Complete Commitment
New Orleans City Directories, 1896–1947

Monographs

American Library Association. Office for Literacy and Outreach Services. *Different Voices, Common Quest: Adult Literacy & Outreach in Libraries!* [Chicago: The Office], 2002.

Barker, Tommie Dora. *Libraries of the South: A Report on Developments, 1930–1935.* Chicago: American Library Association, 1936.

Barry, John M. *Rising Tide: The Great Mississippi Flood of 1927 and How It Changed America.* New York: Simon & Schuster, 1997.

Becker, Patti Clayton. *Books and Libraries in American Society during World War II: Weapons in the War of Ideas.* New York: Routledge, 2005.

Conrad, Glenn R., ed. *A Dictionary of Louisiana Biography.* 2 vols. New Orleans: Louisiana Historical Association, 1988.

Current Biography: Who's News and Why, 1940. New York: H. W. Wilson, 1940.

Daniel, Hawthorne. *Public Libraries for Everyone: The Growth and Development of Library Services in the United States, Especially since the Passage of the Library Services Act.* Garden City, NY: Doubleday, 1961.

Dawson, Alma, and Florence M. Jumonville, eds. *A History of the Louisiana Library Association.* Baton Rouge: Louisiana Library Association, 2003.

Dixon, Margaret, and Nantelle Gittinger. *The First Twenty-Five Years of the Louisiana State Library, 1925–1950.* Baton Rouge: Louisiana State Library, 1950.

Duffus, R. L. *Books, Their Place in a Democracy.* New York: Houghton Mifflin, 1930.

Dunlap, Leslie W. "Introduction." In *"Your Affectionate Husband, J. F. Culver": Letters Written during the Civil War,* ed. Leslie W. Dunlap, notes by Edwin C. Bearss. Iowa City: Friends of the University of Iowa Libraries, 1978.

Fortier, Alcée, ed. *Louisiana: Comprising Sketches of Parishes, Towns, Events, Institutions, and Persons, Arranged in Cyclopedic Form.* 3 vols. New York: Century Historical Association, 1914.

Gleason, Eliza. *The Southern Negro and the Public Library: A Study of the Government and Administration of Public Library Service to Negroes in the South.* Chicago: University of Chicago Press, 1941.

Hair, William Ivy. *The Kingfish and His Realm: The Life and Times of Huey P. Long.* Baton Rouge: Louisiana State University Press, 1991.

Held, Ray E. *The Rise of the Public Library in California.* Chicago: American Library Association, 1973.

Himmel, Ethel E., and William J. Wilson, comps. *The Functions and Roles of State Library Agencies.* Chicago: American Library Association, 2000.

History of Vermilion Parish, Louisiana. [Abbeville, LA?]: Vermilion Historical Society, 1983.

Holley, Edward G., and Robert F. Schremser. *The Library Services and Construction Act: An Historical Overview from the Viewpoint of Major Participants.* Greenwich, CT: JAI Press, 1983.

Holtman, Wilbur C. *The Second Twenty-Five Years of the Louisiana State Library, 1950–1975.* Baton Rouge, 1975.

Humble, Marion. *Rural America Reads: A Study of Rural Library Service*. New York: American Association for Adult Education, 1938.

Humphry, John A., and James Humphry III. *Library Service in Louisiana: Keeping Pace with Progress in the State*. New York: [s.n.], 1968.

Kappler, Charles J., comp. and ed. *Indian Affairs: Laws and Treaties*. Vol. IV: *Laws*. Washington: Government Printing Office, 1929.

Long, Harriet Catherine. *County Library Service*. Chicago: American Library Association, 1925.

Louisiana Library Commission. *Report on the Louisiana Library Demonstration, 1925–1930*. New York: League of Library Commissions, 1931.

Luxenberg, Steve. *Separate: The Story of* Plessy v. Ferguson, *and America's Journey from Slavery to Segregation*. New York: Norton, 2019.

Megraw, Richard B. *Confronting Modernity: Art and Society in Louisiana*. Jackson: University Press of Mississippi, 2008.

Mims, Mary, with Georgia Williams Moritz. *The Awakening Community*. New York: Macmillan, 1932.

Morse, Walter D. *The Birth of Jennings and Jennings Firsts*. [S.l.: s.n., 1959?]

Parsons, Edward A. *The Wonder and the Glory: Confessions of a Southern Bibliophile*. New York: Thistle Press, 1962.

Passet, Joanne E. *Cultural Crusaders: Women Librarians in the American West, 1900–1917*. Albuquerque: University of New Mexico Press, 1994.

Schenk, Gretchen K. *County and Regional Library Development*. Chicago: American Library Association, 1954.

Scott, Anne Firor. *Natural Allies: Women's Associations in American History*. Urbana: University of Illinois Press, 1991.

Statistical Abstract of the United States, 1920. Washington, DC: Government Printing Office, 1921.

Taylor, David A. *Soul of a People: The WPA Writers' Project Uncovers Depression America*. Hoboken, NJ: Wiley, 2009.

U.S. House of Representatives, 80th Cong., 1st sess. *Demonstration of Public Library Service: Hearings before Subcommittee No. 1 of the Committee on Education and Labor . . . on H.R. 2465, a Bill to Provide for the Demonstration of Public Library Service in Areas without Such Service or with Inadequate Library Facilities*. Washington, DC: Government Printing Office, 1948.

Van Slyck, Abigail A. *Free to All: Carnegie Libraries & American Culture, 1890–1920*. Chicago: University of Chicago Press, 1995.

Wall, Bennett H., ed. *Louisiana: A History*. 2nd ed. Wheeling, IL: Forum Press, 1990.

Wiegand, Wayne A. *Part of Our Lives: A People's History of the American Public Library*. New York: Oxford University Press, 2015.

Wiegand, Wayne A., and Donald G. Davis, Jr., eds. *Encyclopedia of Library History.* New York: Garland, 1994.

Wiegand, Wayne A., and Shirley A. Wiegand. *The Desegregation of Public Libraries in the Jim Crow South: Civil Rights and Local Activism.* Baton Rouge: Louisiana State University Press, 2018.

Wilson, Louis Round, and Edward A. Wight. *County Library Service in the South: A Study of the Rosenwald County Library Demonstration.* Chicago: University of Chicago Press, 1935.

Articles and Book Chapters

Adams, Kathryn J. "Bookmobile Service in Louisiana's Demonstration Libraries." In *The Bookmobile—A New Look,* ed. Lois G. Pennell, 1–9. Chicago: American Library Association, 1969.

Aucoin, Sharilynn. "State Library of Louisiana: Special Services Branch." *Louisiana Libraries* 62.1 (Summer 1999), 9.

Bader, Barbara. "Treasure Island by the Roadside." *Horn Book Magazine* 75 (Jan./Feb. 1999), 4–6.

Baldwin, Clara F. "League of Library Commissions." *Bulletin of the American Library Association* 21.10 (Oct. 1927), 426–31.

"The Bookmobile as a Demonstration Book Truck." *Library Journal* 55 (Feb. 1, 1930), 110.

"Bookmobiles Turn 100." *Library Journal* 130.16 (Oct. 1, 2005), 24.

Brady, Patricia. "Literary Ladies of New Orleans in the Gilded Age." *Louisiana History* 33 (Spring 1992), 147–56.

Butler, Kari. "Webster Parish Library." *LLA Bulletin* 61.2 (Fall 1998), 109–12.

Carmichael, James V., Jr. "Southern Librarianship and the Culture of Resentment." *Libraries & Culture* 40.3 (Summer 2005), 324–52.

Cazayoux, Vivian. "Sallie Johnson Farrell." *LLA Bulletin* 50.1–2 (Summer/Fall 1987), 19–23.

Cazayoux, Vivian, et al. "Inside Louisiana's Correctional Institution Libraries." *LLA Bulletin* 32.4 (Winter 1970), 156–63.

Choate, Jackie. "Vermilion Parish Library." *Louisiana Libraries* 62.3 (Winter 2000), 19+.

"Citation for University Honors Essae Martha Culver." *Bulletin of the Louisiana Library Association* 22.4 (Winter 1959), 106.

Clayton, Ronnie W. "The Federal Writers' Project for Blacks in Louisiana." *Louisiana History* 19 (Summer 1978), 327–35.

Cmiel, Kenneth. "Libraries, Books, and the Information Age." In *The History of the*

Book in America, Vol. 5: *The Enduring Book: Print Culture in Post-War America,* ed. David Paul Nord, Joan Shelley Rubin, and Michael Schudson, 325–46. Chapel Hill: Published in association with the American Antiquarian Society by the University of North Carolina Press, 2009.

Connor, John M. "The Victory Book Campaign." *ALA Bulletin* 36.6 (June 1942), 377–78.

Culver, Essae M. "A Call to Action." *ALA Bulletin* 34.6 (June 1940), 377–79.

———. "A County Librarian at Work." *Bulletin of the American Library Association* 19.4 (1925), 354–57.

———. "The Emergence of Libraries." *ALA Bulletin* 35.7 (July 1941), 410–13.

———. "Federal Aid to Libraries." *Bulletin of the Louisiana Library Association* 20.4 (Fall 1957), 177–78.

———. "The Functions of State Supported Library Agencies." In Southeastern Library Association, *Addresses,* 12–14. [S.l.: Southeastern Library Association, 1928].

[Culver, Essae M.?] "James Oliver Modisette." *Bulletin of the Louisiana Library Association* 6 (Sept.-Dec. 1942), 2–4.

Culver, Essae M. "James Oliver Modisette: Friend of Libraries." *ALA Bulletin* 36.14, pt. 1 (Dec. 1, 1942), 817–18.

———. "The Louisiana State Library." *Bulletin of the Louisiana Library Association* 16 (Spring 1953), 41–48.

———. "State Planning in Louisiana." *Library Journal* 60 (May 1, 1935), 381–83.

———. "Webster Parish Library." *Louisiana Teachers' Association Journal* (Oct. 1929), 24–25.

Culver, Essae M., and Nantelle M. Gittinger. "A History of the Citizens' Library Movement." *Bulletin of the Louisiana Library Association* 17 (Winter 1954), 18–23.

Cummings, Jennifer. "'How Can We Fail?': The Texas State Library's Traveling Libraries and Bookmobiles, 1916–1966." *Libraries & the Cultural Record* 44 (2009), 299–325.

Currier, Lura Gibbons. "The Lengthened Shadow: Essae M. Culver and the Louisiana State Library." *ALA Bulletin* 53.1 (Jan. 1959), 35–37.

Dawson, Alma. "Awards." In *A History of the Louisiana Library Association, 1925–2000,* ed. Alma Dawson and Florence M. Jumonville, 55–82. Baton Rouge: Louisiana Library Association, 2003.

———. "The Participation of African Americans in the Louisiana Library Association." In *A History of the Louisiana Library Association, 1925–2000,* ed. Alma Dawson and Florence M. Jumonville, 101–20. Baton Rouge: Louisiana Library Association, 2003.

Dixon, Margaret. "LSU Library Dedication." *Bulletin of the Louisiana Library Association* 22.4 (Winter 1959), 107–9+.

Dixon, Margaret R. "The Webster Parish Library." *Louisiana Teachers Association Journal* (May 1930), in LLC Scrapbook, 1930–1935.

Dodd, Helen Wells. "What a State Library Commission Can Do for Louisiana." In *Louisiana State Library Association, 1911, Proceedings of the Meeting Held April 21–22, at Louisiana State University,* 6–10. Baton Rouge: Louisiana State University, 1911.

Douglas, Emily Taft. "Library Demonstration Bill Introduced." *ALA Bulletin* 40.4 (April 1946), 122–23.

———."Rural Libraries in America." *ALA Bulletin* 40.8 (Sept. 1, 1946), 269–72.

Evans, Luther H. "The Library Demonstration Bill." *ALA Bulletin* 41.4 (April 1947), 107–8.

"Extension of Library Services." *ALA Bulletin* 42.11 (Oct. 15, 1948), 415–23.

Fabian, Ann. "Laboring Classes, New Readers, and Print Cultures." In *Perspectives on American Book History: Artifacts and Commentary,* ed. Scott E. Casper, Joanne D. Chaison, and Jeffrey D. Graves, 285–310. Amherst: University of Massachusetts Press in Association with American Antiquarian Society and the Center for the Book, Library of Congress, 2002.

Ferguson, Milton J. "Oh! Just Judge." *Library Journal* 61 (Mar. 15, 1936), 226.

———."A Quarter of a Century After." *Bulletin of the Louisiana Library Association* 13 (Spring 1950), 35–36.

———."Second Battle of New Orleans." *Library Journal* 61 (Apr. 15, 1936), 314.

———."The Trend toward County Libraries." *Proceedings of the Pacific Northwest Library Association* (1920), 40–45.

———."Why Louisiana?" In Louisiana Library Commission, *Report on the Louisiana Library Demonstration, 1925–1930,* 7–11. New York: League of Library Commissions, 1931.

Fielder, Clara. "Library Demonstration Bill Introduced." *ALA Bulletin* 43.2 (Feb. 1949), 76.

Fontaine, Sue (Mrs. Henry A. Fontaine). "Talk of Many Things." *Bulletin of the Louisiana Library Association* 25 (Summer 1962), 58–63+.

"Foreign Visitor Praises Louisiana Library System." *Bulletin of the Louisiana Library Association* 24 (Fall 1961), 109–10.

"From a New Orleans Diary." *Bulletin of the American Library Association* 26.5 (May 1932), 339.

Fry, James W. "LSA and LSCA, 1956–1973: A Legislative History." *Library Trends* 24.1 (July 1975), 7–26.

Fultz, Michael. "Black Public Libraries in the South in the Era of De Jure Segregation." *Libraries & the Cultural Record* 41.3 (Summer 2006), 337–59.

Gardner, O. Max. "The Significance of the Citizens' Library Movement." *High School Journal* 12 (Dec. 1939), 301.

Hamilton, Rebecca. "The State Library of Louisiana and Public Libraries' Response to Hurricanes: Issues, Strategies, and Lessons." *Public Library Quarterly* 30.1 (Jan. 2011), 40–53.

Hansen, Debra Gold. "Depoliticizing the California State Library." *Information & Culture* 48.1 (2013), 68–90.

Hart, Andrew. "Librarians Despise Censorship. How Can Prison Librarians Handle That? It's Complicated." *Washington Post,* Jan. 16, 2018.

Hawk, Michelle. "Bookmobile Services in Rural America: Past, Present, and Future." *Bookmobile and Outreach Services* 11.2 (2008), 57–78.

Healey, Paul D. "Go and Tell the World: Charles R. McCarthy and the Evolution of the Legislative Reference Movement, 1901–1917." *Law Library Journal* 99 (Winter 2007), 33–53.

Hill, Sue. "Conferences of the Louisiana Library Association." In *A History of the Louisiana Library Association, 1925–2000,* ed. Alma Dawson and Florence M. Jumonville, 45–54. Baton Rouge: Louisiana Library Association, 2000.

Holden, Edna. "The Cost of Book Truck Service—Is It Worth While?" *Library Journal* 55 (Feb. 1, 1930), 102–5.

Holloway, Glenn H. "Trustees Section." *Bulletin of the American Library Association* 26.8 (Aug. 1962), 662.

James, K. B. "Australian Librarian Commends Louisiana State Library's Demonstration Plan." *Bulletin of the Louisiana Library Association* 21 (Fall 1958), 111–17.

Jaques, Thomas F. "State Library of Louisiana: The Purpose and Focus." *Louisiana Libraries* 62.1 (Summer 1999), 3.

Jarred, Ada D., and Thurlow Mayeux. "An Interview with Sallie Farrell." *LLA Bulletin* 56.2 (Fall 1993), 87–92.

Jumonville, Florence M. "In Memoriam: Sallie Farrell, Second State Librarian of Louisiana." *Louisiana Libraries* 72.4 (Spring 2010), 17–22.

——. "The Role of the State in the Organization of Statewide Library Service: Essae M. Culver, Louisiana's First State Librarian." *Library Trends* 52.4 (Spring 2004), 853–76.

——. "When We First Met: Conferences, Officers, and Activities of LSLA and LLA, 1909–1932." *Louisiana Libraries* 73.2 (Fall 2010), 7–16.

Kaestle, Carl F. "Seeing the Sites: Readers, Publishers, and Local Print Cultures in 1880." In *The History of the Book in America,* Vol. 4: *Print in Motion: The Expansion of Publishing and Reading in the United States, 1880–1940,* ed. Carl F. Kaestle and Janice A. Radway, 22–45. Chapel Hill: Published in association with the American Antiquarian Society by the University of North Carolina Press, 2009.

Kaestle, Carl F., and Janice A. Radway. "Epilogue." In *The History of the Book in*

America, Vol. 4: *Print in Motion: The Expansion of Publishing and Reading in the United States, 1880–1940,* ed. Carl F. Kaestle and Janice A. Radway, 528–35. Chapel Hill: Published in association with the American Antiquarian Society by the University of North Carolina Press, 2009.

"Libraries for Louisiana." *Bulletin of the Louisiana Library Association* 23.3 (Fall 1960), 90.

"The Library Demonstration Bill." *ALA Bulletin* 40.5 (May 1946), 157–59.

"Library Demonstration Bill, S. 48—H.R. 2465." *ALA Bulletin* 41.5 (May 1947), 134.

Long, Elizabeth. "Aflame with Culture: Reading and Social Mission in the Nineteenth-Century White Women's Literary Club Movement." In *The History of the Book in America,* Vol. 4: *Print in Motion: The Expansion of Publishing and Reading in the United States, 1880–1940,* ed. Carl F. Kaestle and Janice A. Radway, 476–90. Chapel Hill: Published in association with the American Antiquarian Society by the University of North Carolina Press, 2009.

"A Look at the Trail Blazer Library System." *LLA Bulletin* 35.3 (Fall 1973), 115–18.

Lorenz, John G. "Library Services Act—The First Three Years." *ALA Bulletin* 54.1 (Jan. 1960), 17–27.

"LSU Library Dedication." *Bulletin of the Louisiana Library Association* 22.4 (Winter 1959), 107.

Maestri, Helen. "The New Orleans Public Library in the Nineteenth Century." *Bulletin of the Louisiana Library Association* 15.2 (Spring 1952), 35–43.

"Manual for State and Local Directors, Victory Book Campaign." *ALA Bulletin* 36.1, pt. 2 (Jan. 1942), 1–12.

McHenry, Elizabeth. "Reading and Race Pride: The Literary Activism of Black Clubwomen." In *The History of the Book in America,* Vol. 4: *Print in Motion: The Expansion of Publishing and Reading in the United States, 1880–1940,* ed. Carl F. Kaestle and Janice A. Radway, 491–510. Chapel Hill: Published in association with the American Antiquarian Society by the University of North Carolina Press, 2009.

McKann, Michael R. "The Same Building, But a New Look: State Library of Louisiana." *Louisiana Libraries* 62.1 (Summer 1999), 4–5.

McMonagle, Sharin. "Rapides Parish Library." *LLA Bulletin* 61. 2 (Fall 1998), 106–8.

Milam, Carl H. "Executive Secretary's Report." *ALA Bulletin* 40.11 (Oct. 15, 1946), 323–33.

Modisette, J. O. "Rural Libraries and the Schools." *Louisiana Club Woman* ([Sept.?] 1928), 14+.

"New Hospital Library Opens." *LLA Bulletin* 33.2 (Summer 1970), 59.

"New Library at DeQuincy Correctional and Industrial School." *LLA Bulletin* 32 (Spring 1969), 45–46.

Owen, Dolores B. "The Lafayette Public Library: Its Origin and Development." *LLA Bulletin* 56 (Fall 1993), 63–75.

"Papers and Proceedings of the Forty-Seventh Annual Meeting of the American Library Association (July 1925)." *Bulletin of the American Library Association* 19.4 (1925), 353–63.

Parker, Wyman W. "1959 ALA Awards, Citations, and Scholarships." *ALA Bulletin* 53.8 (Sept. 1959), 697–702.

Pawley, Christine. "Advocate for Access: Lutie Stearns and the Traveling Libraries of the Wisconsin Free Library Commission, 1895–1914." *Libraries & Culture* 35 (Summer 2000), 435–58.

Phelps, Connie. "Louisiana Parish Libraries and World War II: A Survey." *LLA Bulletin* 56.3 (Winter 1994), 137–42.

Phillips, Faye. "'To Build upon the Foundation': Charles Gayarré's Vision for the Louisiana State Library." *Libraries & the Cultural Record* 43 (2008), 56–76.

Phillips, Gary. "The LSL Processing Center in Action." *LLA Bulletin* 42.3 (Winter 1980), 63–65.

Porter, Eva L. "The Louisiana Union Catalog." *Bulletin of the Louisiana Library Association* 22.4 (Winter 1959), 117–18+.

"Presenting Essae M. Culver." *Bulletin of the Louisiana Library Association* 8 (March–June 1945), 5.

Redding, Joan. "The Dillard Project: The Black Unit of the Louisiana Writers' Project." *Louisiana History* 32 (Winter 1992), 47–62.

Reed, Margaret McD. "Early History of the Library Movement in Louisiana." In Louisiana Library Commission, *Seventh Biennial Report of the Louisiana Library Commission, 1936–1937.* Baton Rouge: The Commission, 1933.

Richardson, Cary J. "Pomona College Honors Essae M. Culver." *Bulletin of the Louisiana Library Association* 17.4 (Fall 1954), 131–32.

Richardson, E. S. "Book Service Free to All." *Bulletin of the American Library Association* 27.5 (May 1933), 212–17.

———. "Ducks and Geese Are Flying South." *Nation's Schools* 8.1 (July 1931), 49–56.

Rothstein, Samuel. "The Origins of Legislative Reference Services in the United States." *Legislative Studies Quarterly* 5 (Aug. 1990), 401–11.

"Rural Public Library Service." *Bulletin of the Louisiana Library Association* 9.3 (Mar. 1946), 89.

Scott, John W. "Highway Building in Louisiana before Huey Long: An Overdue Re-Appraisal." *Louisiana History* 44 (Winter 2003), 5–38.

Shaw, Thomas Shuler. "Miss Essae Martha Culver: First Lady of Louisiana Librarians." *LLA Bulletin* 50 (Summer/Fall 1987), 11–17.

Smith, Virginia R. "'Give Good Books, Give More Books': The Victory Book Campaign." *LLA Bulletin* 56.3 (Winter 1994), 133–35.

———."User Services Branch of the State Library of Louisiana." *Louisiana Libraries* 62.1 (Summer 1999), 5–9.

Spooner, Gloria. "Establishment of African American Public Library Service in Louisiana." *Louisiana Libraries* 23.3 (Winter 2001), 23–25.

Stielow, Frederick J. "Librarian Warriors and Rapprochement: Carl Milam, Archibald MacLeish, and World War II." *Libraries & Culture* 25 (Fall 1990), 513–33.

Stone, Charles H. "Library Objectives in the Southeast." *Library Quarterly* 9.1 (Jan. 1939), 17–31.

"Suggested Activities for Wartime Library Service." *ALA Bulletin* 36.1, pt. 1 (Jan. 1942), 6–10.

Taylor, Velma J. "The Louisiana State Recruitment Project." *ALA Bulletin* 56.4 (Apr. 1962), 352–54.

"Trail Blazer System Is Underway." *LLA Bulletin* 33.2 (Summer 1970), 60.

[Untitled editorial]. *Library Journal* 50 (Feb. 15, 1925), 176.

[Untitled news item]. *Library Journal* 42 (Jan. 1917), 65.

[Untitled news item]. *Library Journal* 50 (Apr. 15, 1925), 346.

Violette, Rachel. "The Value of a Public Library." *Louisiana* (Apr. 1929), 23–24.

Watson, Paula D. "Founding Mothers: The Contribution of Women's Organizations to Public Library Development in the United States." *Library Quarterly* 64 (July 1994), 233–69.

"Where Have All the Systems Gone?" *LLA Bulletin* 44.3 (Winter 1981), 129–33.

Wiegand, Wayne A. "The American Public Library: Construction of a Community Reading Institution." In *The History of the Book in America*, Vol. 4: *Print in Motion: The Expansion of Publishing and Reading in the United States, 1880–1940*, ed. Carl F. Kaestle and Janice A. Radway, 430–51. Chapel Hill: Published in association with the American Antiquarian Society by the University of North Carolina Press, 2009.

Wright, Marion A. "The Citizens Library Movement." *Bulletin of the American Library Association* 30 (July 1936), 530–33.

Online Sources

American Library Association. "Interlibrary Loan Code for the United States" (2001), http://www.ala.org/Content/NavigationMenu/RUSA/Professional_Tools4/Reference_Guidelines/Interlibrary_Loan_Code_for_the_United_States.htm. Accessed Nov. 22, 2003.

———."League of Library Commissions File, 1904–1944," https://archives.library.illinois.edu/alaarchon/?p=collections/controlcard&id=7034. Accessed Aug. 20, 2017.

Bradshaw, Jim. "Great Flood of 1927." In *knowlouisiana.org Encyclopedia of Louisiana,* http://www.knowlouisiana.org/entry/great-flood-of-1927. Accessed Sept. 11, 2017.

Desmond, J. Michael. "John Jacob Desmond." In *knowlouisiana.org Encyclopedia of Louisiana,* http://www.knowlouisiana.org/entry/john-jacob-desmond. Accessed July 14, 2018.

"Find a Grave." https://www.findagrave.com. First accessed Oct. 18, 2017.

Galbi, Douglas A. "Book Circulation per U.S. Public Library User Since 1856," www.galbithink.org/libraries/circulation.htm. Accessed Sept. 2, 2017.

Louisiana Digital Library. http://louisianadigitallibrary.org. First accessed July 25, 2017.

Police Jury Association of Louisiana. *Parish Government Structure* [data file], 1999, http://www.lpgov.org/facts.htm. Accessed Feb. 13, 2018.

Readex. *America's Historical Newspapers.* First accessed Dec. 26, 2009.

State Library of Louisiana. "Message from the State Library," http://www.state.lib.la.us/about-the-state-library/message-from-the-state-librarian. Accessed Aug. 1, 2018.

INDEX